iPad For Seniors

2022–2023 Edition

by Dwight Spivey

for
d**ımmies**®
y Brand

iPad For Seniors For Dummies®, 2022–2023 Edition

Published by: **John Wiley & Sons, Inc.**, 111 River Street, Hoboken, NJ 07030-5774, www.wiley.com

Copyright © 2022 by John Wiley & Sons, Inc., Hoboken, New Jersey

Published simultaneously in Canada

No part of this publication may be reproduced, stored in a retrieval system or transmitted in any form or by any means, electronic, mechanical, photocopying, recording, scanning or otherwise, except as permitted under Sections 107 or 108 of the 1976 United States Copyright Act, without the prior written permission of the Publisher. Requests to the Publisher for permission should be addressed to the Permissions Department, John Wiley & Sons, Inc., 111 River Street, Hoboken, NJ 07030, (201) 748-6011, fax (201) 748-6008, or online at http://www.wiley.com/go/permissions.

Trademarks: Wiley, For Dummies, the Dummies Man logo, Dummies.com, Making Everything Easier, and related trade dress are trademarks or registered trademarks of John Wiley & Sons, Inc. and may not be used without written permission. iPad is a registered trademark of Apple, Inc. All other trademarks are the property of their respective owners. John Wiley & Sons, Inc. is not associated with any product or vendor mentioned in this book. *iPad For Seniors For Dummies®, 2022–2023 Edition* is an independent publication and has not been authorized, sponsored, or otherwise approved by Apple Inc.

For general information on our other products and services, please contact our Customer Care Department within the U.S. at 877-762-2974, outside the U.S. at 317-572-3993, or fax 317-572-4002. For technical support, please visit https://hub.wiley.com/community/support/dummies.

Wiley publishes in a variety of print and electronic formats and by print-on-demand. Some material included with standard print versions of this book may not be included in e-books or in print-on-demand. If this book refers to media such as a CD or DVD that is not included in the version you purchased, you may download this material at http://booksupport.wiley.com. For more information about Wiley products, visit www.wiley.com.

Library of Congress Control Number: 2022930648

ISBN: 978-1-119-86323-6 (pbk)

ISBN 978-1-119-86325-0 (ebk); ISBN 978-1-119-86324-3 (ebk)

SKY10032667_021922

Contents at a Glance

Table of Contents

Introduction

I f you bought this book (or are even thinking about buying it), you've probably already made the decision to buy an iPad. The iPad is designed to be easy to use, but you can still spend hours exploring the preinstalled apps, configuring settings, and learning out how to sync the device to your computer or through iCloud. I've invested those hours so that you don't have to — and I've added advice and tips for getting the most from your iPad.

This book helps you get going with your iPad quickly and painlessly so that you can move directly to the fun part.

About This Book

If you are a mature person who is relatively new to using a tablet, or you want to update to iPadOS 15 and learn about all the new features of that version, you need this book. In this book, you discover the basics of buying an iPad, working with its preinstalled apps, getting on the Internet, and using social media.

This book uses a few conventions to assist you:

» **Bold:** I use bold type to make figure references stand out in the text.

» **Italics:** I use italics for emphasis and for placeholder text that substitutes for what you might be seeing onscreen, such as *Price* when the actual price is what you would be seeing.

» **Command sequences:** When you need to follow a series of actions, you might see it presented like this: Tap Settings ➪ General ➪ Display Date & Time. That means to first tap the Settings icon, and then tap General on the screen that appears, and then tap the Date & Time option.

» **URLs:** Web addresses appear in monofont type in the printed book and as clickable links in the e-book, like this: `www.dummies.com`.

The Tip icon in the margin of a page alerts you to brief pieces of advice to help you to take a skill further, provide an alternative way of doing something, or, occasionally, to be aware of a problem an action might cause.

Like all *For Dummies* books, this book uses nontechnical language as it guides you through basic steps of working with your iPad. To make the content of this book easily accessible, it's organized into sets of tasks within the following parts:

» **Part 1: Getting to Know Your iPad:** The first chapter in this part guides you through buying an iPad, in case you don't have one yet, as well as any accessories you might need with it. Also in this part, you learn what buttons to push and what movements to make to turn on and use your iPad effectively. If you need to update your iPad to the latest version, you can find out about that and more in this part.

» **Part 2: Beginning to Use Your iPad:** This part begins by showing you how to enable accessibility features that may help you to more easily use your iPad. You then learn more about Apple's virtual assistant, Siri, and how to manage apps and contacts and use communication tools such as FaceTime and social media apps. Finally, I give you a good start on surfing the web and sending and receiving email.

» **Part 3: Enjoying Media:** Your iPad will quickly become indispensable for all things media related. From reading books to watching movies and television shows to listening to your favorite tunes and podcasts, this part shows you the ropes for acquiring new content and enjoying it. You also find out how to take stunning pictures and videos using your iPad's built-in cameras.

>> **Part 4: Living with Your iPad:** Finally, this part of the book helps you to stay on top of your busy life by setting reminders of important items on your to-do lists, calendar events, and appointments, and by taking notes. You'll also explore several utilities that come with iPadOS 15 and learn how to troubleshoot and maintain your iPad.

Foolish Assumptions

This book assumes that you are a mature iPad user who wants to get straight to the basics of using an iPad. It assumes that you may not be familiar with using a tablet, or that you are updating to iPadOS 15 and want to discover all the new features that come with that update. In writing this book, I've tried to consider the types of activities that might interest someone who is 50 years old or older.

Beyond the Book

Like every *For Dummies* book, this one comes with a free Cheat Sheet that brings together some of the most commonly needed information for people learning to use, in this case, the iPad. To get the Cheat Sheet, head for www.dummies.com and enter *iPad For Seniors For Dummies Cheat Sheet* in the Search box.

Where to Go from Here

You can work through this book from beginning to end or simply open a chapter to solve a problem or acquire a specific new skill whenever you need it. The steps in every task quickly get you to where you want to go without a lot of technical explanation.

At the time I wrote this book, all the information it contained was accurate for the 12.9-inch iPad Pro (1st, 2nd, 3th, 4th, and 5th generations), 11-inch iPad Pro (1st, 2nd, and 3rd generations), 10.5-inch iPad Pro, 9.7-inch iPad Pro, iPad (5th, 6th, 7th, 8th, and 9th generations), iPad Air 2, iPad Air (3rd and 4th generations), iPad mini (5th and 6th generations), iPad mini 4, version 15 of iPadOS (the operating system used by the iPad), and version 12.8 (for Macs) or 12.12 (for PCs) or later of iTunes. Apple may introduce new iPad models and new versions of iOS and iTunes between book editions. If you've bought a new iPad and found that its hardware, user interface, or the version of iTunes on your computer looks a little different, be sure to check out what Apple has to say at www.apple.com/iPad. You'll no doubt find updates there on the company's latest releases.

1

Getting to Know Your iPad

Chapter **1**
Buying Your iPad

You've read about it. You've seen the lines at Apple Stores on the day a new version of the iPad is released. You're so intrigued that you've decided to get your own iPad. Perhaps you're not new to tablet computers but are ready to make the switch to the ultimate in such devices. Your iPad offers lots of fun apps, such as games and exercise trackers; allows you to explore the online world; lets you read e-books, magazines, and other periodicals; allows you to take and organize photos and videos; plays music and movies; and a lot more.

Trust me: You've made a good decision, because the iPad redefines the tablet computing experience in an exciting way. It's also an absolutely perfect fit for seniors.

In this chapter, you learn about the advantages of the iPad, as well as where to buy this little gem and associated data plans from providers for iPads that support cellular data. After you have one in your hands, I help you explore what's in the box and get an overview of the little buttons and slots you'll encounter. Luckily, the iPad has very few of them.

Discover the Newest iPads and iPadOS 15

Apple's iPad gets its features from a combination of hardware and its software operating system (called iPadOS; the term is short for iPad operating system). As of this writing, the most current version of the operating system is iPadOS 15. It's helpful to understand which features the newest iPad models and iPadOS 15 bring to the table (all of which are covered in more detail in this book).

The iPad is currently available in various sizes, depending on the version of iPad. Here are the five basic sizes, by iPad type:

» **iPad:** The ninth-generation iPad features a touchscreen that measures 10.2 inches diagonally and sports a super-fast 64-bit desktop-class A13 Bionic processor.

» **iPad Air:** The fourth-generation iPad Air employs a touchscreen measuring 10.9 inches diagonally and features a 64-bit A14 Bionic processor.

» **iPad mini:** The iPad mini 6's screen measures 8.3 inches diagonally and uses a 64-bit A13 Bionic processor to do the behind-the-scenes work.

» **iPad Pro:** The two iPad Pro models are the fastest of the bunch. One measures 11 inches diagonally, and the other is 12.9 inches; they both come with blazing-fast M1 processors, which are the same processors used in many of Apple's newest Mac desktop and laptop computers.

TIP

Dimensions of devices are typically shown in the units of measurement commonly used in a region. This means, for example, that the basic iPad is shown on Apple's U.S. site as being 9.8 inches (250.6mm) high and 6.8 inches (174.1mm) wide. In metric–system countries, both dimensions are given, but the order is reversed. When it comes to screen sizes, however, the dimensions are given in inches.

In addition to the features of previous iPads, the latest iPad models offer

» **Screen resolution:** In addition to screen size, screen resolution has evolved so that Apple's Retina and Liquid Retina displays, both of which support very high-resolution graphics, now appear across the line. The name derives from the concept that individual pixels on the screen are so small that at normal viewing distance, they can't be distinguished.

» **Apple Pencil:** Originally designed exclusively for use with iPad Pro models, the Apple Pencil now works with all the latest iPad models. (Be sure to check which version of Apple Pencil will work with your iPad by visiting www.apple.com/apple-pencil.) Apple Pencil lets you draw and write on the screen with a familiar pencil-style tool rather than with your finger. The Apple Pencil contains a battery and sophisticated processing powers that make the experience of using it very much like (and sometimes better than) traditional pencils. Third-party pencils and drawing tools exist, but Apple's integration of Apple Pencil is remarkably smooth; the product has taken off quickly among graphic artists, illustrators, and designers. As other people have discovered its usability for marking up documents, it is becoming more and more common in business environments.

» **Neural Engine:** The Neural Engine is a component of the processor in every iPad that focuses on handling specialized tasks related to artificial intelligence, image and speech processing, and more cool things.

» **Touch ID:** This security feature is included on several newer iPad models that have a Home button. Sensors in the Home button allow you to train the iPad to recognize your fingerprint and grant you access with a finger press. Touch ID also allows you to use the Apple Pay feature to buy items without having to enter your payment information every time.

» **Facial recognition:** Touch ID is replaced with Face ID on iPad models that don't have a Home button. Using Face ID and the front-facing camera, your iPad unlocks when it recognizes your face.

» **Barometric sensor:** On all iPad models, this sensor makes it possible for your iPad to sense air pressure around you. This feature is especially cool when you're hiking a mountain, where the weather may change as you climb. Perhaps more to the point, the changes in barometric pressure can be sensed on a smaller scale so that elevation can be sensed and measured as you move normally.

» **More keyboard options:** The iPad Pro has a full-size onscreen keyboard. Because the screen has more space, the top of the keyboard can contain extra commands for filling in passwords and using more advanced input techniques.

» **Smart Connector for Smart Keyboard**: In addition to the onscreen keyboard, you can use a Smart Connector to hook up a Smart Keyboard, an external keyboard that makes getting complex work done much easier.

» **Live photos:** Using the 3D Touch feature, you can press a photo on the screen to make it play like a short video. The Camera app captures 1.5 seconds on either side of the moment when you capture the photo, so anything moving in the image you photographed, such as water flowing in a stream, seems to move when you press and hold the still photo.

The iPadOS 15 update to the operating system adds many features, including (but definitely not limited to)

» **Performance enhancements:** Apple promises that iPadOS 15 will increase the speed and performance of your iPad, including older models going back as far as iPad Air 2. From apps to keyboards to taking pictures, everything gets a speed upgrade.

» **Focus:** Think of Focus as an extension of the Do Not Disturb feature. You can customize a focus to filter notifications based on what you're doing at the moment. The default focus modes are personal, work, and sleep, and notifications are filtered based on their settings.

» **Safari:** iPadOS 15 gives Safari a whole new look and makes navigation easier. Tab groups are a welcome new feature that allow you to group your open web pages any way you like.

» **Maps:** Like Safari, Maps got a nice interface overhaul. Three-dimensional items like mountain ranges, buildings, trees, and more are rendered to make them more lifelike, making it easier to follow directions and recognize locations. A more detailed driving map is also a great enhancement.

» **FaceTime:** You can now schedule calls using FaceTime (this one falls into the "it's about time" category . . .) and send links to participants. Also, the interface got a refresh, and the enhancements to sound technologies make hearing call participants much easier.

» **Siri improvements:** Siri just keeps getting better. Siri can now speak in more natural tones and cadence, thanks to new software rendering capabilities. Siri can also give you more personalized information, including the ability to find event information and reminders in other apps. And Siri can now play audio files from third-party app providers.

» **Live text:** Live text lets you interact with text in images. For example, if the text is an address, you can tap it to open the address in Maps. Or you can select text from a photo and copy it into a document. Live text is a great addition to iPadOS 15.

» **Built-in apps have been updated:** iPadOS 15 provides performance enhancements and interface upgrades for all the apps that come preinstalled with it.

TIP

Don't need or use all the built-in apps? If so, you can remove them from your Home screen. When you remove a built-in app from your Home screen, you aren't deleting it — you're hiding it. This is due to security reasons that are beyond the scope of this book. However, the built-in apps take up very little of your iPad's storage space, and you can easily add them back to your Home screen by searching for them in the App Store and tapping the Get button.

These are but a very few of the improvements made to the latest version of iPadOS. I highly suggest visiting www.apple.com/ipados to find out more.

Choose the Right iPad for You

The most obvious differences among iPad models (shown together in **Figure 1-1**) are their thickness and weight, with the Pro being biggest, followed by iPad Air, then iPad, and finally the smallest, iPad mini. All models come in Space Gray, with iPad Air, iPad, and iPad Pro also offering Silver. iPad mini may not have Silver, but alongside Space Gray does offer Pink, Purple, and Starlight. iPad Air also gives you the choices of Rose Gold, Green, and Sky Blue.

Image courtesy of Apple, Inc.

FIGURE 1-1

All four models come in Wi-Fi only, so you access a Wi-Fi network for Internet access, or Wi-Fi + Cellular for connecting to the Internet through Wi-Fi or a cellular network (as your cellphone does).

The iPad models also differ slightly in available memory and price based on that memory (prices are accurate as of this writing and are subject to change):

» **iPad Pro 11-inch:** Wi-Fi models come in 128GB for $799, 256GB for $899, 512GB for $1,099, 1TB for $1,499, and 2TB for $1,899; Wi-Fi + Cellular models of each memory configuration cost $200 more than their Wi-Fi–only counterparts.

» **iPad Pro 12.9-inch:** Wi-Fi models come in 128GB for $1,099, 256GB for $1,199, 512GB for $1,399, 1TB for $1,799, and 2TB for $2,199; Wi-Fi + Cellular models of each memory configuration cost $200 more than their Wi-Fi–only counterparts.

» **iPad Air:** Wi-Fi models come in 64GB for $599 and 256GB for $749; Wi-Fi + Cellular models come in 64GB for $729 and 256GB for $879.

» **iPad:** Wi-Fi models come in 64GB for $329 and 256GB for $479; Wi-Fi + Cellular models come in 64GB for $459 and 256GB for $609.

» **iPad mini:** The Wi-Fi model comes in 64GB for $499 and 256GB for $649, and the Wi-Fi + Cellular model comes in 64GB for $649 and 256GB for $799.

Finally, the iPad models vary in screen quality and resolution, camera quality, and so on. Logically, the bigger the iPad, the bigger the price and higher the quality.

Decide How Much Storage Is Enough

Storage is a measure of how much information — for example, movies, photos, and software applications (apps) — you can store on a computing device. Storage can also affect your iPad's performance when handling such tasks as streaming favorite TV shows from the web or downloading music.

Streaming refers to playing video or music content from the web (or from other devices) rather than playing a file stored on your iPad. You can enjoy a lot of material online without ever down-loading its full content to your iPad.

Your storage options with the various iPad models range from 64 gigabytes (GB) to 2 terabytes (TB), which is equivalent to 2,000GB. You must choose the right amount of storage because you can't open the unit and add more as you typically can with a desktop computer. However, Apple has thoughtfully provided iCloud, a service you can use to back up content to the Internet. (You can read more about iCloud in Chapter 3.)

How much storage is enough for your iPad? Here's a guideline:

» If you regularly work with large media files, such as movies or TV shows, you might need 512GB or higher. For example, if you shoot 4K video at 60 frames per second, that will take roughly 1GB of storage space for every two-and-a-half minutes of foot-age. In light of this fact, at least 1TB of storage may be more appealing if you shoot a lot of video.

» If you like lots of media, such as movies or TV shows, you may need at least 256GB.

» For most people who manage a reasonable number of photos, download some music, and watch heavy-duty media, such as movies online, 128GB is probably sufficient.

» If you simply want to check email, browse the web, and write short notes to yourself, 64GB likely is plenty.

Do you know how big a gigabyte (GB) is? Consider this: Just about any computer you buy today comes with a minimum of 256GB of storage. Computers have to tackle larger tasks than iPhones, so that number makes sense. The iPad, which uses a technology called flash storage for storing data, is meant (to a great extent) to help you experience online media and email; it doesn't have to store much because it pulls lots of content from the Internet.

In the world of storage, 64GB for any kind of storage is puny if you keep lots of content (such as audio, video, and photos) on the device.

Know What Else You May Need: Internet and Computer

Although you can use your iPad on its own without any Internet or Wi-Fi access and without a computer to pair it with, it's easier if you have Internet access and a computer that you can (occasionally) use with your iPad.

Use basic Internet access for your iPad

You need to be able to connect to the Internet to take advantage of most iPad features. If you have an Apple ID, you can have an iCloud account, Apple's online storage service, to store and share content online, and you can use a computer to download photos, music, or applications from non-Apple online sources (such as stores, sharing sites, or your local library) and transfer them to your iPad through a process called syncing, which you learn about in Chapter 3. You can also use a computer or iCloud to register your iPad the first time you start it, although you can have the folks at the Apple Store handle registration for you if you have an Apple Store nearby. If you don't have a store nearby, visit www.apple.com/shop/help for assistance.

You can set up your iPad without an Internet connection and without going to an Apple Store: The best way to find out more information is to contact http://support.apple.com through an Internet connection on another device or at a public library or Internet cafe.

Can you use your iPad without owning a computer and just use public Wi-Fi hotspots to go online (or a cellular connection, if you have such a model)? Yes. To go online using a Wi-Fi–only iPad and to use many of its built-in features at home, however, you need to have a home Wi-Fi network available.

Pair your iPad with a computer

For syncing with a computer, Apple's iPad User Guide recommends that you have

» A Mac or PC with a USB 2.0 or 3.0 port and one of these operating systems:

- macOS version 10.11.6 (El Capitan) or newer
- Windows 10 or newer

» iTunes 12.8 or newer on a Mac running macOS El Capitan (10.11.6) through macOS Mojave (10.14.6), the Finder on Mac's running macOS Catalina (10.15) and newer, and iTunes 12.12 or newer on a PC, available at www.itunes.com/download

» An Apple ID

» Internet access

» An iCloud account

Apple has set up its iTunes software and the iCloud service to give you two ways to manage content for your iPad — including movies, music, or photos you've downloaded — and specify how to sync your calendar and contact information.

There are a lot of tech terms to absorb here (iCloud, iTunes, syncing, and so on). Don't worry: Chapters 2 and 3 cover those settings in more detail.

Choose Wi-Fi Only or Wi-Fi + Cellular

You use Wi-Fi to connect to a wireless network at home or at locations such as an Internet cafe, a library, a grocery store, or any public transportation that offers Wi-Fi. This type of network uses short-range radio to connect to the Internet; its range is reasonably limited, so if you leave home or walk out of the coffee shop, you can't use it anymore. (These limitations may change, however, because some towns are installing community-wide Wi-Fi networks.)

The cellular technologies allow an iPad to connect to the Internet via a widespread cellular network. You use it in much the same way that you make calls from just about anywhere with your cellphone. A Wi-Fi + Cellular iPad costs additional money when compared to the basic Wi-Fi–only model, but it also includes GPS (Global Positioning System) service, which pinpoints your location so that you can get more accurate driving directions.

Also, to use your cellular network in the United States, you must pay a monthly fee. The good news is that no carrier requires a long-term contract, which you probably had to have when you bought your cellphone and its service plan. You can pay for a connection during the month you visit your grandkids or friends, for example, and get rid of it when you arrive home. Features, data allowance (which relates to accessing email or downloading items from the Internet, for example), and prices vary by carrier and could change at any time, so visit each carrier's website to see what it offers. Note that if you intend to stream videos (watch them on your iPad from the Internet), you can eat through your data plan allowance quickly.

How do you choose? If you want to wander around the woods or town — or take long drives with your iPad continually connected to the Internet to get step-by-step navigation info from the Maps app — get Wi-Fi + Cellular and pay the additional costs. Don't bother with cellular if you'll use your iPad mainly at home or via a Wi-Fi hotspot (a location where Wi-Fi access to the Internet is available, such as a local coffee shop or bookstore).You can find lots of hotspots at libraries, restaurants, hotels, airports, and other locations.

If you have a Wi-Fi–only iPad, you can use the hotspot feature on a smartphone, which allows the iPad to use your phone's cellular connection to go online if you have a data-use plan that supports hotspot use with your phone service carrier. Check out the features of your phone to turn on the hotspot feature.

Consider iPad Accessories

At present, Apple and many other companies offer some accessories that you may want to check out when you purchase your iPad, including the following:

» **iPad cases and covers:** Your iPad isn't cheap, and unlike a laptop computer, it has a constantly exposed screen that can be damaged if you drop or scratch it. Investing in a good iPad case or cover is a good idea if you intend to take your iPad out of your house.

» **Printers:** Several HP, Brother, Canon, and Epson printers support the wireless AirPrint feature. At this writing, prices range from $129 to $399, and discounts are often available.

» **Smart Keyboards:** You can buy an attachable keyboard for certain iPad models which will make working with productivity apps much easier. These keyboards connect to your iPad to provide power and transmit data between the devices. Also, the Magic Keyboard from Apple for iPad Pro includes a trackpad for easy navigation without using your finger on the screen.

» **Apple Pencil:** For $99 (first generation) or $129 (second generation), you can buy the highly sophisticated stylus for use with the iPad. The Apple Pencil makes it easy to draw on your iPad screen or manage complex interactions more precisely.

» **Apple Digital AV Adapter:** To connect devices to output high-definition media, you can buy this adapter for about $40 and use it with an HDMI cable. More and more devices that use this technology are coming out, such as projectors and TVs. But remember that wireless connections such as Bluetooth and Wi-Fi are less expensive and can eliminate all those cables and cords. In some circumstances, a wired connection is faster and more effective than wireless.

Explore What's in the Box

After you fork over your hard-earned money for your iPad, you'll be holding one box. Besides your iPad and a small documentation package, here's a rundown of what you'll find when you take off the shrink wrap and open it up:

» **iPad:** Your iPad is covered in a thick plastic sleeve-film that you can take off and toss (unless you think there's a chance that you'll return the device, in which case you may want to keep all packaging for 14 days — Apple's standard return period).

» **Documentation:** Under the iPad itself is a small, white envelope about the size of a half-dozen index cards. Open it and you'll find some Apple stickers and some very brief instructions on how to use your iPad. Apple feels that using an iPad should be so intuitive that you don't really need instructions. But this book exists and folks are buying it (thanks!), so Apple may not be right about that.

» **A Lightning-to-USB-C cable:** Use this cable to connect the iPad to your computer or use it with the last item in the box: the USB power adapter.

» **USB-C power adapter:** The power adapter attaches to the cable so that you can plug it into the wall and charge the battery.

That's it. That's all you'll find in the box. It's kind of a study in Zen-like simplicity.

Take a First Look at the Gadget

The little card contained in the documentation that comes with your iPad gives you a picture of the iPad with callouts to the buttons you'll find on it. In this section, I give you a bit more information about those buttons and other physical features of the iPad. **Figure 1-2** shows you the layout for the iPad model, and **Figure 1-3** gives you the rundown for features pertaining to the iPad Air. **Figure 1-4** lays out the iPad mini, and the iPad Pro models are described in **Figure 1-5**.

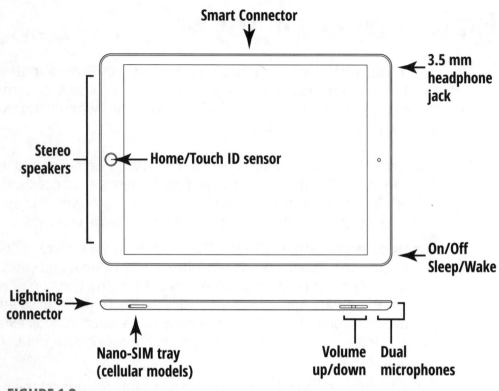

Smart Connector

3.5 mm headphone jack

Stereo speakers

Home/Touch ID sensor

On/Off Sleep/Wake

Lightning connector

Nano-SIM tray (cellular models)

Volume up/down

Dual microphones

FIGURE 1-2

Here's the rundown on what the various hardware features are and what they do:

» **Home/Touch ID button:** On the iPad, press this button to go back to the Home screen to find just about anything. The Home screen displays all your installed and preinstalled apps and gives you access to your iPad settings. No matter where you are or what you're doing, press the Home button, and you're back at home base. You can also double-press the Home button to pull up a scrolling list of apps so that you can quickly move from one app to another. (Apple refers to this as multitasking.) If you press and hold the Home button, you open Siri, the iPhone voice assistant. Finally, on the newest iPads, the Home button contains a fingerprint reader used with the Touch ID feature.

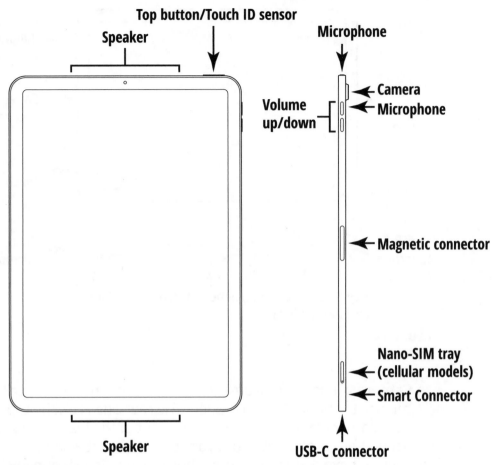

Speaker

Top button/Touch ID sensor

Microphone

← Camera

Volume up/down ← Microphone

← Magnetic connector

Nano-SIM tray ← **(cellular models)**

← Smart Connector

Speaker

USB-C connector

FIGURE 1-3

» **Sleep/Wake button:** You can use this button (whose functionality I cover in more detail in Chapter 2) to power up your iPad, put it in Sleep mode, wake it up, or power it down.

» **Lightning/USB-C Connector slot:** Plug in the Lightning or USB-C connector (depending on your iPad model) at the USB end to the power adapter to charge your battery or use it without the power adapter to sync your iPad with your computer (which you find out more about in Chapter 3).

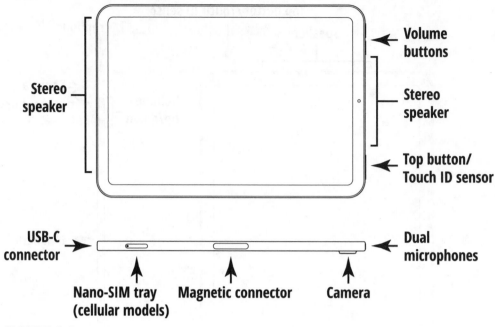

Stereo speaker

Volume buttons

Stereo speaker

Top button/ Touch ID sensor

USB-C connector

Dual microphones

Nano-SIM tray (cellular models)

Magnetic connector

Camera

FIGURE 1-4

>> **Cameras:** iPads offer front- and rear-facing cameras, which you can use to shoot photos or video. The rear one is on the top-right corner (if you're looking at the front of the iPad), and you need to be careful not to put your thumb over it when taking shots. (I have several very nice photos of my fingers already.)

>> **Smart Connector:** iPad Pro, iPad Air, and iPad include this feature to support accessories such as the Smart Keyboard.

>> **Nano-SIM tray:** This tray comes only with Wi-Fi + Cellular models. The Nano-SIM is what allows your iPad to connect and authenticate to a cellular network.

>> **(Tiny, mighty) speakers:** One nice surprise when I first got my iPad was hearing what a great little stereo sound system it has, and how much sound can come from these tiny speakers.

>> **Volume:** Tap the volume switch, called a rocker, up for more volume and down for less.

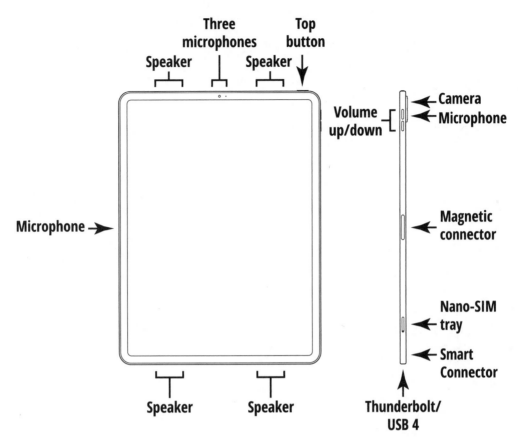

FIGURE 1-5

TIP

You can use this rocker as a camera shutter button when the camera is activated.

» **Headphone jack (not available in all models) and microphone(s):** If you want to listen to your music in private, you can plug in a 3.5mm mini-jack headphone (including an older iPhone headset, if you have one, which gives you bidirectional sound). Microphones make it possible to speak into your iPad to deliver commands or enter content using the Siri personal-assistant feature. Using Siri, you can do things such as make phone calls using the Internet, use video-calling services, dictate your keyboard input, or work with other apps that accept audio input.

Chapter **2**

Exploring Your iPad

G ood news! Getting anything done on the iPad is simple when you know the ropes. In fact, using your fingers to do things is a very intuitive way to communicate with your computing device, which is just what the iPad is.

In this chapter, you turn on your iPad and then take your first look at the Home screen. You also practice using the onscreen keyboard, see how to interact with the touchscreen in various ways, learn how to use Touch ID or Face ID, get pointers on working with cameras, get an overview of built-in applications (more commonly referred to as apps), and more.

See What You Need to Use the iPad

You need to be able, at a minimum, to connect to the Internet to take advantage of most iPad features, which you can do using a Wi-Fi network (a network that you set up in your own home or access in a public place such as a library) or a cellular data connection from your cellular provider (if your iPad model supports cellular data).

You may want to have a computer so that you can connect your iPad to it to download photos, videos, music, or applications and transfer them to or from your iPad through a process called *syncing* (see Chapter 3 for more about syncing). An Apple service called iCloud syncs content from all your Apple iOS devices (such as the iPad or iPhone), so anything you buy on your iPhone that can be run on an iPad, for example, will automatically be pushed to your iPad. In addition, you can sync without connecting a cable to a computer using a wireless Wi-Fi connection to your computer.

Your iPad will probably arrive registered and activated, or if you buy it in a store, the person helping you can handle that procedure.

Turn On Your iPad for the First Time

When you're ready to get going with your new toy, be sure you're within range of a Wi-Fi network that you can connect with, and then hold the iPad with one hand on either side, oriented like a pad of paper. Plug the charging cable that came with your device (which kind depends on the iPad model you have) into your iPad and plug the other end into a USB port on your computer or into the charging block that came with your iPad, just in case you lose your battery charge during the setup process.

Now follow these steps to set up and register your iPad:

1. Press and hold the Sleep/Wake button or Top button (depending on your iPad model) on the top of your iPad until the Apple logo appears. In another moment, a screen appears with a cheery Hello on it.

2. Follow the series of prompts to make choices about your language and location, using iCloud (Apple's online sharing service), and so on.

3. After you deal with all the setup screens, a Welcome to iPad screen appears; tap Get Started to display the Home screen.

TIP If you set up iCloud during or after registering (see Chapter 3), updates to your operating system will be downloaded to your iPad without plugging it into a computer. Apple refers to this feature as *PC Free*, simply meaning that your device has been liberated from having to use a physical connection to a computer to get upgrades.

TIP You can choose to have personal items transferred to your iPad from your computer when you sync the two devices using iTunes or Finder (depending on your computer's operating system), including music, videos, downloaded apps, audiobooks, e-books, podcasts, and browser bookmarks. Contacts and Calendars are downloaded via iCloud, or (if you're moving to iPad from an Android phone) you can download an app from the Google Play Store called Move to iOS (developed by Apple) to copy your current Android settings to your iPad. (See this support article from Apple for more info: https://support.apple.com/en-us/HT201196.) You can also transfer to your computer any content you download directly to your iPad by using iTunes, the App Store, or non-Apple stores.

Meet the Multitouch Screen

The iPad has more than one Home screen. By default, the first Home screen contains preinstalled apps, and the second contains a few more preinstalled apps. After those initial screens are fully populated with app icons, other screens are created to contain any further apps you download or sync to your iPad.

When the initial iPad Home screen appears (see **Figure 2-1**), you see a pretty background and two sets of icons.

FIGURE 2-1

One set of icons appears in the Dock, along the bottom of the screen. The *Dock* contains the Messages, Safari, Music, Mail, Calendar, Photos, and Notes app icons by default, though you can swap out one app for another. The Dock appears on every Home screen and can even be accessed from within apps. You can add new apps to your iPad to populate additional Home screens, too.

Other icons appear above the Dock and are closer to the top of the screen. Some of these icons are for widgets, which are snippets of information from apps and other sources; see the section "Wonderful Widgets," later in this chapter. Other icons above the Dock are for apps. I cover all these icons in the "Take Inventory of Preinstalled Apps" task, later in this chapter. Different icons appear in this area on each Home screen. You can also nest apps in folders, which gives you the possibility of storing almost limitless apps on your iPad. You are, in fact, limited — but only by your iPad's memory.

TIP

Treat the iPad screen carefully. It's made of glass and will break if an unreasonable amount of force is applied, or if it's dropped, or if the kids in your life throw it against the wall (yes, that's actually happened in our house).

The iPad uses *touchscreen technology*: When you swipe your finger across the screen or tap it, you're providing input to the device just as you do to a computer using a mouse or keyboard. You hear more about the touchscreen in the next task, but for now, go ahead and play with it for a few minutes — really, you can't hurt anything. Use the pads of your fingertips (not your fingernails) and try these tasks:

» **Tap the Settings icon.** The various settings (which you read more about throughout this book) appear, as shown in **Figure 2-2.**

TIP

To return to the Home screen, press the Home button (if your iPad has one), or swipe up from the very bottom of the screen (if your iPad does not have a Home button).

» **Swipe a finger from right to left on the Home screen.** This action moves you to the next Home screen.

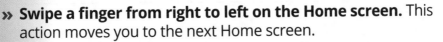

TIP

The little white dots at the bottom of the screen, above the Dock icons, indicate which Home screen is displayed.

» **To experience the screen rotation feature, hold the iPad firmly while turning it sideways.** The screen flips to the landscape (horizontal) orientation, if the app you're in supports it.

To flip the screen back to portrait (vertical) orientation, just turn the device so that it's oriented like a pad of paper again. (Some apps force iPad to stay in one orientation or the other.)

» **Drag your finger down from the very top edge of the screen to reveal items such as notifications, reminders, and calendar entries.** Drag up from the very bottom edge of the Home screen to hide these items.

» **Drag your finger down from the top-right corner of the screen to display Control Center (containing commonly used controls and tools and discussed later in this chapter).** Swipe up from the bottom of the screen to hide Control Center.

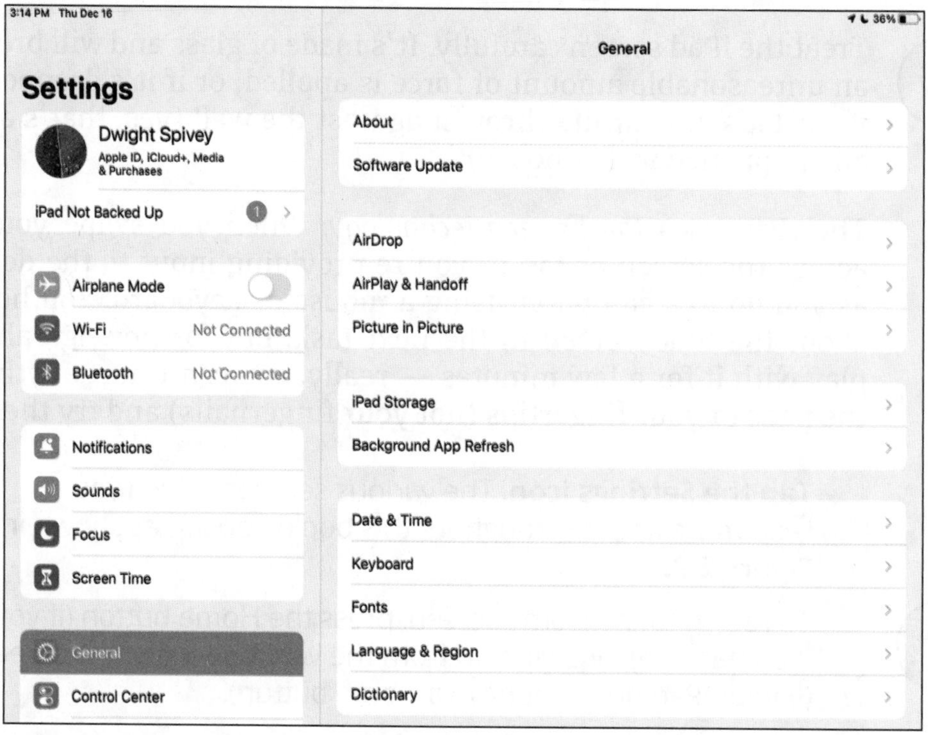

FIGURE 2-2

TIP

You can customize the Home screen by changing its *wallpaper* (background picture) and brightness. You can read about making these changes in Chapter 4.

TIP

Although the iPad's screen has been treated to repel oils, you're about to deposit a ton of fingerprints on your iPad — one downside of a touchscreen device. A soft cloth, like the one you might use to clean your eyeglasses, is usually all you need to clean things up, though. Having said that, third-party cleaners and screen protectors are available should you opt to use them; just be sure they're compatible with your particular iPad model, because materials used in each model may vary.

Say Hello to Tap and Swipe

You can use several methods for getting around and getting things done with your iPad using its multitouch screen, including

» **Tap once.** To open an app, choose a field (such as a search box), choose an item in a list, use an arrow to move back or forward one screen, or follow an online link, simply tap the item once with your finger.

» **Tap twice.** Use this method to enlarge or reduce the display of a web page (see Chapter 9 for more about using the Safari web browser) or to zoom in or out in the Maps app.

» **Pinch.** As an alternative to the tap-twice method, you can pinch your fingers together or move them apart on the screen (see **Figure 2-3**) when you're looking at photos, maps, web pages, or email messages to quickly reduce or enlarge them, respectively. This method allows you to grow or contract the image on the screen to a variety of sizes rather than a fixed size, as with the double-tap method.

TIP

You can use the three-finger tap to zoom your screen to be even larger or use multitasking gestures to swipe with four or five fingers. This method is handy if you have vision challenges. Go to Chapter 4 to discover how to turn on this feature using Accessibility settings.

» **Drag to scroll (known as *swiping*).** When you touch your finger to the screen and drag to the right or left, the screen moves (see **Figure 2-4**). Swiping to the left on the Home screen, for example, moves you to the next Home screen. Swiping down while reading an online newspaper moves you down the page; swiping up moves you back up the page.

» **Flick.** To scroll more quickly on a page, quickly flick your finger on the screen in the direction you want to move.

» **Tap the status bar.** To move quickly to the top of a list, web page, or email message, tap the status bar at the top of the iPad screen. (For some sites, you have to tap the status bar twice to get this to work.)

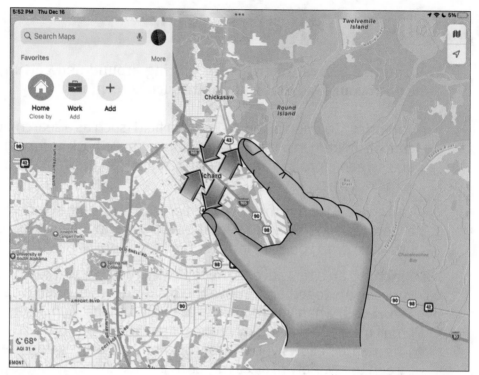

FIGURE 2-3

> » **Press and hold.** If you're using Notes or Mail or any other appli-
> cation that lets you select text, or if you're on a web page, press-
> ing and holding text selects a word and displays editing tools
> that you can use to select, cut, or copy and paste the text. You
> can also press and hold icons on the Home screen to view a list
> of options you can use with it.

When you rock your iPad backward or forward, the background
moves as well (a feature called *parallax*). You can disable this feature if it makes you nauseous. From the Home screen, tap Settings ➪
Accessibility ➪ Motion and then tap and turn on the Reduce Motion
setting by tapping the toggle switch (it turns green when the option
is enabled).

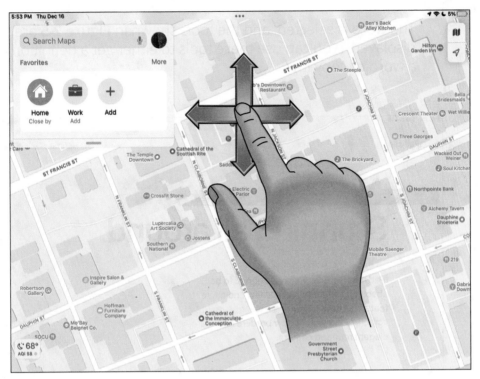

FIGURE 2-4

You can try these methods now:

» Tap the Safari button in the Dock at the bottom of any iPad Home screen to display the web browser.

» Tap a link to move to another page.

» Double-tap the page to enlarge it; then pinch your fingers together on the screen to reduce its size.

» Drag one finger up and down the page to scroll.

» Flick your finger quickly up or down on the page to scroll more quickly.

» Press and hold your finger on a word that isn't a link (links take you to another location on the web).

The word is selected, and the tools shown in **Figure 2-5** are displayed. (You can use these tools to either get a definition of a word or copy it.)

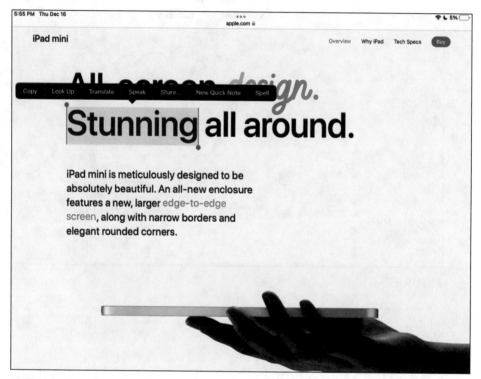

FIGURE 2-5

» Press and hold your finger on a link or an image.

A menu appears (shown in **Figure 2-6**) with commands that you select to open the link or picture, open it in a new tab or window, open it in a new tab group, download a linked file, add it to your Reading List, copy it, or share it. If you press and hold an unlinked image, the menu also offers the Add to Photos command.

Tap outside the menu to close it without making a selection.

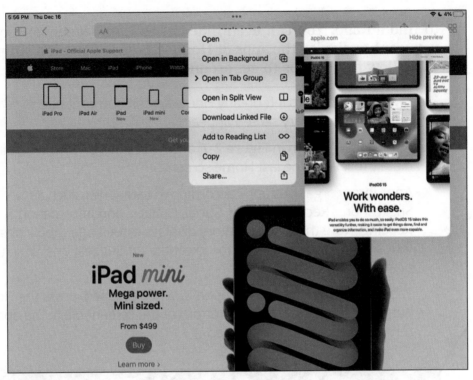

FIGURE 2-6

» Position your fingers slightly apart on the screen, and then pinch your fingers together to reduce the page; with your fingers already pinched together on the screen, move them apart to enlarge the page.

» Press the Home button or swipe up from the bottom of the screen (depending on your iPad model) to go back to the Home screen.

Introducing App Library

App Library is an organizational tool that houses every app on your iPad and organizes them automatically, according to categories (defined by Apple). This tool allows you to hide apps from your Home screens, reducing the number of them that you have to scroll through to find an app. You can even hide entire Home screens, too! And if you want to display the apps or Home screens again, it's simple to do so. Follow these steps to get around in App Library:

1. Swipe from right to left on any Home screen and continue to swipe until the App Library screen appears.

   App Library (shown in **Figure 2-7**) always resides on the screen immediately following the last Home screen.

   App Library organizes apps according to categories, such as Suggestions, Recently Added, Social, Utilities, and Information & Reading. Note that each category displays three larger app icons and four smaller app icons, with the exception of Suggestions, which displays four larger icons.

2. Tap one of the large apps to open it. When finished, press the Home button or swipe up from the bottom of the screen to exit the app and return to the App Library screen.

FIGURE 2-7

3. Tap one of the smaller apps to expand the category, and then tap the app you want to open. Tap near the top or bottom of the screen when viewing an expanded category to return to the App Library's main screen.

4. Tap the search field at the top of App Library to see all apps listed alphabetically, as shown in **Figure 2-8.** To find a specific app, type its name using the keyboard.

FIGURE 2-8

5. To perform a quick action on an app icon in App Library, press and hold an app icon to open the quick actions menu, the contents of which will vary depending on which options the app offers.

For example, **Figure 2-9** shows the Instagram quick actions menu, which offers some options that aren't available in the Camera app's quick actions menu.

FIGURE 2-9

6. To remove an app from your Home screen (leaving it in App Library) or delete it from your iPad, press and hold an app's icon on the Home screen until the quick actions menu appears. Tap Remove App and then tap one of the selections shown in **Figure 2-10.** Tap Delete App to delete the app from your iPad altogether, or tap Remove from Home Screen to remove the app from the Home screen but retain it in App Library.

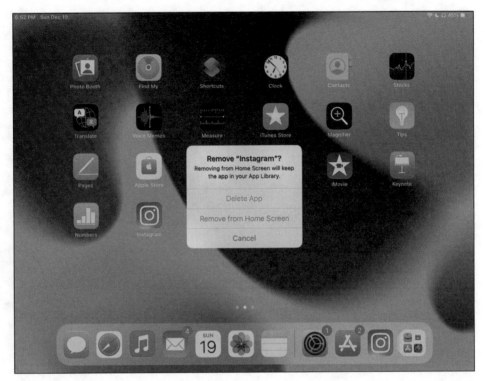

FIGURE 2-10

7. To hide an entire Home screen, press and hold any area on a Home screen until all the icons begin to jiggle. Tap one of the small white dots just above the Dock to view thumbnails of each of your Home screens, as shown in **Figure 2-11.** Tap the circle below a Home screen to hide or display it. (A visible Home screen displays a check mark in the circle.) Tap Done when you're finished.

The Home screen remains in App Library, and you can display it again later.

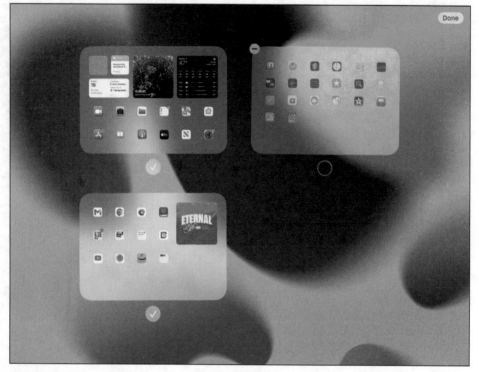

FIGURE 2-11

The Dock

The Dock at the bottom of your iPad's screen houses apps you use most often. You can remove or add apps from it simply by dragging and dropping their icons in or out of the Dock. You can also reorder icons within the Dock using the same drag-and-drop method. To drag and drop, press and hold an app icon until it pulsates (essentially tagging it to your finger) and then drag to a new location and drop it by removing your finger from the screen.

The Dock is divided between left and right sides by a thin gray line. The icons on the right side of the Dock are for those you use often but don't keep in the Dock at all times. This makes it easier to access these apps while you're using them more heavily. You can enable or disable this behavior by going to Settings ➪ Home Screen & Dock and toggling the Show Suggested and Recent Apps in Dock switch to On (green) or Off.

Display and Use the Onscreen Keyboard

The built-in iPad keyboard appears whenever you're in a text-entry location, such as a search field or a text message. Follow these steps to display and use the keyboard:

1. Tap the Notes icon on the Home screen to open the Notes app.

2. Open a note to work in:

- Tap the New Note icon in the top-right to create a new note.
- If you've already created some notes, tap one to display the page and then tap anywhere on the note.

3. Type a few words using the keyboard, as shown in **Figure 2-12**.

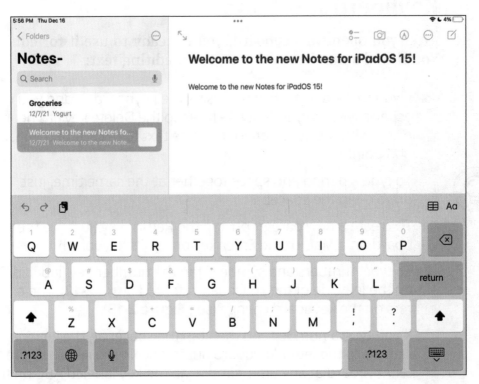

FIGURE 2-12

TIP

To make the keyboard display as wide as possible, rotate your iPad to landscape (horizontal) orientation. (If you've locked the screen orientation in Control Center, you have to unlock the screen to do this; just swipe down from the right corner of the screen to open Control Center, and then tap the Lock icon)

TIP

QuickType provides suggestions above the keyboard as you type. You can turn this feature off or on by pressing and holding either the Emoji (the smiley face) or International icon (looks like a globe) on the keyboard to display a menu. Tap Keyboard Settings and toggle the Predictive switch to turn the feature to Off or On (green). To quickly return to Notes from Keyboard Settings, tap the word Notes in the upper left of your screen.

Keyboard shortcuts

After you open the keyboard, you're ready to use it for editing text. You'll find a number of shortcuts for editing text:

» If you make a mistake while using the keyboard — and you will, especially when you first use it — tap the Delete key (it's near the *p* key, with the little *x* on it) to delete text to the left of the insertion point.

TIP

To type a period and space together at the same time, just double-tap the spacebar.

» To create a new paragraph, tap the Return key (just like the keyboard on a Mac, or the Enter key on a PC's keyboard).

» To type numbers and symbols, tap the number key (labeled .?123) on the left side of the spacebar (refer to **Figure 2-12**). The characters on the keyboard change (see **Figure 2-13**).

If you type a number and then tap the spacebar, the keyboard returns to the letter keyboard automatically. To return to the letter keyboard at any time, simply tap the key labeled ABC on the left side of the spacebar.

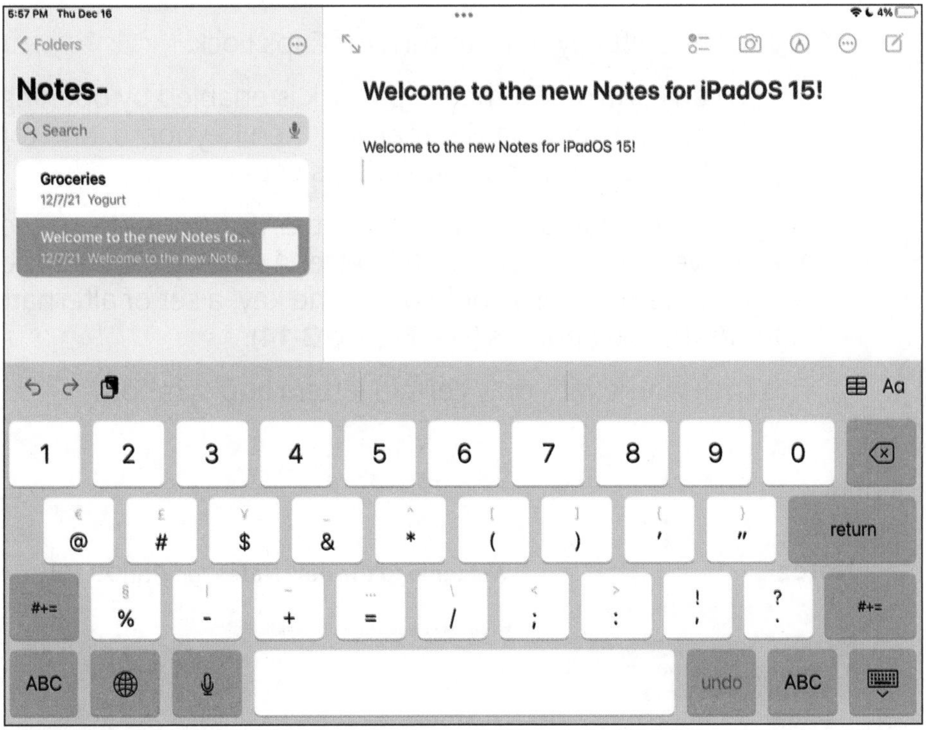

FIGURE 2-13

TIP

You can easily access an alternative character on a key by tapping and dragging down on the key. For example, if you need an exclamation mark (!), simply tap and drag the comma (,) key downward, and an exclamation mark will be inserted (because it's the alternate character on the comma key).

» Use the Shift key (it's a wide, upward-facing arrow in the lower-left corner of the keyboard) to type capital letters:

- Tapping the Shift key once causes only the next letter you type to be capitalized.

- Double-tap (rapidly tap twice) the Shift key to turn on the Caps Lock feature so that all letters you type are capitalized until you turn off the feature.

- Tap the Shift key once to turn off Caps Lock.

  You can control whether Caps Lock is enabled by opening the Settings app, tapping General and then Keyboard, and toggling the switch called Enable Caps Lock.

» To type a variation on a symbol or letter (for example, to see alternative presentations for the letter *A* when you press the A key on the keyboard), hold down the key; a set of alternative letters/symbols appears (see **Figure 2-14**).

  This trick works with only certain letters and symbols.

TIP

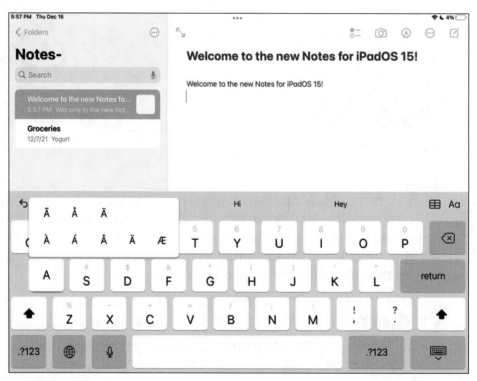

FIGURE 2-14

» Tap the smiley-faced Emoji button to display the Emoji keyboard containing symbols that you can insert, including numerical, symbol, and arrow keys, as well as a row of symbol sets along the bottom of the screen.

Tapping one of these displays a portfolio of icons from smiley faces and hearts to pumpkins, cats, and more. Tap the ABC button to close the Emoji keyboard and return to the letter keyboard.

A small globe symbol appears instead of the Emoji button on the keyboard if you've enabled multilanguage functionality in the iPad Settings app.

» Press the Home button or swipe up from the bottom of the screen (iPad Pro models only) to return to the Home screen.

You can buy a Smart Keyboard Folio to go with iPad Pro models, or a Smart Keyboard for iPad Air and iPad. This physical keyboard from Apple attaches to your iPad and allows both power and data exchange. The connection for your keyboard is magnetic, so it's a snap to put it and the iPad together.

QuickPath

QuickPath allows you to quickly zip your finger from key to key to quickly spell words without ever lifting your finger from the screen. For example, spell the word *path* by touching *p* on the keyboard and then quickly moving to *a* and then *t* and then *h.* Ta-da! You've spelled *path* without leaving the screen.

Use the Small Keyboard

The *small keyboard* feature allows you to shrink the keyboard to make more of the rest of the screen visible and to assist with one-handed typing. Open an application such as Notes in which you can use the onscreen keyboard and then follow these steps:

1. Tap an entry field or page to display the onscreen keyboard.

2. Spread two fingers apart, place them on the keyboard, and then quickly pinch your fingers together on the keyboard to shrink it, as shown in **Figure 2-15.** (This feature can be finicky, so you may have to try it a few times.)

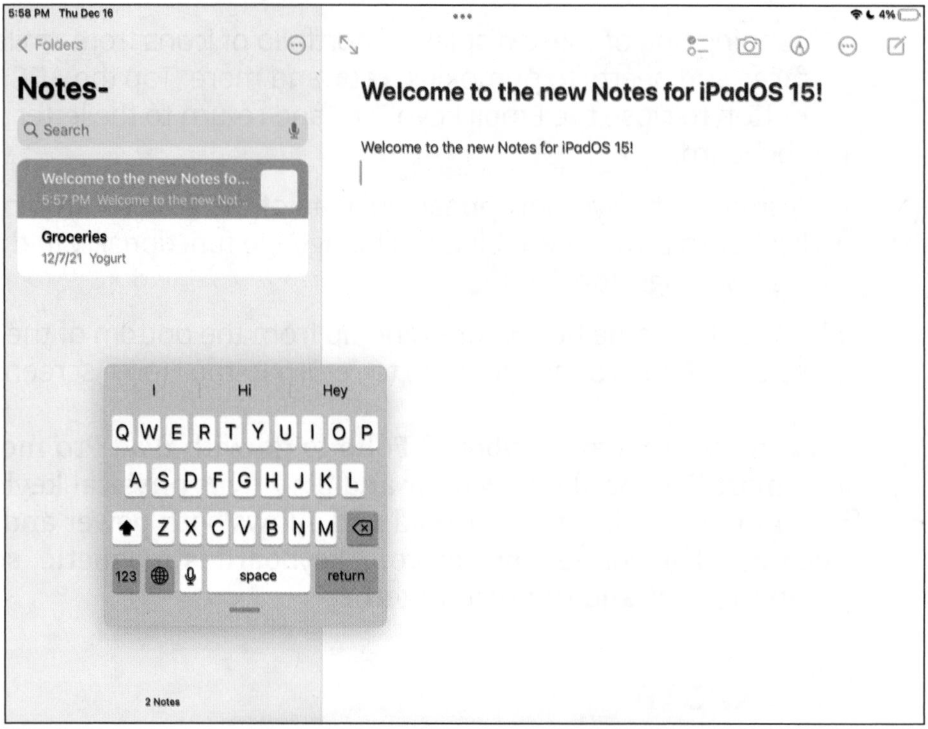

FIGURE 2-15

3. Now hold the iPad with a hand on either side and practice using your thumbs to enter text. You may also move the small keyboard around the screen by tapping and dragging the dark-gray handle at the bottom of the keyboard (under the spacebar).

4. To restore the original keyboard, pinch two fingers together, place them on the keyboard, and then quickly spread them apart.

Be sure to double-check that you didn't inadvertently type unnecessary characters in your text when pinching.

TIP

Flick to Search

The Search feature in iPadOS helps you find suggestions from the web, Music, iTunes, and the App Store as well as suggestions for nearby locations and more. Here's how to use Search:

1. Swipe down on any area of any Home screen (except the far edges) to reveal the Search feature (see **Figure 2-16**).

FIGURE 2-16

2. Begin entering a search term.

   In the example in **Figure 2-17,** after I typed the word *coffee,* the Search feature displayed maps and other search results. As you continue to type a search term or phrase, the results narrow to match it.

3. Scroll down to view more results.

4. Tap an item in the search results to open it in its appropriate app or player.

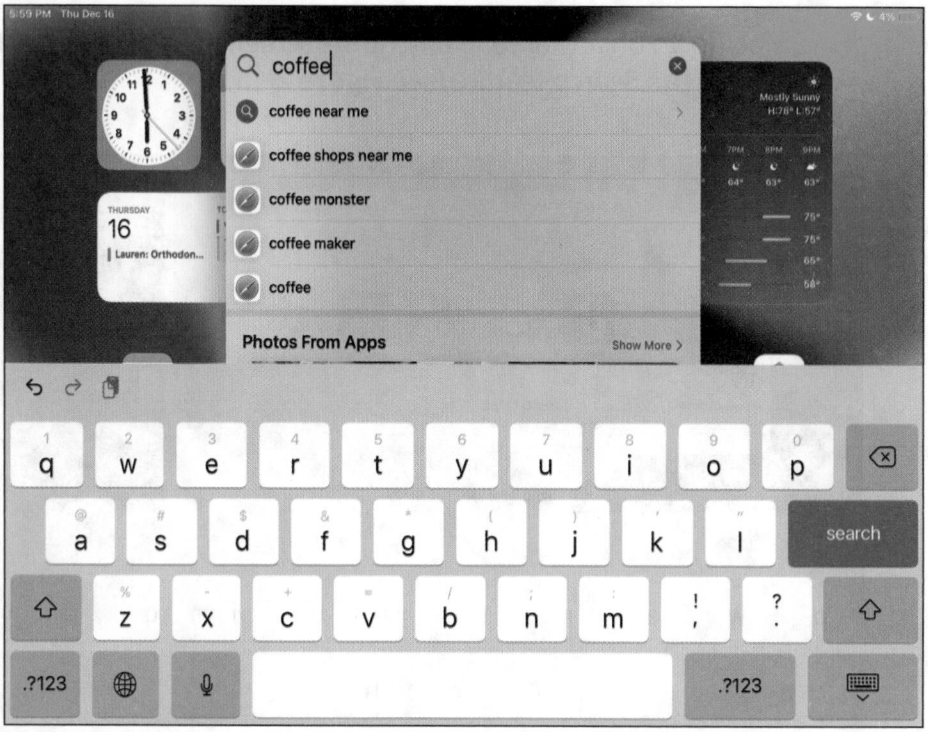

FIGURE 2-17

Easily Switch Between Apps

iPadOS 15 lets you easily switch from one app to another without closing the first one and returning to the Home screen. With iPadOS 15, you accomplish this task by previewing all open apps and jumping from one to another; you quit an app by simply swiping upward (apps you've opened remain open in the background unless you quit them this way). To find out the ropes of basic app switching, follow these steps:

1. Open the App Switcher by doing one of the following, depending on your iPad model:

- Press the Home button twice.

- Swipe up from the bottom edge of any screen with one finger, pause in the middle of the screen, and then lift your finger.

2. The App Switcher appears (see **Figure 2-18**).

FIGURE 2-18

3. To locate another app that you want to switch to, flick to scroll to the left or right.

4. Tap an app to open it.

TIP

Press the Home button once or swipe up from the bottom of the screen (depending on your iPad model) to return to the app that you were working in.

Use Slide Over and Split View

iPadOS 15 allows you to be more productive than ever before with your iPad with features like Slide Over and Split View.

Slide Over lets you view one app in a floating panel, while viewing and working with other apps behind it. Split View allows two apps to share the screen between them, splitting the screen so that one app is on the left and the other is on the right. You can even adjust the amount of space each app is allocated by dragging a divider between them.

Starting with Slide Over

To use the Slide Over feature, follow these steps:

1. From within an app you're already using, swipe up from the bottom edge of the screen to open the Dock.

2. Touch the icon of the app you want in the Dock to slide over the app you're already working in, hold it for a brief moment, and then drag it above the Dock.

3. The second app will open "floating" above the first app; it's now in Slide Over mode, as illustrated with Notes and Safari in **Figure 2-19.**

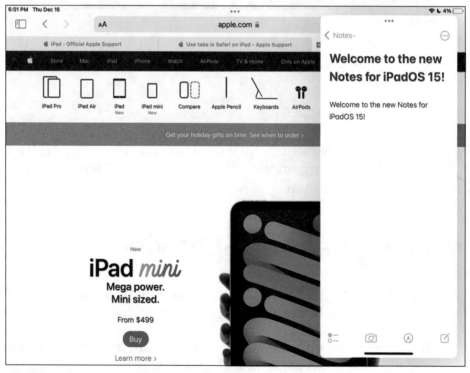

FIGURE 2-19

4. Simply tap the Home button or swipe up from the bottom of the screen (depending on your iPad model) to close Slide Over. You can also tap and hold the top of the floating app and then slide it off the screen to the right or left.

Moving to Split View

If you want to use both apps at the same time, you can move on to Split View. With Slide Over open, tap and drag the small gray dots at the top of the floating window toward the edge of the screen to open Split View, as shown in **Figure 2-20.** Simply tap the Home button or swipe up on one of the apps to exit Split View.

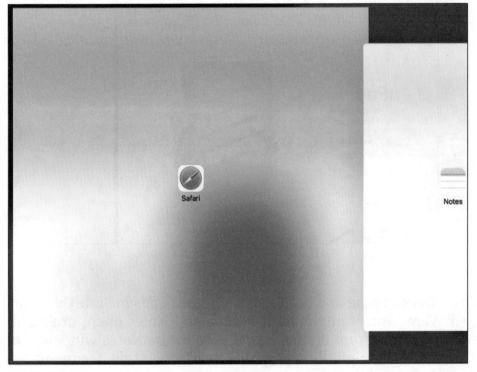

FIGURE 2-20

You can also move between Slide Over, Split View, and even Full Screen, by tapping the three gray dots at the top of a window and then tapping the icon for one of the aforementioned options.

While you're in Split View, you can drag the heavy black divider (see **Figure 2-21**) left or right to change the sizes of the panes, or you can have equal space for both apps. Both apps are fully functional, although in some special cases, the app may not show certain noncritical elements to adjust to the narrower width of the split view when compared to the full screen.

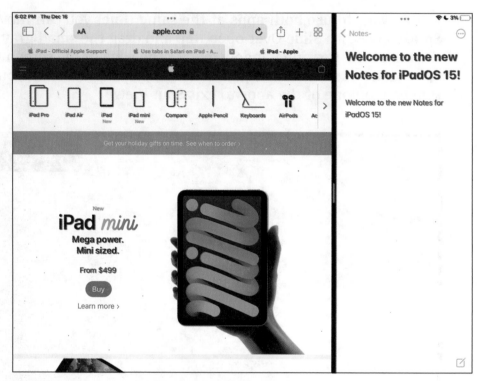

FIGURE 2-21

TIP

You can drag and drop items between apps in Slide Over and Split View. For example, with Photos and Notes open, drag and drop a picture from Photos into a note in the Notes window. Another example might be dragging a link from a text document into the Safari web browser to open it.

Examine the iPad Cameras

iPads have front- and back-facing cameras. You can use the cameras to take still photos (covered in more detail in Chapter 14) or shoot videos (covered in Chapter 15).

For now, take a quick look at your camera by tapping the Camera app icon on the Home screen. You can use the controls on the screen to take pictures and video, switch between front and rear cameras, turn the flash on and off, and so much more. See Chapters 14 and 15 for more detail about using the iPad cameras.

Discover Control Center

Control Center is a one-stop screen for common features and settings, such as connecting to a network, increasing screen brightness or volume, and more. Here's how to use it:

1. To display Control Center, swipe down from the upper-right corner of the screen. The Control Center screen appears to the right.

2. In Control Center (highlighted in **Figure 2-22**), tap a button or press and drag a slider to access or adjust a setting.

3. After you make a change, tap anywhere on the screen outside of Control Center to exit it.

Some options in Control Center are hidden from initial view but may be accessed by tapping and holding a button in Control Center. For example, press and hold on the Brightness slider to reveal the True Tone, Dark Mode, and Night Shift buttons (as shown in **Figure 2-23**).

TIP

Try pressing and holding other buttons in Control Center to see what other options are waiting for you to discover. If you press and hold an item and its icon just bounces, no further options are available for the item.

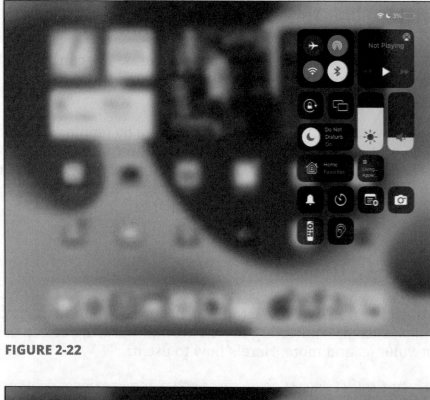

FIGURE 2-22

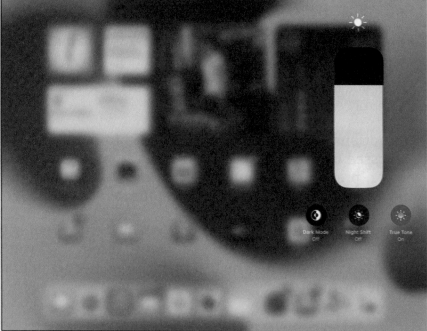

FIGURE 2-23

iPadOS 15 allows you to customize Control Center (a feature I love):

1. Tap Settings.

2. Tap Control Center and take a gander at the items in the Included Controls and More Controls sections (see **Figure 2-24**).

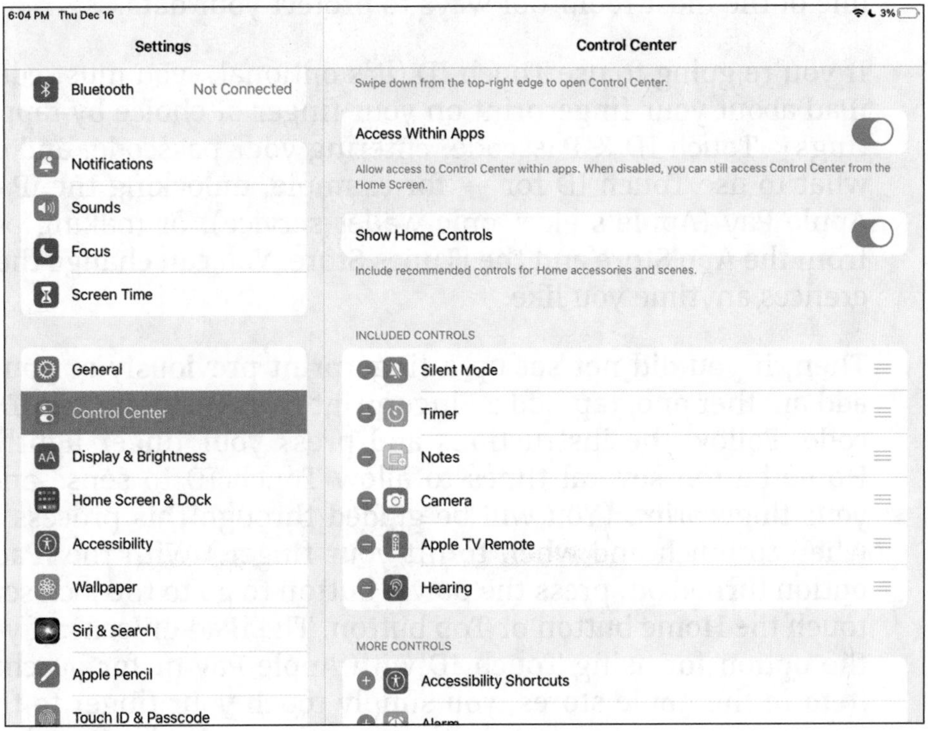

FIGURE 2-24

3. Remove items from Control Center by tapping the minus sign (–) to the left, and then tap the Remove button that appears to the right.

4. To add an item to Control Center, tap the plus sign (+) to the left. You'll see the item in Control Center the next time you visit it. Don't forget to press and hold an item to reveal any extras the item may afford.

Understand Touch ID

Certain iPad models sport a feature called Touch ID, which allows you to unlock your iPad by touching the Home button or Top button (depending on the model). The button contains a sophisticated fingerprint sensor. Because your fingerprint is unique, this feature is one of the most foolproof ways to protect your data.

If you're going to use Touch ID (it's optional), you must educate the iPad about your fingerprint on your finger of choice by tapping Settings ⇨ Touch ID & Passcode, entering your passcode, and choosing what to use Touch ID for — for example, unlocking the iPad, using Apple Pay (Apple's electronic wallet service), or making purchases from the App Store and the iTunes Store. You can change these preferences anytime you like.

Then, if you did not set up a fingerprint previously or you want to add another one, tap Add a Fingerprint from inside Touch ID & Passcode. Follow the instructions and press your finger lightly on the Home button several times to allow Touch ID to sense and record your fingerprint. (You will be guided through this process and told when to touch and when to lift your finger.) With the iPad Unlock option turned on, press the power button to go to the lock screen and touch the Home button or Top button. The iPad unlocks. If you chose the option for using Touch ID with Apple Pay or for purchasing an item in the Apple stores, you simply touch your finger to the Home button or Top button rather than enter your Apple ID and password to complete a purchase.

Take a Look at Face ID

Many iPad models use a different — and very cool — method of authenticating a user: Face ID. Face ID uses your iPad's built-in cameras and scanners to scan your face and save a profile of it. It then remembers the information and compares it to whoever is facing the iPad. If the face doesn't match the profile, the person can't access the iPad (unless they know and use your passcode, which you have to set up to use Face ID). Face ID is so advanced that it can even work in total darkness.

To set up Face ID:

1. Go to Settings and tap Face ID & Passcode.
2. Tap Set Up Face ID.
3. Hold the iPad in front of your face (in portrait mode, not landscape).
4. Tap the Get Started button and then follow the prompts to slowly move your head in a complete circle. If you have difficulty moving your head, tap the Accessibility Options button at the bottom of the screen and follow the prompts from there.
5. Tap Continue and follow the prompts to perform the circle step again.
6. Tap Done when finished.

The next time you want to use your iPad, simply hold it up in front of you, swipe up from the bottom of the screen when the lock icon unlocks, and you'll jump right into the Home screen or whatever app you were last using.

For more information on using Face ID and its capabilities, visit `https://support.apple.com/en-us/HT208109`.

Lock Screen Rotation

Sometimes you don't want your screen orientation to flip when you move your iPad around. Use these steps to lock the iPad into portrait orientation (narrow and tall, not low and wide):

1. Swipe down from the upper-right corner of any screen to open Control Center.
2. Tap the Lock Screen button. (It's the button that looks like a padlock with an arrow encircling it.)
3. Tap anywhere on the screen outside Control Center to exit it.

Perform the steps again to unlock the screen, if desired.

Explore the Status Bar

Across the top of the iPad screen is the status bar. Tiny icons in this area can provide useful information, such as the time, battery level, and wireless-connection status. **Table 2-1** lists some of the most common items you find on the status bar.

TABLE 2-1 **Common Status Bar Icons**

Icon	Name	What It Indicates
(Wi-Fi icon)	Wi-Fi	You're connected to a Wi-Fi network.
(Activity icon)	Activity	A task is in progress — a web page is loading, for example.
2:30 PM	Time	You guessed it: You see the time.
(Lock icon)	Screen Rotation Lock	The screen is locked in portrait orientation and doesn't rotate when you turn the iPad.
(Moon icon)	Do Not Disturb	Your iPad's communications are disabled during scheduled times.
(Battery icon)	Battery Life	This shows the charge percentage remaining in the battery. The indicator changes to a lightning bolt when the battery is charging.

TIP

If you have GPS, cellular (if your iPad supports it), Bluetooth service, or a connection to a virtual private network (VPN), a corresponding symbol appears on the status bar whenever a feature is active. (If you don't already know what a virtual private network is, there's no need to worry about it.)

Wonderful Widgets

Widgets are snippets of information, such as the weather and calendar appointments, that are provided at a glance so that you don't have to open individual apps. You can add widgets to any Home screen.

To add a widget:

1. Press and hold down on any Home screen until all the icons are jiggling.

2. Tap the plus sign (+) in the upper-left corner of the screen.

3. When the list of widgets opens, scroll through and tap the widget you want to add, or use the Search Widgets field at the top to find a specific widget.

4. If the widget has several styles (as indicated by dots at the bottom of the screen), like Forecast in **Figure 2-25,** swipe right or left to see those styles. Then tap to select one.

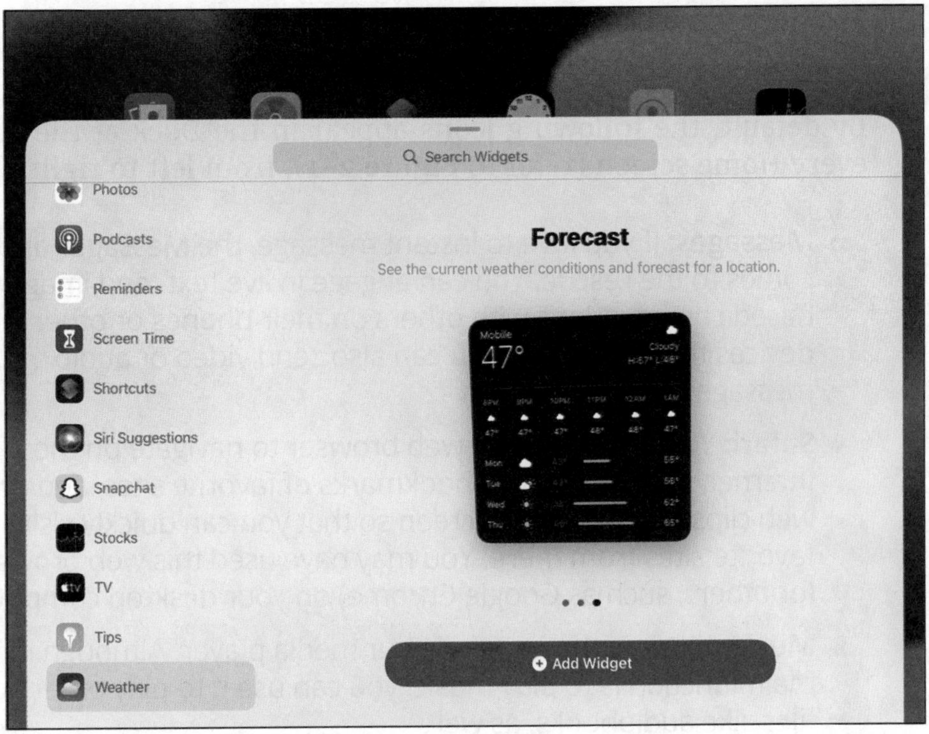

FIGURE 2-25

5. Tap the blue Add Widget button.

You can move your widget to another location by dragging it, or remove it and start over by tapping the minus sign (–) button in the upper-left corner of the widget.

6. When you're finished, tap Done in the upper right.

Take Inventory of Preinstalled Apps

The iPad comes with certain functionality and applications — or apps, for short — built in. When you look at the Home screen, you see icons for each app. This task gives you an overview of what each app does. (You can find out more about every one of them as you read different chapters in this book.)

By default, the following icons appear in the Dock at the bottom of every Home screen (refer to **Figure 2-1**), from left to right:

» **Messages:** If you love to instant message, the Messages app comes to the rescue. You can engage in live text- and image-based conversations with others on their phones or other devices that use email. You can also send video or audio messages.

» **Safari:** You use the Safari web browser to navigate on the Internet, create and save bookmarks of favorite sites, and add web clips to your Home screen so that you can quickly visit favorite sites from there. You may have used this web browser (or others, such as Google Chrome) on your desktop computer.

» **Music:** Music is the name of your media player. Although its main function is to play music, you can use it to play other audio files, like audiobooks, as well.

» **Mail:** Use this application to access email accounts that you have set up. You can use tools to move among a few preset mail folders, read and reply to email, and download attached photos to your iPad. Read more about email accounts in Chapter 10.

- » **Calendar:** Use this handy onscreen daybook to set up appoint-ments and send alerts to remind you about them.

- » **Photos:** Organize pictures in folders, send photos in email, use a photo as your iPad wallpaper, and assign pictures to contacts. You can also run slide shows of your photos, open albums, pinch or unpinch to shrink or expand photos, and scroll photos with a simple swipe.

- » **Notes:** Enter text, format text, or cut and paste text and objects (such as images) from a website into this simple notepad app.

Apps with icons above the Dock on the Home screen include the following:

- » **FaceTime:** Engage in phone calls using video of the sender and receiver.

- » **Camera:** The Camera app is Control Center for the still and video cameras built into the iPad.

- » **Files:** This app allows you to browse files that you've stored not only on your iPad but also on other services, such as iCloud Drive, Google Drive, Dropbox, and the like.

- » **Clock:** Display clocks from around the world, set alarms, and use timer and stopwatch features.

- » **Maps:** View classic maps or aerial views of addresses and get directions from one place to another whether traveling by car, foot, or public transportation. You can even get your directions read aloud by a spoken narration feature.

- » **TV:** This media player is similar to Music but specializes in play-ing videos, and it offers a few features specific to this type of media, such as chapter breakdowns and information about a movie's plot and cast.

- » **Contacts:** In this address-book feature, you can enter contact information (including photos, if you like, from your Photos or Cameras app) and share contact information by email. You can also use the search feature to find your contacts easily.

» **Reminders:** This useful app centralizes all your calendar entries, creates alerts to keep you on schedule, and allows you to create to-do lists.

» **News:** News is a customizable aggregator for stories from your favorite news sources.

» **iTunes Store:** Tapping this icon takes you to the iTunes store, where you can shop 'til you drop (or until your iPad battery runs out of juice) for music, movies, TV shows, and audiobooks and then download them directly to your iPad. (See Chapter 11 for more about how the iTunes Store works.)

» **App Store**: Buy and download apps that do everything from enabling you to play games to building business presentations. Many of these apps and games are free!

» **Books**: The Books app (formerly known as iBooks) is bundled with the iPad out of the box. Because the iPad has been touted as being a good small screen e-reader — a device that enables you to read books on an electronic device, similar to the Amazon Kindle Fire HD — you should definitely check this one out. (To work with the Books e-reader application itself, go to Chapter 12.)

» **Home**: Control most (if not all) of your home automation devices in one convenient app.

» **Photo Booth:** Enjoy snapping fun pictures of yourself and others with this app that adds a little flare to the standard Camera app.

» **Stocks:** Keep track of the stock market, including stocks that you personally follow, in real time.

» **Translate:** The Translate app translates text or voice between supported languages.

» **Voice Memos:** Record your thoughts and save or share them.

» **Measure:** Use your iPad to measure distances using its built-in camera.

» **Magnifier:** Zoom in on anything to get a better look.

- » **Podcasts:** Use this app to find and listen to recorded informational programs.

- » **Find My:** The Find My app combines the Find iPhone and Find Friends apps to help you locate Apple devices that you own (see Chapter 19 for more info) and track down friends who also own an Apple device.

- » **Shortcuts:** This app helps you string together multiple iPad actions into single commands that you can run either manually or by using Siri.

- » **Settings:** Settings is the central location on the iPad where you can specify settings for various functions and do administrative tasks, such as set up email accounts or create a password.

Lock iPad, Turn It Off, or Unlock It

Sleep is a state in which the screen goes black, though you can quickly wake up the iPad. You can also turn off the power to give your new toy a rest.

Here are the procedures you use to put the iPad to sleep or turn it off:

- » **Sleep:** Press the Sleep/Wake or Top button (depending on your iPad model), and the iPad goes to sleep. The screen goes black and is locked.

TIP

    The iPad automatically enters Sleep mode after a brief period of inactivity. You can change the time interval at which it sleeps by adjusting the Auto-Lock feature in Settings ⇨ Display & Brightness.

- » **Power Off:** From any app or Home screen, press and hold the Sleep/Wake or Top button until the Slide to Power Off bar appears at the top of the screen, and then swipe the bar. You've just turned off your iPad.

» **Force Off:** For models with a Home button, if the iPad becomes unresponsive, hold the Sleep/Wake or Top button and Home button simultaneously until the iPad shuts itself off. For iPad models without a Home button, press and release the Volume Up button, press and release the Volume Down button, and then press and hold the Top button to achieve the same result. Let go of all buttons, regardless of model, when the Apple logo appears on the screen.

To wake the iPad up from Sleep mode, simply press the Home button once or tap the screen (iPad models without a Home button).

If you have the Passcode feature enabled, you need to enter your passcode before proceeding to unlock your screen after pressing the Home button. However, if you have Touch ID enabled, you need to press the Home button only once and rest your finger on it for it to scan your fingerprints; the iPad will automatically unlock. If you have Face ID, your iPad will scan your face and unlock when you swipe up from the bottom of the screen.

TIP

Want a way to shut down your iPad without having to press buttons? Go to Settings ➪ General and scroll all the way to the bottom of the screen. Tap the Shut Down button, slide the Power Off slider, and your iPad will turn off.

Chapter **3**

Beyond the Basics

I n this chapter, I look at updating your iPad OS version (the operating system that your iPad uses) and making sure that your iPad's battery is charged.

Next, if you want to find free or paid content for your iPad from Apple, from movies to music to e-books to audiobooks, you'll need to have an iTunes account.

You can also use the wireless sync feature to exchange content between your computer and iPad over a wireless network.

Another feature you might take advantage of is the iCloud service from Apple to store and push all kinds of content and data to all your Apple devices — wirelessly. You can pick up where you left off from one device to another through iCloud Drive, an online storage service that enables sharing content among devices so that edits that you make to documents in iCloud are reflected on all of your iPadOS and iOS devices, and Macs running OS X Yosemite or later.

TIP

The operating system for Apple's Mac computers used to be called OS X. These days, it's referred to as macOS. The Mac operating system is mentioned a few times throughout this book, and you should know that OS X and macOS are different names for different versions of the same thing.

Update the Operating System to iPadOS 15

This book is based on the latest version of the iPad operating system at the time: iPadOS 15. To be sure that you have the latest and greatest features, update your iPad to the latest iPadOS now (and do so periodically to receive minor updates to iPadOS 15 or future versions of iPadOS). If you've set up an iCloud account on your iPad, you'll receive an alert and can choose to install the update or not, or you can update manually:

1. Tap Settings.

Be sure that you have Wi-Fi enabled and that you're connected to a Wi-Fi network to perform these steps.

2. Tap General.

3. Tap Software Update.

Your iPad checks to find the latest iPadOS version and walks you through the updating procedure if an update is available.

TIP

You can also allow your iPad to perform automatic updates overnight. Go to Settings ➪ General ➪ Software Update ➪ Automatic Updates and toggle the switch to On (green). Your iPad must be connected to Wi-Fi and its charger to automatically update.

Charge the Battery

My iPad showed up in the box fully charged, and I hope yours did, too. Because all batteries run down eventually, one of your first priorities is to know how to recharge your iPad's battery.

Gather your iPad along with its charging cable and power adapter (be sure to use the proper cable and adapter).

Here's how to charge your iPad:

1. Gently plug the correct end of the charging cable into the iPad. What kind of connector it is depends on which model iPad you have.

2. Plug the other end of the charging cable into the Apple power adapter.

3. Plug the adapter into an electric outlet.

   The charging icon appears onscreen, indicating that your phone is getting power.

 You can also charge your iPad using your Mac, assuming it has the correct ports to match your charging cable.

TIP

Sign into an iTunes Account for Music, Movies, and More

The terms *iTunes Account* and *Apple ID* are interchangeable: Your Apple ID *is* your iTunes Account, but you'll need to be signed in with your Apple ID to download items from the App Store and the iTunes Store.

 If you've never set up an Apple ID or iTunes Account, please visit https://support.apple.com/en-us/HT204316 on your computer, iPhone, or iPad for help in doing so.

TIP

To be able to buy or download free items from the iTunes Store or the App Store on your iPad, you must open an Apple ID. Here's how to sign in to an account after you've created it:

1. Tap Settings on your iPad.

2. Tap Sign In to Your iPad at the top-left of the Settings list, as shown in **Figure 3-1.**

TIP

You must be connected to a Wi-Fi or cellular network to sign in.

3. Enter your Apple ID and password in the fields provided (see **Figure 3-2**) and then tap the Sign In button.

TIP

If you prefer not to leave your credit card info with Apple, one option is to buy an iTunes gift card and provide that as your payment information. You can replenish the card periodically through the Apple Store.

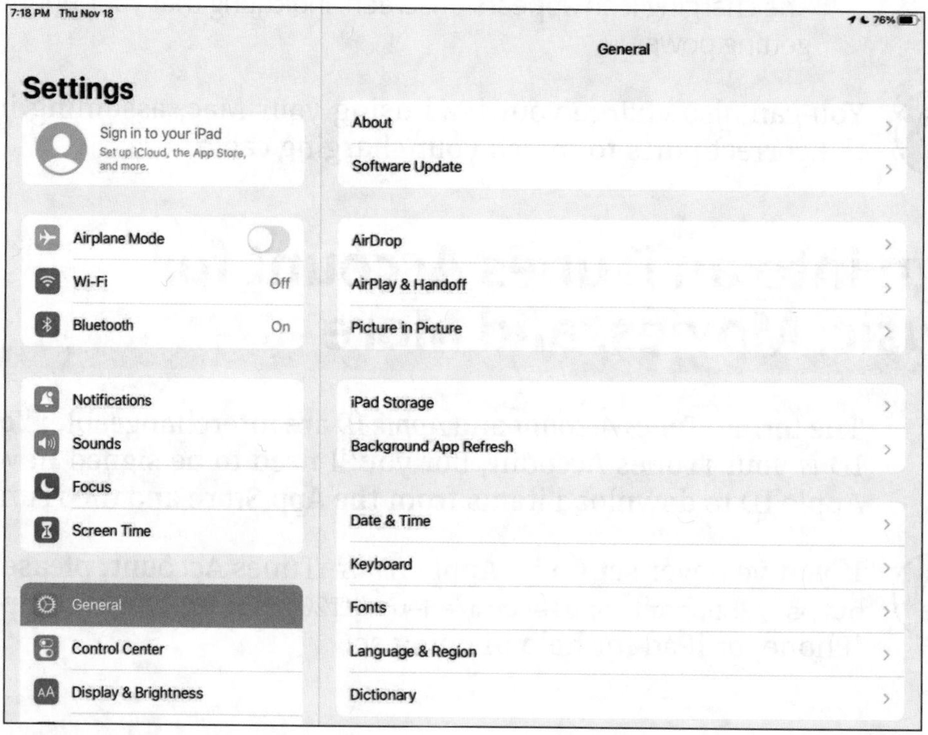

FIGURE 3-1

FIGURE 3-2

SIGN IN WITH APPLE

Sign in with Apple is a relatively new privacy feature introduced in iPadOS 13 that allows you to use your Apple ID to sign in to many social media accounts or websites. This service provides a simple and secure way to sign in to accounts without having to remember a unique password for each one. Think of it as Apple's more secure replacement for Sign in with Google or Sign in with Facebook, both of which you've probably seen online. The Sign in with Apple button will show up in apps and websites when an account log in is required. Check out `https://support.apple.com/en-us/HT210318` for more information on what I consider to be an important privacy feature from Apple.

Sync Wirelessly

You can connect your iPad to a computer and use the tools there to sync content on your computer to your iPad. Also, with Wi-Fi turned on in Settings, use the iTunes Wi-Fi Sync setting to allow cordless syncing if you're within range of a Wi-Fi network that has a computer connected to it with Finder open or iTunes installed and open.

TIP

If you have a Mac running macOS Mojave (10.14.x) or earlier, or a Windows-based PC, you'll need iTunes installed on your computer to sync content with your iPad. You can download iTunes by visiting www.apple.com/itunes. If you have a Mac running macOS Catalina (10.15) or later, you use Finder to sync with your iPad.

Before you can perform a wireless sync, you need to perform a few steps with your iPad connected to your computer:

1. If you're charging with an electrical outlet, remove the power adapter.

2. Use your iPad's charging cable to connect your iPad to your computer.

3. If you have a Mac running macOS Mojave or earlier, or a Windows-based PC running iTunes:

   a. Open iTunes and click the icon of your iPad, which appears in the tools in the upper-left corner of the window.

   b. Select the Sync with This iPad over Wi-Fi check box. You may need to scroll down a bit to see the Sync with This iPad over Wi-Fi option.

TIP

You can click any item on the left side of the screen to handle settings for syncing such items as Movies, Music, and Books. You can also tap the list of items in the On My Device section on the left side to view and even play content directly from your iPad.

4. If you have a Mac running macOS Catalina or later:

   a. Open a Finder window and then click the icon of your iPad, which appears in the left sidebar.

   b. Select the Show This iPad When on Wi-Fi check box.

5. Click Apply in the lower-right corner of the iTunes or Finder window.

6. Disconnect your iPad from your computer.

After you complete the preceding steps, you'll be able to wirelessly sync your iPad with your computer. Follow these steps:

1. Back up your iPad. See Chapter 20 to find out how.

2. On the iPad, tap Settings ⇨ General ⇨ iTunes Wi-Fi Sync. The iTunes Wi-Fi Sync settings appear.

3. In the iTunes Wi-Fi Sync settings, tap Sync Now to sync with a computer connected to the same Wi-Fi network.

4. If you need to connect your iPad to a network, tap Settings ⇨ Wi-Fi and then tap a network to join.

TIP

If you have your iPad set up to sync wirelessly to your Mac or PC and both are within range of the same Wi-Fi network, your iPad will appear in your devices list. This setup allows you to sync and manage syncing from iTunes or Finder (depending on which is required for your computer).

Your iPad will automatically sync with iTunes once a day if both are on the same Wi-Fi network, iTunes is running (on computers that require iTunes), and your iPad is charging.

Understand iCloud

There's an alternative to syncing content by using iTunes. iCloud is a service offered by Apple that allows you to back up most of your content to online storage. That content is then pushed automatically to all your Apple devices through a wireless connection. All you need to do is get an iCloud account, which is free (again, this is simply using your Apple ID), and make settings on your devices and in iTunes for which types of content you want pushed to each device. After you've done that, content that you create or purchase on one device — such as music, apps, and TV shows, as well as documents created in Apple's iWork apps (Pages, Keynote, and Numbers), photos, and so on — is synced among your devices automatically.

You can stick with iCloud's default storage capacity, or you can increase it if you need more capacity.

>> Your iCloud account includes 5GB of free storage. You may be fine with the free 5GB of storage.

Content that you purchase from Apple (such as apps, books, music, iTunes Match content, Photo Sharing contents, and TV shows) isn't counted against your storage.

>> If you want additional storage, you can buy an upgrade. Currently, 50GB costs only 99 cents per month, 200GB is $2.99 per month, and 2TB (which is an enormous amount of storage) is $9.99 per month. (All prices are in U.S. dollars.) Most likely, 50GB will satisfy the needs of folks who just like to take and share pictures, but if videos are your thing, you may eventually want to consider the larger capacities.

WHAT INFORMATION DOES iCLOUD BACK UP?

It's understandable to question what iCloud backs up on your iPad or other Apple devices, such as your iPhone or Mac. Apple's happy to share that with us iPad fans:

- Device settings
- Home screen settings and app organization
- Photos and videos
- Text messages
- Data from the apps you've installed
- Your purchase history from Apple: apps, music, ringtones, movies, and TV shows
- Apple Watch data
- Your Visual Voicemail password

For more information, please see Apple's support site at https://support.apple.com/en-us/HT207428.

To upgrade your storage, go to Settings, tap your Apple ID at the top of the screen, go to iCloud ⇨ Manage Storage, and then tap Change Storage Plan, Buy More Storage, or Upgrade next to iCloud Storage. On the next screen, tap the amount you need and then tap Buy (in the upper-right corner), as shown in **Figure 3-3.**

TIP

If you change your mind, you can get in touch with Apple within 15 days to cancel your upgrade.

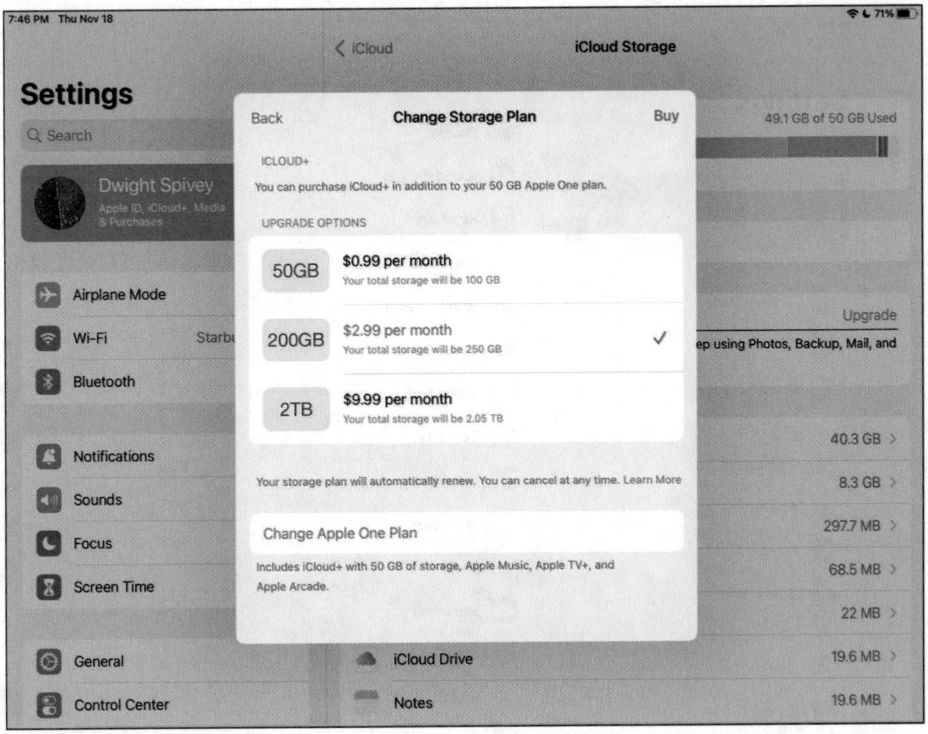

FIGURE 3-3

Turn on iCloud Drive

iCloud Drive is the online storage space that comes free with iCloud (as covered in the preceding section).

Before you can use iCloud Drive, you need to be sure that iCloud Drive is turned on. Here's how to turn on iCloud Drive:

1. Tap Settings and then tap your Apple ID at the top of the screen.

2. Tap iCloud to open the iCloud screen.

3. Scroll down in the iCloud screen until you see iCloud Drive.

4. Tap the On/Off switch to turn on (green) iCloud Drive (see **Figure 3-4**).

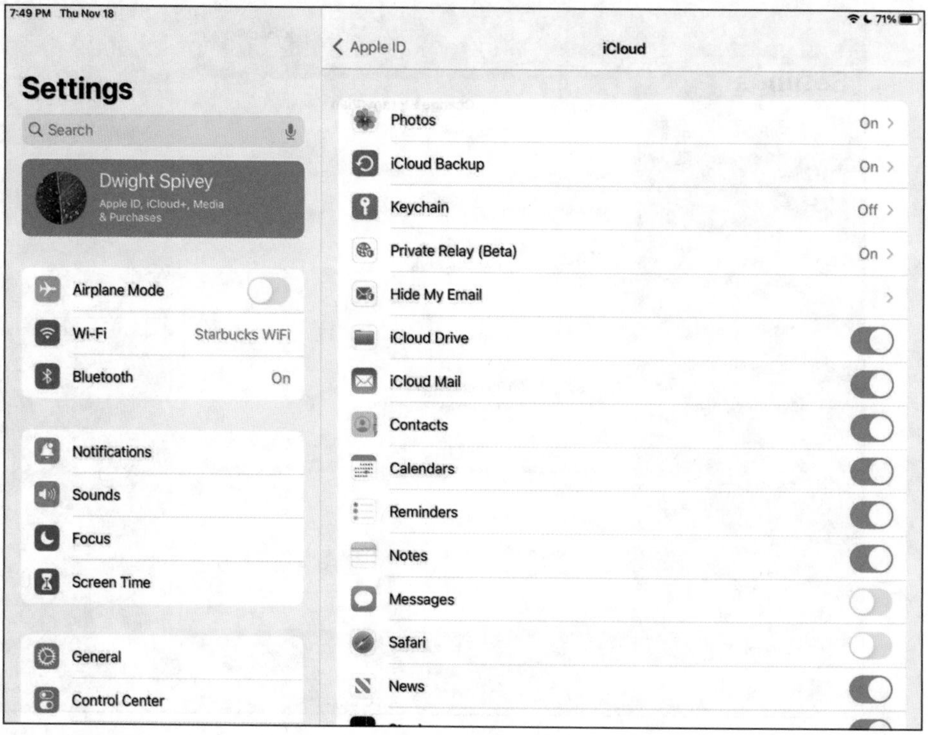

FIGURE 3-4

Set Up iCloud Sync Settings

When you have an iCloud account up and running, you have to specify which type of content iCloud should sync with your iPad. Follow these steps:

1. Tap Settings, tap your Apple ID at the top of the screen, and then tap iCloud.

2. In the iCloud settings shown in **Figure 3-5**, tap the On/Off switch for any item that's turned off that you want to turn on (or vice versa).

   You can sync Photos, Mail, Contacts, Calendars, Reminders, Safari, Notes, News, Wallet, Keychain (an app that stores all your passwords and even credit card numbers across all Apple devices), and more. The listing of apps on this screen isn't alphabetical, so scroll down if at first you don't see what you're looking for.

TIP

   If you want to allow iCloud to provide a service for locating a lost or stolen iPad, tap your Apple ID in Settings, tap Find My, tap Find My iPad, and then toggle the On/Off switch in the Find My iPad field to On (green) to activate it.

   This service helps you locate, send a message to, or delete content from your iPad if it falls into other hands.

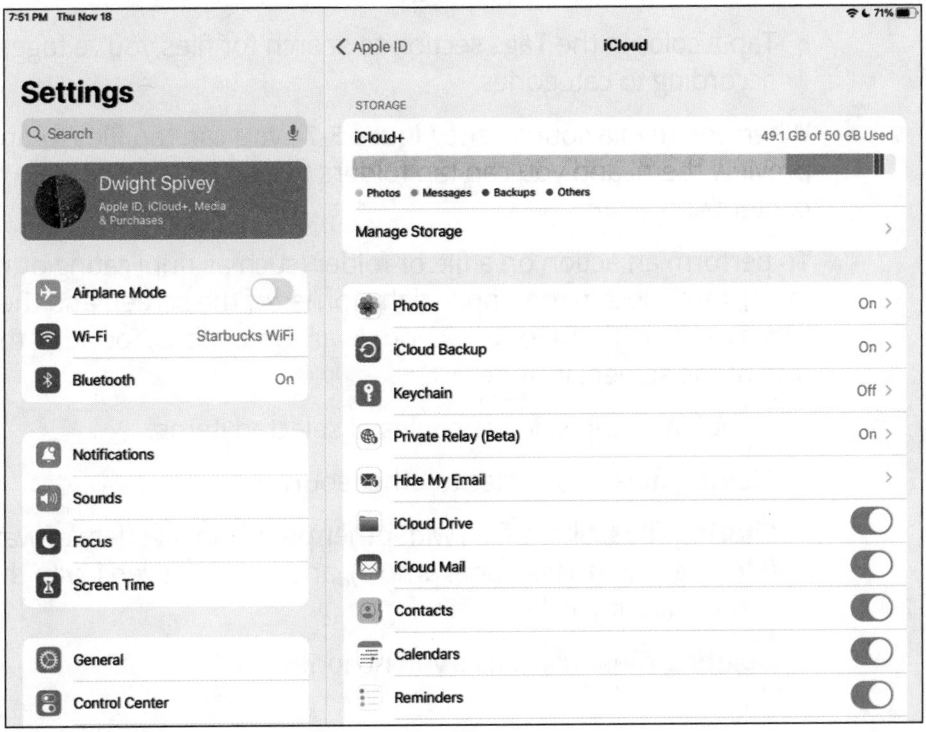

FIGURE 3-5

Browse Your iPad's Files

Longtime iPad users have pined for a way to browse files stored on their devices, as opposed to being limited to finding documents and other files within the apps they're intended for or created by. Finally, a few iPadOS iterations back, the Files app came along to allow you to browse not only for files stored on your iPad but also for stuff you've stored on other online (cloud) services, such as Google Drive, Drop-box, and others.

You'll find the Files app on the first Home screen, by default.

1. Tap the Files icon to open the app.

2. On the Browse screen (see **Figure 3-6**):

    - Tap the Search field to search for items by title or content.

    - Tap a source in the Locations or Favorites sections to browse a particular service or your iPad.

    - Tap a color in the Tags section to search for files you've tagged according to categories.

3. When you're in a source (see **Figure 3-7**), you can tap files to open or preview them, and you can tap folders to open them and view their contents.

4. To perform an action on a file or folder (such as duplicating or moving it), tap Select in the upper-right corner of the screen and then tap items to select them for an action. Available actions, found at the bottom of the screen, include

    - **Duplicating files:** Make copies of selected items.

    - **Moving files:** Move files to other sources.

    - **Sharing files:** Share files with other people in a variety of ways (Messages and Mail, for example), and you can even invite them to make edits, if you like.

    - **Deleting files:** Trash files you no longer need.

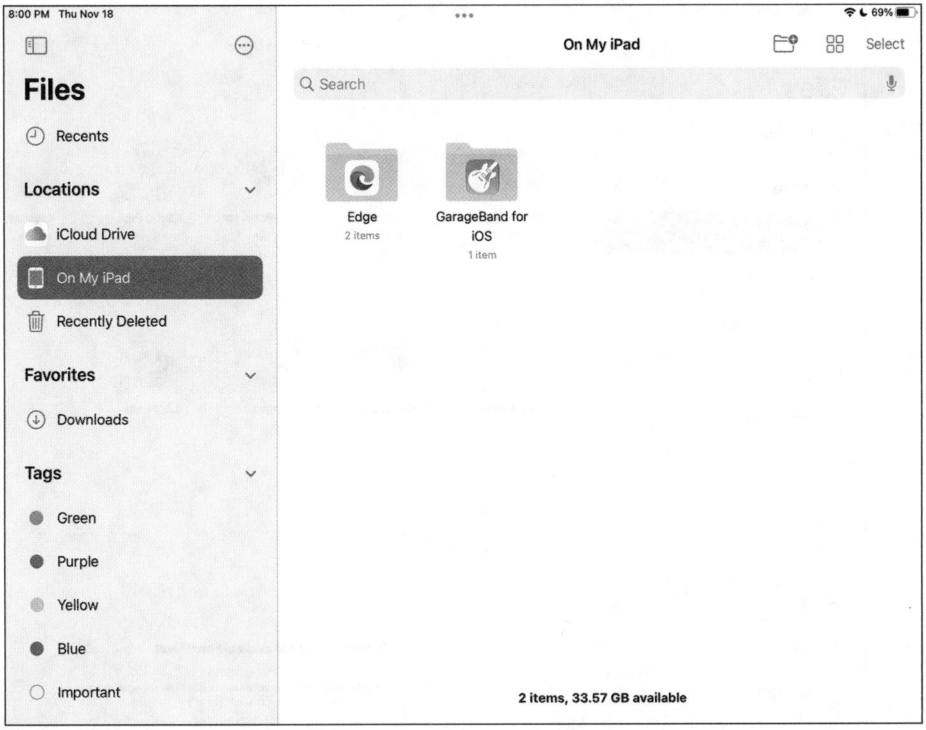

FIGURE 3-6

USE EXTERNAL STORAGE

iPhone and iPad users have been asking Apple for quite a while to allow the use of external storage devices, such as SD cards, USB devices, or hard drives. You can connect such devices to your iPad now using your iPad's Lightning port. You'll need to make sure that your external device will connect to the charging port on your iPad, usually requiring an adapter. Apple has a Lightning-to-SD Card adapter that will enable you to use SD cards (from your camera, for example) with your iPad (if it has a Lightning connector).

Every external storage device uses a file format, and Apple supports ExFAT, FAT32, HFS+, and APFS formats in the Files app. Be sure your external devices support one of those file formats before attempting to use them with your iPad. Also, some devices may need to be connected to an external power source. Again, check with the manufacturer of the device to find out if this is necessary.

FIGURE 3-7

TIP

If you need to retrieve a file you've deleted (you have 30 days to do so before it disappears forever into the digital ether), go to the Browse screen (if you're not already there) and tap Recently Deleted in the left toolbar. Tap Select in the upper-right corner, tap the file you'd like to retrieve, and tap the Recover button at the bottom of the screen. The file will be placed back in the location it was originally deleted from. Please note that some services may not allow you to retrieve a file you've deleted, so if you don't see the file you're looking for, contact that particular service for help.

2

Beginning to Use Your iPad

Chapter **4**

Making Your iPad More Accessible

iPad users are a very diverse group, and some face visual, motor, or hearing challenges. If you're one of these folks, you'll be glad to know that Apple offers some handy accessibility features for your iPad.

To make your screen easier to read, you can use the Magnifier, adjust the brightness, or change the wallpaper. You can also set up the VoiceOver feature to read onscreen elements out loud. Voice Control, Numbers, and Grids are welcome accessibility features to help you navigate more easily. Then there is a slew of features that you can turn on or off, including Zoom, Invert Colors, Speak Selection, Large Type, and more.

If hearing is your challenge, you can do the obvious thing and adjust the system volume. The iPad also allows you to use mono audio (useful when you're wearing headphones) and an LED flash when an alert sounds.

Features that help you deal with physical and motor challenges include an AssistiveTouch feature for those who have difficulty using the iPad touchscreen, Switch Control for working with adaptive accessories, and the Home Button and Call Audio Routing settings, which allow you to adjust how quickly you have to tap the iPad screen to work with features and whether you can use a headset or speaker to answer calls.

The Guided Access feature helps if you have difficulty focusing on one task. It also provides a handy mode for showing presentations of content in settings where you don't want users to flit off to other apps, as in school or a public kiosk.

This chapter covers these and more accessibility features of iPadOS 15.

Use Magnifier

The Magnifier app uses your iPad's camera to help you magnify objects. Magnifier is considered an accessibility feature, but almost everyone needs a magnifier at one time or another. To utilize Magnifier:

1. Tap the Magnifier app icon to open it. By default, it resides on the second Home screen.

2. Point your iPad's camera at the object you want to magnify.

3. Drag the magnification slider (shown in **Figure 4-1**) to increase or decrease magnification.

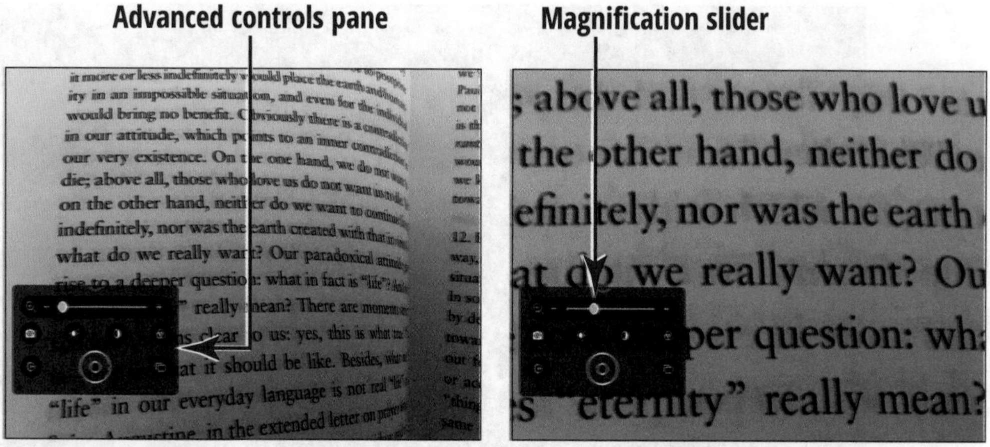

Advanced controls pane   **Magnification slider**

FIGURE 4-1

By default, Magnifier offers an advanced controls pane (refer to **Figure 4-1**) with more controls to help customize your experience. You can select which camera to use, adjust brightness and contrast levels, and apply color filters. You can also take freeze frames if you want to freeze something onscreen momentarily by tapping the large round button.

TIP

Freeze frames are not saved to Photos. They disappear into the ether when you close the Magnifier app.

Tap the Customize Controls button (looks like a gear and is in the lower left of the advanced controls pane) to open the Customize Controls dialog, as shown in **Figure 4-2**. From here, you can determine which controls appear in the advanced controls pane. To remove a control, tap the red circle containing the, minus sign (–) found to the left of the control name; then tap the Remove button that appears on the right. To add a control you've removed, simply tap the green circle containing the plus sign (+).

TIP

You can combine magnification with your iPad's portability so that you can reach up to (or behind) an object and magnify something that would not only be too small to see otherwise but would be out of view entirely.

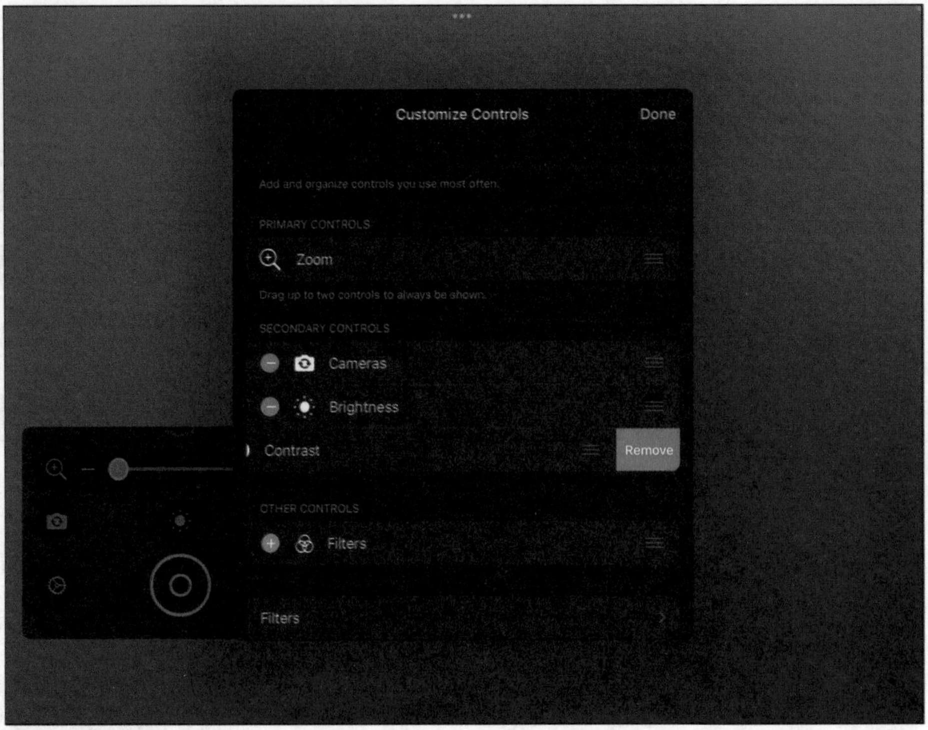

FIGURE 4-2

Set Brightness and Night Shift

Especially when using your iPad as an e-reader, you may find that a slightly less bright screen reduces strain on your eyes. To manually adjust screen brightness, follow these steps:

1. Tap the Settings icon on the Home screen.

> **TIP**
>
> If glare from the screen is a problem for you, consider getting a screen protector. This thin film both protects your screen from damage and reduces glare. You can easily find them on Amazon, and just about any cellphone dealer or tech store carries them.

2. In Settings, go to Accessibility ➪ Display & Text Size.

3. Tap the Auto-Brightness On/Off switch (see **Figure 4-3**) to turn off this feature (the button turns white when off). You may need to scroll down to the bottom of the Display & Text Size list to find this option.

Settings	‹ Accessibility	Display & Text Size

Sounds

Focus

Screen Time

General

Control Center

Display & Brightness

Home Screen & Dock

Accessibility

Wallpaper

Siri & Search

Apple Pencil

Touch ID & Passcode

Battery

Privacy

Increase Contrast

Increase color contrast between app foreground and background colors.

Differentiate Without Color

Replaces user interface items that rely solely on color to convey information with alternatives.

Smart Invert

Smart Invert reverses the colors of the display, except for images, media and some apps that use dark color styles.

Classic Invert

Classic Invert reverses the colors of the display.

Color Filters   Off ›

Color filters can be used to differentiate colors by users who are color blind and aid users who have difficulty reading text on the display.

Reduce White Point

Reduce the intensity of bright colors.

Auto-Brightness

Turning off auto-brightness may affect battery life.

FIGURE 4-3

4. Tap Display & Brightness on the left side of the screen, and then tap and drag the Brightness slider (see **Figure 4-4**) to the right to make the screen brighter or to the left to make it dimmer.

5. Press the Home button or swipe up on the screen (for iPad models without a Home button) to close Settings.

TIP

In the Apple Books e-reader app, you can set a sepia tone for the page. This might be easier on your eyes. See Chapter 12 for more about using Apple Books.

Night Shift is another option in Display & Brightness that you can use during hours of darkness. It changes the screen colors to reduce the amount of blue in the images on your iPad. Bright blue light seems to interfere with sleep in some people, so turning on Night Shift if you read before bed (or in bed) may help you sleep better.

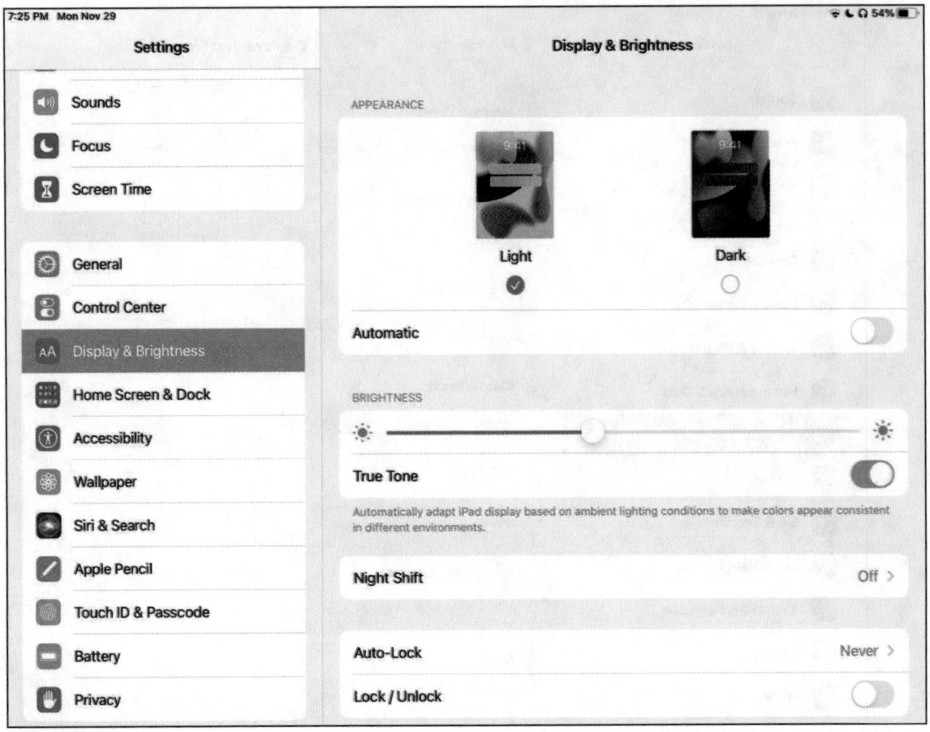

FIGURE 4-4

TIP

You can schedule Night Shift to be automatically enabled at certain times, or you can manually enable it when needed.

Change the Wallpaper

The default iPad background image on your iPad may be pretty, but it may not be the one that works best for you. Choosing different wallpaper may help you to more easily see all the icons on your Home screen. Follow these steps:

1. Tap the Settings icon on the Home screen.

2. In Settings, tap Wallpaper.

3. In the Wallpaper settings, tap Choose a New Wallpaper.

4. Tap a wallpaper category, shown in **Figure 4-5,** to view choices.

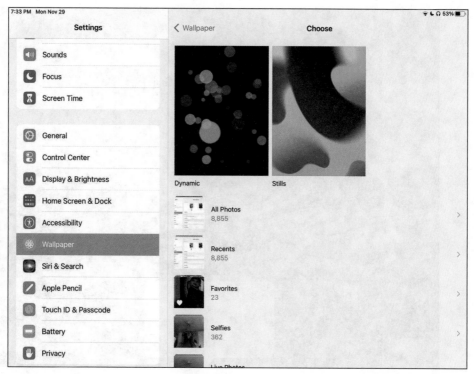

FIGURE 4-5

5. Tap a sample to select it.

TIP

If you prefer to use a picture that's on your iPad, tap an album in the lower part of the Wallpaper screen to locate a picture; tap to use it as your wallpaper.

6. In the preview that appears (see **Figure 4-6**), tap the Set button in the lower right, and then tap your choice of

- Set Lock Screen (the screen that appears when you lock the iPad by tapping the power button)

- Set Home Screen

- Set Both

Some wallpaper may allow you to select one of the following:

- Still (the picture is static)

- Perspective (the picture seems to move when you move your iPad)

FIGURE 4-6

7. Press the Home button or swipe up from the bottom of the screen (for iPad models without a Home button).

You return to your Home screen with the new wallpaper set as the background.

Set Up VoiceOver

VoiceOver reads the names of screen elements and settings to you, but it also changes the way you provide input to the iPad. In Notes, for example, you can have VoiceOver read the name of the Notes buttons to you, and when you enter notes, it reads words or characters that you've entered. It can also tell you whether such features as Auto-Correction are on.

VoiceOver is even smarter in iPadOS 15 than in previous incarnations. It includes support for apps and websites that may not have built-in accessibility support. It can read descriptions of images in apps and on the web, and it can identify and speak text it finds in images.

To turn on VoiceOver, follow these steps:

1. Tap the Settings icon on the Home screen.

2. In Settings, tap Accessibility.

3. In the Accessibility pane, tap VoiceOver.

4. In the VoiceOver pane, shown in **Figure 4-7,** tap the VoiceOver On/ Off switch to turn on this feature (the button becomes green). With VoiceOver on, you must first single-tap to select an item such as a button, which causes VoiceOver to read the name of the button to you. Then you double-tap the button to activate its function.

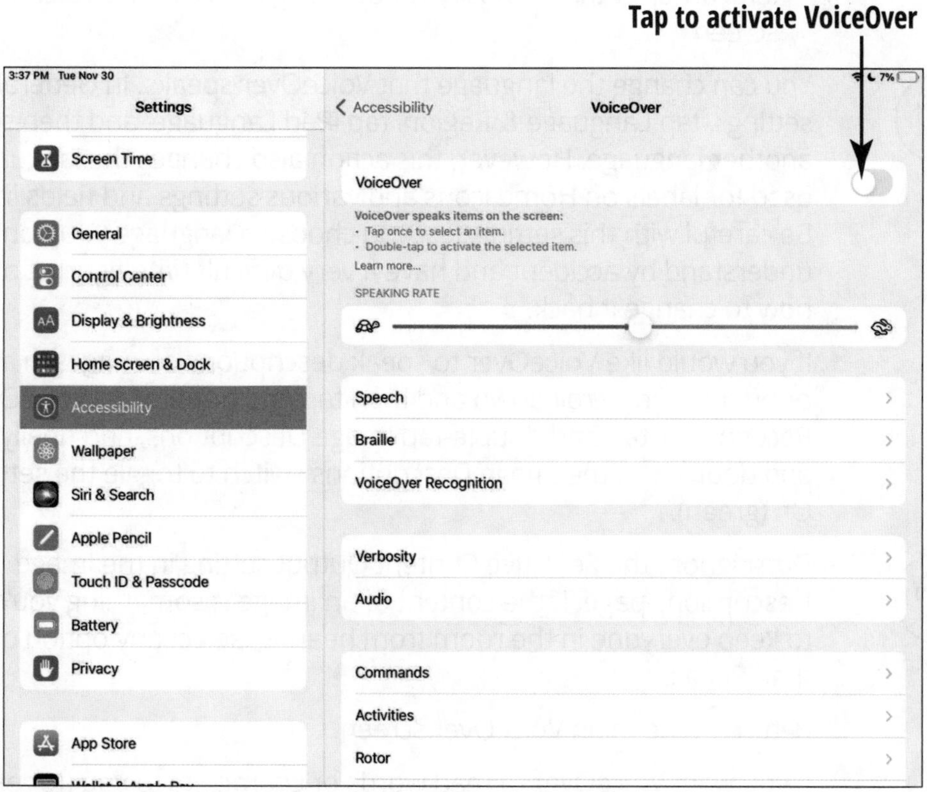

FIGURE 4-7

5. Tap the VoiceOver Practice button to select it and then double-tap the button to open VoiceOver Practice. (This is the new method of tapping that VoiceOver activates.) Practice using gestures (such as pinching or flicking left), and VoiceOver tells you what action each gesture initiates.

6. Tap the Done button and then double-tap the same button to return to the VoiceOver dialog.

7. Tap the Verbosity button once and then double-tap to open its options:

- Tap the Speak Hints On/Off switch and then double-tap the switch to turn the feature on (or off). VoiceOver speaks the name of each tapped item.

- Tap once and then double-tap the VoiceOver button in the upper-left corner of the Verbosity window to go back to the VoiceOver screen.

TIP

You can change the language that VoiceOver speaks. In General settings, tap Language & Region, tap iPad Language, and then select another language. However, this action also changes the language used for labels on Home icons and various settings and fields in iPad. Be careful with this setting, lest you choose a language you don't understand by accident and have a very difficult time figuring out how to change it back.

8. If you would like VoiceOver to speak descriptions of images in apps or on the web, scroll down and then tap and double-tap VoiceOver Recognition, tap and double-tap Image Descriptions, and finally tap and double-tap the Image Descriptions switch to toggle the setting to On (green).

TIP

Don't ignore the Sensitive Content Output setting in the Image Descriptions page. If the content of an image is something you'd like to keep everyone in the room from hearing, select any option other than Speak.

9. Return to the main VoiceOver screen.

10. If you want VoiceOver to read words or characters to you (for example, in the Notes app), scroll down, tap and double-tap Typing, and then tap and double-tap Typing Feedback.

11. In the Typing Feedback dialog, tap and then double-tap to select the option you prefer in both the Software Keyboards section and the Hardware Keyboards section.

The Words option causes VoiceOver to read words to you but not characters, such as the "dollar sign" ($). The Characters and Words option causes VoiceOver to read both characters and words.

12. Press the Home button or swipe up from the bottom of the screen (iPad models without a Home button) to return to the Home screen.

The following section shows how to navigate your iPad after you've turned on VoiceOver.

You can use the Accessibility Shortcut setting to help you more quickly turn the VoiceOver, Zoom, Switch Control, Grayscale, AssistiveTouch, or Invert Colors features on and off:

1. In the Accessibility screen, tap Accessibility Shortcut (near the very bottom of the screen).

2. In the screen that appears, choose what you want three presses of the Home button (or Top button, for iPads without a Home button) to activate. Now three presses with a single finger on the Home button or Top button (depending on your iPad model) provide you with the option you selected wherever you go in iPad.

Use VoiceOver

After VoiceOver is turned on (see preceding section), you need to figure out how to use it. I won't kid you — using it is awkward at first, but you'll get the hang of it.

Here are the main onscreen gestures you should know how to use:

» **Tap an item to select it.** VoiceOver then speaks its name.

» **Double-tap the selected item.** This action activates the item.

» **Flick three fingers.** It takes three fingers to scroll around a page with VoiceOver turned on.

The first time my iPad locked when using VoiceOver, I had no idea how to unlock it. Luckily, I found the answer by consulting Apple's support site from a computer. If your iPad has a Home button, just press it to unlock — simple. However, if your iPad doesn't have a Home button, you need to look at your iPad (for Face ID to recognize you) and then slowly move your finger up from the bottom of the screen until you hear two tones, which indicate that your screen is unlocked.

If tapping with two or three fingers seems difficult for you, try tapping with one finger from one hand and one or two from the other. When double- or triple-tapping, you have to perform these gestures as quickly and as precisely as you can for them to work.

Table 4-1 provides additional gestures to help you use VoiceOver. If you want to use this feature often, I recommend the VoiceOver section of the iPad online User Guide, which goes into great detail about using VoiceOver. You find the User Guide at `https://support.apple.com/manuals/iPad`. When there, just click the model of iPad or the version of iPad OS you have to read its manual. You can also get an Apple Books version of the manual through that app in the Book Store (see Chapter 12 for more information).

Check out some of the settings for VoiceOver, including a choice for Braille, Language Rotor for making language choices, the ability to navigate images, and a setting to have iPad speak notifications.

TABLE 4-1   **VoiceOver Gestures**

Gesture	Effect
Flick right or left	Select the next or preceding item
Tap with two fingers	Stop or continue speaking the current item
Flick two fingers up	Read everything from the top of the screen
Flick two fingers down	Read everything from the current position
Flick three fingers up or down	Scroll one page at a time
Flick three fingers right or left	Go to the next or preceding page
Tap three fingers	Speak the scroll status (for example, line 20 of 100)
Flick four fingers up or down	Go to the first or last element on a page
Flick four fingers right or left	Go to the next or preceding section (as on a web page)

Make Additional Vision Settings

Several Vision features are simple on/off settings that you can turn on or off after you tap Settings ➪ Accessibility:

» **Zoom:** The Zoom feature enlarges the contents displayed on the iPad screen when you double-tap the screen with three fingers. The Zoom feature works almost everywhere in iPad: in Photos, on web pages, on your Home screens, in your Mail, in Music, and in Videos. Give it a try!

» **Spoken Content:** Options here include the ability to have your iPad speak items you've selected or to hear the content of an entire screen, highlight content as it's spoken, and more.

» **Display & Text Size:** Includes such features as

- Color Filters (aids in case of color blindness)
- Reduce White Point (helps reduce the intensity of bright colors)

- Invert Colors (which reverses colors on your screen so that white backgrounds are black and black text is white). Classic Invert inverts all colors, and Smart Invert does not invert colors for items like images, multimedia, and some apps that may use darker color styles.

TIP

The Invert Colors feature works well in some places and not so well in others. For example, in the Photos application, pictures appear almost as photo negatives (which is a really cool trick to try). Your Home screen image likewise looks a bit strange. And don't even think of playing a video with this feature turned on! However, if you need help reading text, White on Black can be useful in several apps.

» **Larger Text (under Accessibility ⇨ Display & Text Size):** If having larger text in such apps as Contacts, Mail, and Notes would be helpful to you, you can turn on the Larger Text feature and choose the text size that works best for you.

» **Bold Text (under Accessibility ⇨ Display & Text Size):** Turning on this setting restarts your iPad (after asking you for permission to do so) and then causes text in various apps and in Settings to be bold.

» **Button Shapes (under Accessibility ⇨ Display & Text Size):** This setting applies shapes to buttons so that they're more easily distinguishable. For an example, check out the Accessibility button near the top of the screen after you enable Button Shapes by toggling its switch to On. Turn it back off and notice the difference (shown in **Figure 4-8;** the button name is underlined).

» **Reduce Transparency (under Accessibility ⇨ Display & Text Size):** This setting helps increase legibility of text by reducing blurring and transparency effects that make up a good deal of the iPad user interface.

» **Increase Contrast (under Accessibility ⇨ Display & Text Size):** Use this setting to set up backgrounds in some areas of the iPad and apps with greater contrast, which should improve visibility.

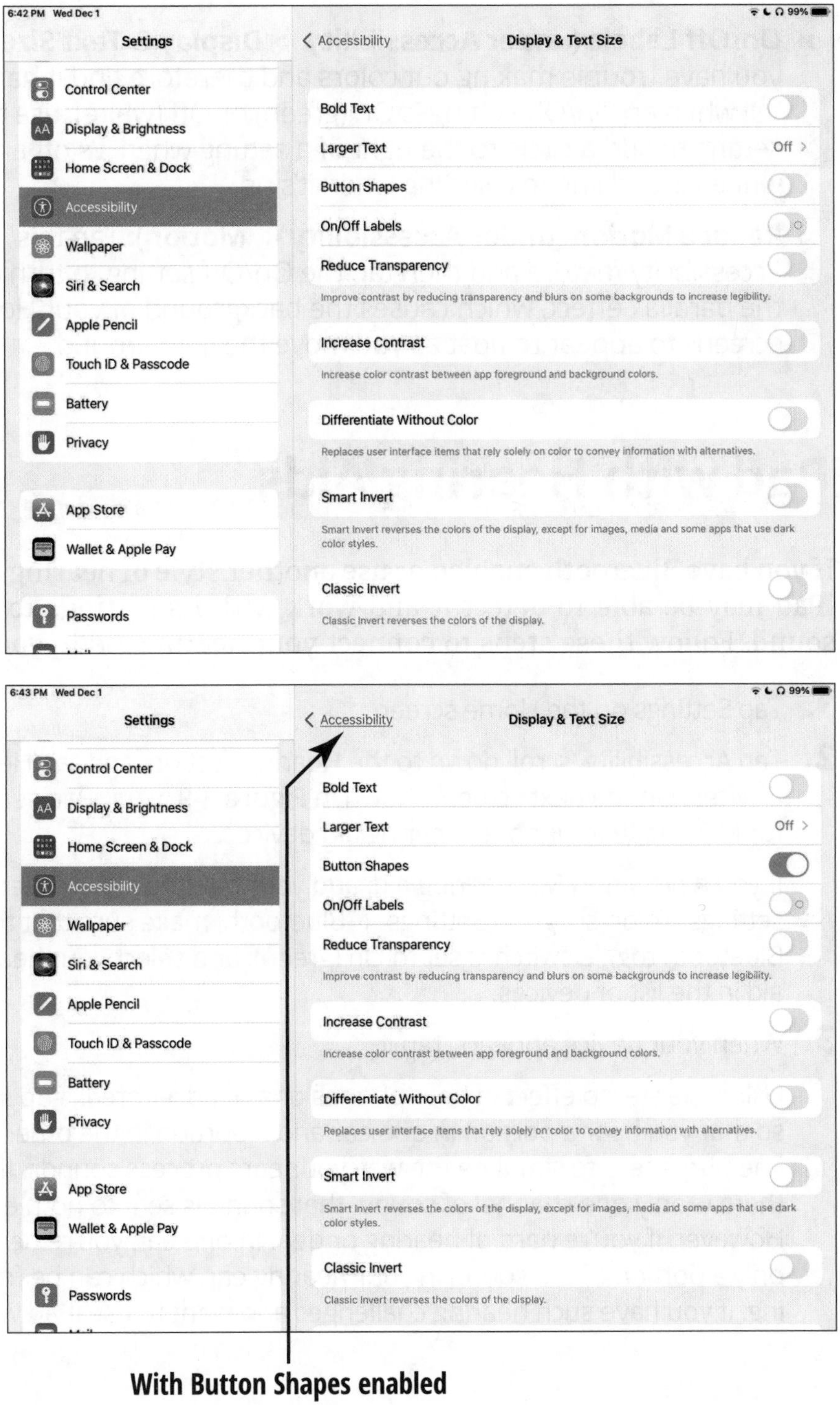

With Button Shapes enabled

FIGURE 4-8

- » **On/Off Labels (under Accessibility ⇨ Display & Text Size):** If you have trouble making out colors and therefore find it hard to tell when an On/Off setting is On (green) or Off (white), use this setting to add a circle to the right of a setting when it's off and a white vertical line to a setting when it's on.

- » **Reduce Motion (under Accessibility ⇨ Motion):** Tap this accessibility feature and then tap the On/Off setting to turn off the parallax effect, which causes the background of your Home screens to appear to float as you move the iPad around.

Use iPad with Hearing Aids

If you have Bluetooth enabled or use another style of hearing aid, your iPad may be able to detect it and work with its settings to improve sound. Follow these steps to connect your hearing aid to your iPad.

1. Tap Settings on the Home screen.

2. Tap Accessibility, scroll down to the Hearing section, and tap Hearing Devices. On the next screen, shown in **Figure 4-9,** your iPad searches for MFi (Made for iPhone) hearing aid devices.

TIP

If you have a non-MFi hearing aid, add your hearing aid in Bluetooth settings. To do so, go to Settings ⇨ Bluetooth, make sure that the Bluetooth toggle switch is set to On (green), and select your hearing aid in the list of devices.

3. When your device appears, tap it.

TIP

Using the stereo effect in headphones or a headset breaks up sounds so that you hear a portion in one ear and a portion in the other ear. The purpose is to simulate the way your ears process sounds. If there is only one channel of sound, that sound is sent to both ears. However, if you're hard of hearing or deaf in one ear, you're hearing only a portion of the sound in your hearing ear, which can be frustrating. If you have such hearing challenges and want to use iPad with a headset connected, you should turn on Mono Audio (go to Settings ⇨ Accessibility ⇨ Audio & Visual). When it's turned on, all sound is combined and distributed to both ears. You can use the slider below Mono Audio to direct more sound to the ear you hear best with.

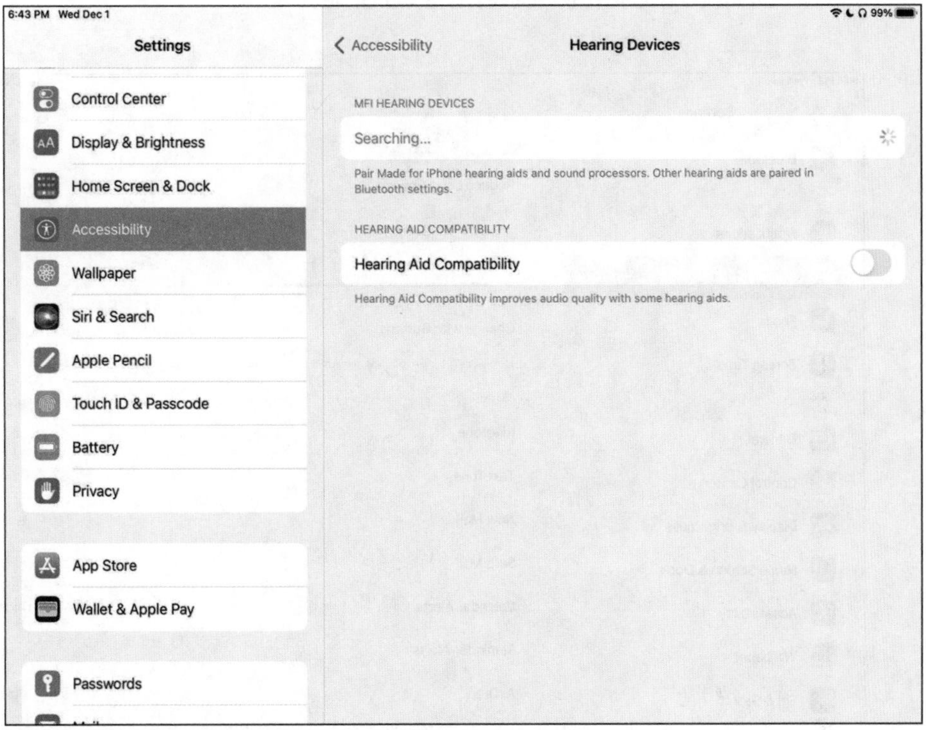

FIGURE 4-9

Adjust the Volume

Though individual apps (such as Music and TV) have their own volume settings, you can set your iPad system volume for your ringer and alerts as well to help you better hear what's going on. Follow these steps:

1. Tap Settings on the Home screen and then tap Sounds.

In the Sounds settings, you can turn on or off the sounds that iPad makes when certain events occur (such as receiving new Mail or Calendar alerts). These sounds are turned on by default.

2. In the Sounds settings that appear (see **Figure 4-10**), tap and drag the Ringer and Alerts slider to adjust the volume of these audible attention grabbers:

- Drag to the right to increase the volume.

- Drag to the left to lower the volume.

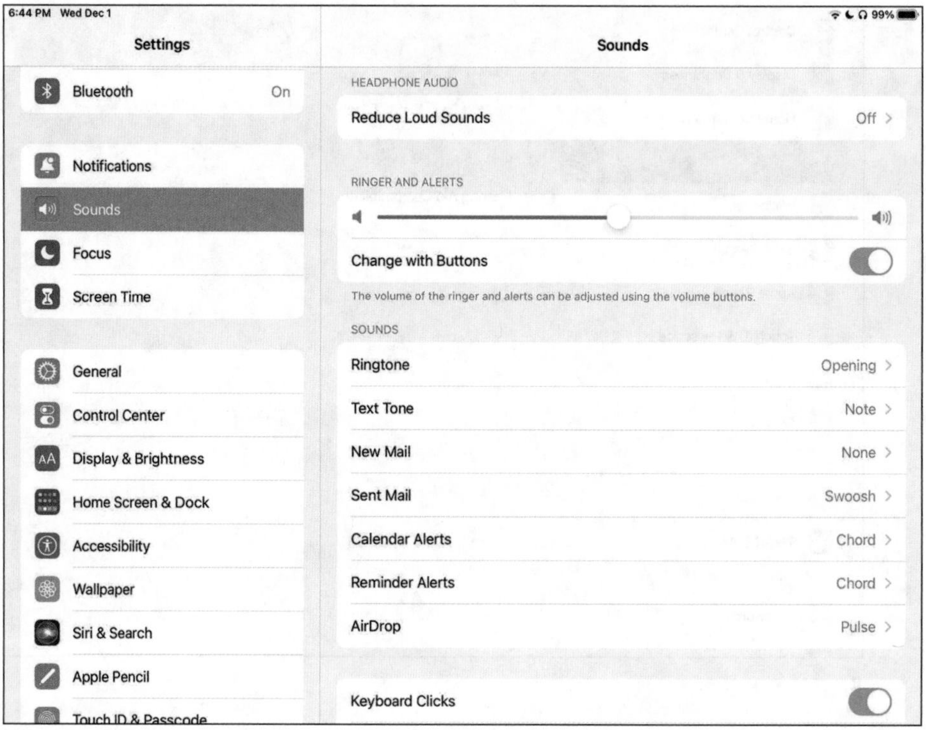

FIGURE 4-10

3. Press the Home button or swipe up from the bottom of the screen to return to the Home screen.

Set Up Subtitles and Captioning

Closed captioning and subtitles help folks with hearing challenges enjoy entertainment and educational content. Follow these steps:

1. Tap Settings on the Home screen and then tap Accessibility.

2. Scroll down to the Hearing section and tap Subtitles & Captioning.

3. On the following screen, tap the On/Off switch to turn on Closed Captions + SDH (Subtitles for the Deaf and Hard of Hearing).

   You can also tap Style and choose a text style for the captions, as shown in **Figure 4-11.** A neat video helps show you what your style will look like when the feature is in use. Tap the black box in the lower right of the video to expand it to full screen. Tap the screen to return to the Style screen.

4. Press the Home button or swipe up from the bottom of the screen to return to the Home screen.

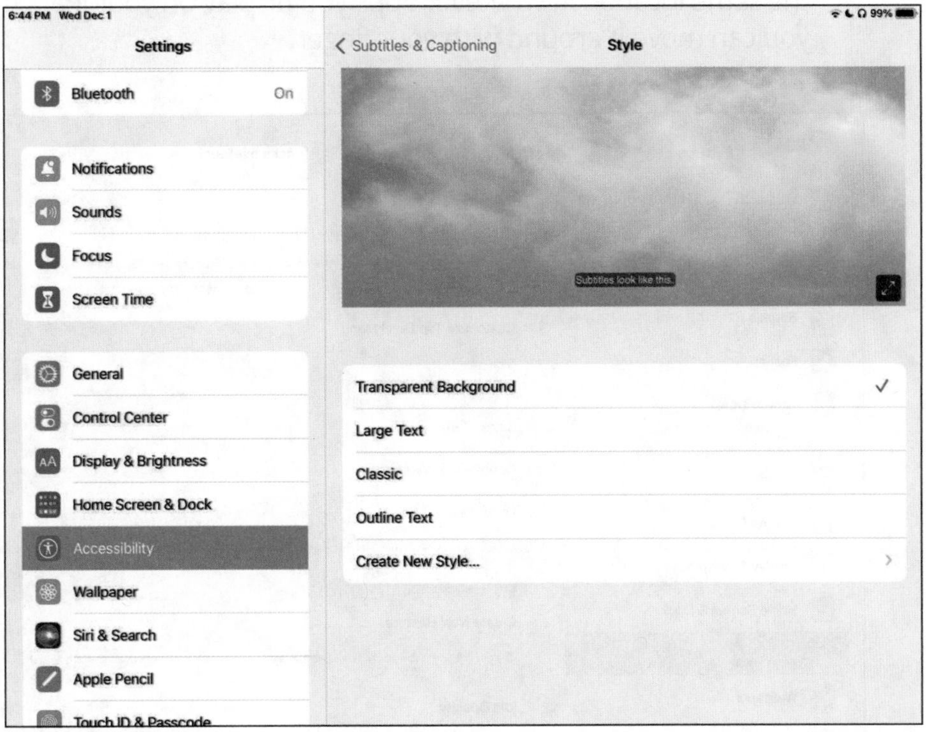

FIGURE 4-11

Turn On and Work with AssistiveTouch

If you have difficulty using buttons, the AssistiveTouch Control Panel aids input using the touchscreen.

1. To turn on AssistiveTouch, tap Settings on the Home screen and then tap Accessibility.

2. In the Accessibility pane, scroll down and tap Touch; then tap AssistiveTouch. In the pane that appears, tap the On/Off switch for AssistiveTouch to turn it to On (see **Figure 4-12**). A black square (called the AssistiveTouch Control Panel) then appears on the right side of the screen; you see it on your iPad's screen, but it doesn't display in screenshots, such as **Figure 4-12.** This square now appears in the same location in whatever apps you display on your iPad, though you can move it around with your finger.

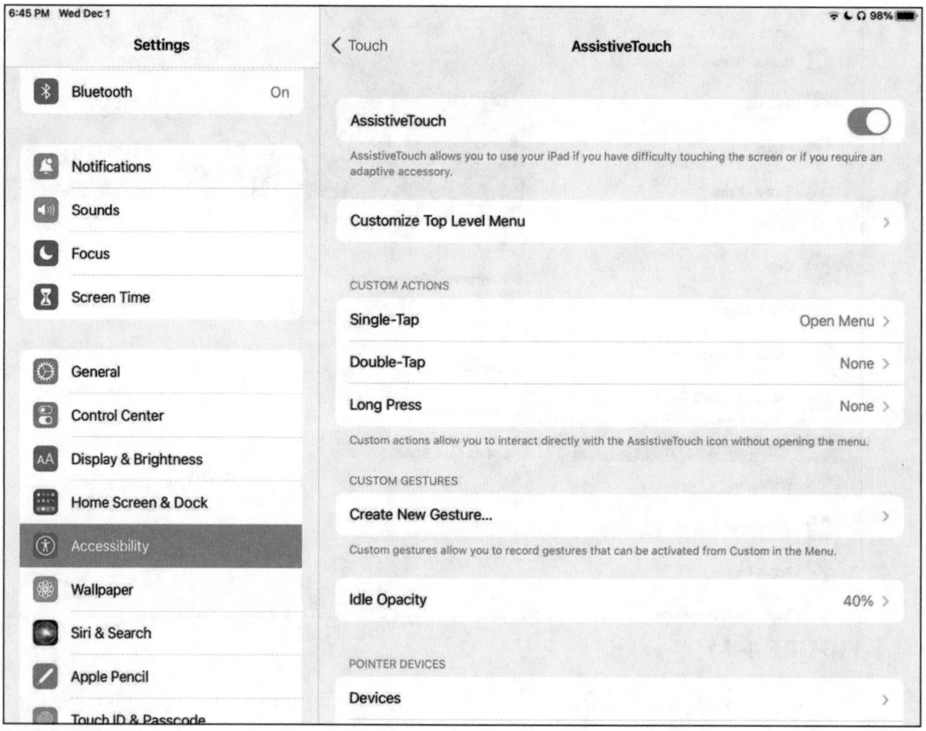

FIGURE 4-12

3. Tap the AssistiveTouch Control Panel to display options, as shown in **Figure 4-13.** The panel includes Notifications and Control Center options.

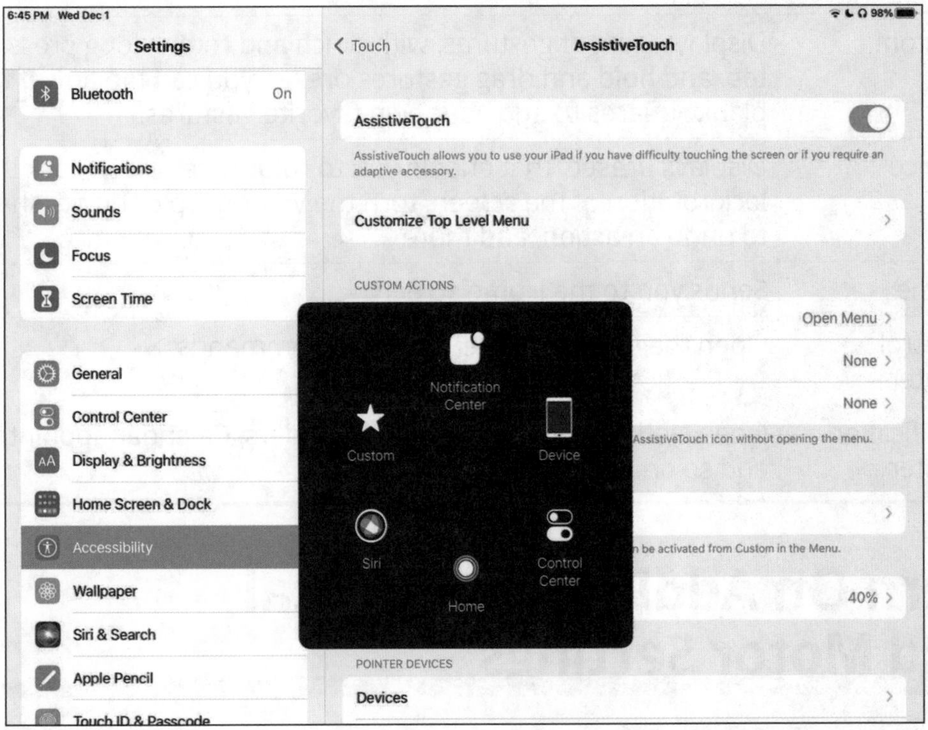

FIGURE 4-13

4. You can tap Custom or Device on the panel to see additional choices; tap Siri to activate the personal assistant feature; tap Notifications or Control Center to display those panels; or tap Home to go directly to the Home screen. After you choose an option, pressing the Home button or swiping up from the bottom of the screen (iPad models without a Home button) takes you back to the Home screen.

Table 4-2 shows the major options available in the AssistiveTouch Control panel and their purposes.

TABLE 4-2   AssistiveTouch Controls

Control	Purpose
Siri	Activates the Siri feature, which allows you to speak questions and make requests of your iPad.
Custom	Displays a set of gestures, with pinch and rotate, long press, double-tap, and hold and drag gestures preset; you can tap any of the other blank squares to add your own favorite gestures.
Device	Displays presets that enable you to rotate the screen, lock the screen, lock rotation of the screen, turn the volume up or down, shake iPad to undo an action, and more.
Home	Sends you to the Home screen.
Control Center	Open the Control Center common commands.
Notification Center	Open Notification Center with reminders, Calendar appointments, and so on.

Turn On Additional Physical and Motor Settings

Use these On/Off settings in the Accessibility settings to help you deal with how fast you tap and how you answer incoming calls:

» **Home Button (appears only for iPad models that have one):** Sometimes if you have dexterity challenges, it's hard to double-press or triple-press the Home button fast enough to make an effect. Choose the Slow or Slowest option when you tap this setting to allow you a bit more time to make that second or third press. Also, the Rest Finger to Open feature at the bottom of the screen is helpful by allowing you to simply rest your finger on the Home button to open your iPad using Touch ID (if enabled), as opposed to needing to press the Home button.

» **Call Audio Routing (under Accessibility ⇨ Touch):** If you prefer to use your speaker phone to receive incoming calls, or you typically use a Bluetooth headset with your iPad that allows you to tap a button to receive a call, tap this option and then choose Bluetooth Headset or Speaker. Speakers and headsets can both provide a better hearing experience for many.

TIP

If you have certain adaptive accessories that allow you to control devices with head gestures, you can use them to control your iPad, highlighting features in sequence and then selecting one of those features. Use the Switch Control feature in the Accessibility settings to turn this mode on and make settings.

Focus Learning with Guided Access

Guided Access is a feature that you can use to limit a user's access to iPad to a single app, and even limit access in that app to certain features. This feature can be useful in a classroom, for someone with attention deficit disorder, and even in a public setting (such as a kiosk where you don't want users to be able to open other apps).

1. Tap Settings and then tap Accessibility.

2. Scroll down and tap Guided Access; then, on the screen that follows, tap the Guided Access switch to turn the feature to On (green).

3. Tap Passcode Settings and then tap Set Guided Access Passcode to activate a passcode so that those using an app can't return to the Home screen to access other apps. You may also activate Touch ID or Face ID (for iPad models without a Home button) to perform the same function.

4. In the Set Passcode dialog that appears (see **Figure 4-14**), enter a passcode using the numeric pad. Enter the number again when prompted.

5. Press the Home button or swipe up from the bottom of the screen (for iPad models without a Home button) to return to the Home screen, then tap an app to open it.

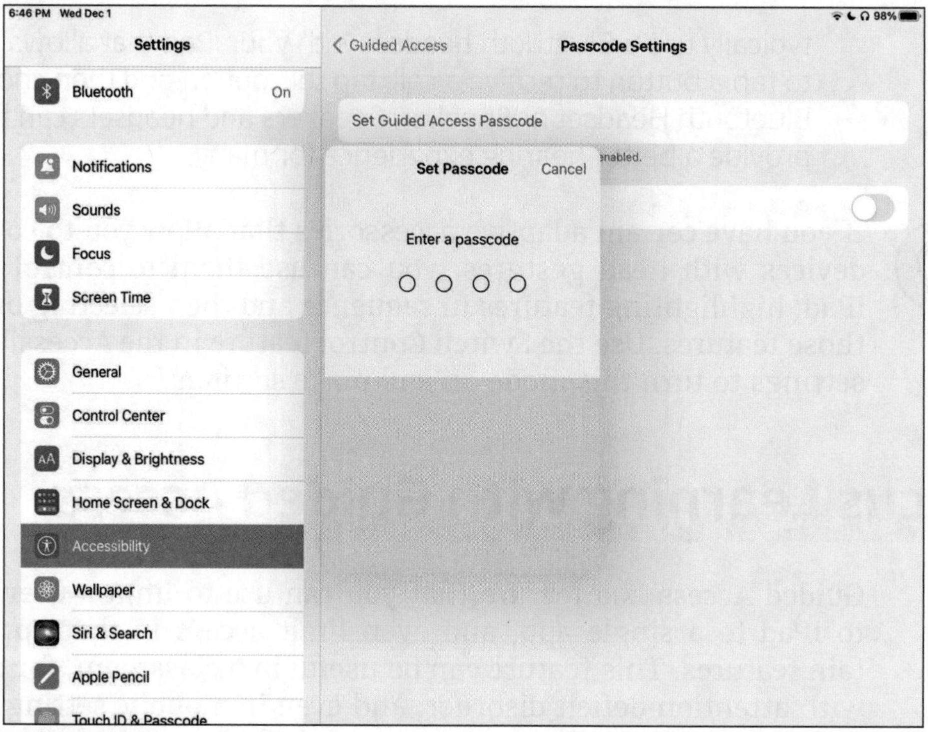

FIGURE 4-14

6. Rapidly press the Home button or Top button (for iPad models without a Home button) three times. You're presented with some Accessibility Shortcuts options on the screen. Tap the Guided Access button, and then tap the Options button along the bottom of the screen to display these options in a dialog window:

- **Sleep/Wake Button or Top Button (depending on your iPad model):** You can put your iPad to sleep or wake it up with three presses of the Home button or Top button.

- **Volume Buttons:** You can tap Always On or Always Off. If you don't want users to be able to adjust volume using the volume toggle on the side of the iPad, for example, use this setting.

- **Motion:** Turn this setting off if you don't want users to move the iPad around or switch viewing orientations — for example, to play a race car driving game in Landscape mode.

- **Keyboards:** Use this setting to prohibit people using this app from entering text using the keyboard.

- **Touch:** If you don't want users to be able to use the touchscreen, turn this off.

- **Time Limit:** Tap this and use settings that are displayed to set a time limit for the use of the app.

7. Tap outside the dialog window to hide the options.

At this point, you can also use your finger to circle areas of the screen that you want to disable, such as a Store button in the Music app.

8. Press the Start button (upper-right corner) and then press the Home button or Top button (for iPad models without a Home button) three times. Enter your passcode, if you set one, and tap End.

9. Tap the Home button or swipe up from the bottom of the screen (for iPad models without a Home button) again to return to the Home screen.

Control Your iPad with Voice Control

iPadOS 15 includes an exciting accessibility innovation: the ability to control your iPad using your voice! The Voice Control also enables you to use numbers and grid overlays to command your iPad to perform tasks. This feature is a real game changer for a lot of folks.

1. Tap Settings and then tap Accessibility.

2. Scroll down and tap Voice Control. Do one of the following:

- If you haven't used Voice Control before, on the screen that follows, tap Set Up Voice Control (shown in **Figure 4-15**). Read through the information screens, tapping Continue to advance through them. At the end, you'll see that the Voice Control toggle switch is set to On (green).

Pay particular attention to the What Can I Say? screen. It tells you in simple terms the commands you can use to get started with Voice Control, such as "Go home" and "Show grid."

- If you've used Voice Control before but have since disabled it, toggle the Voice Control switch to On (green).

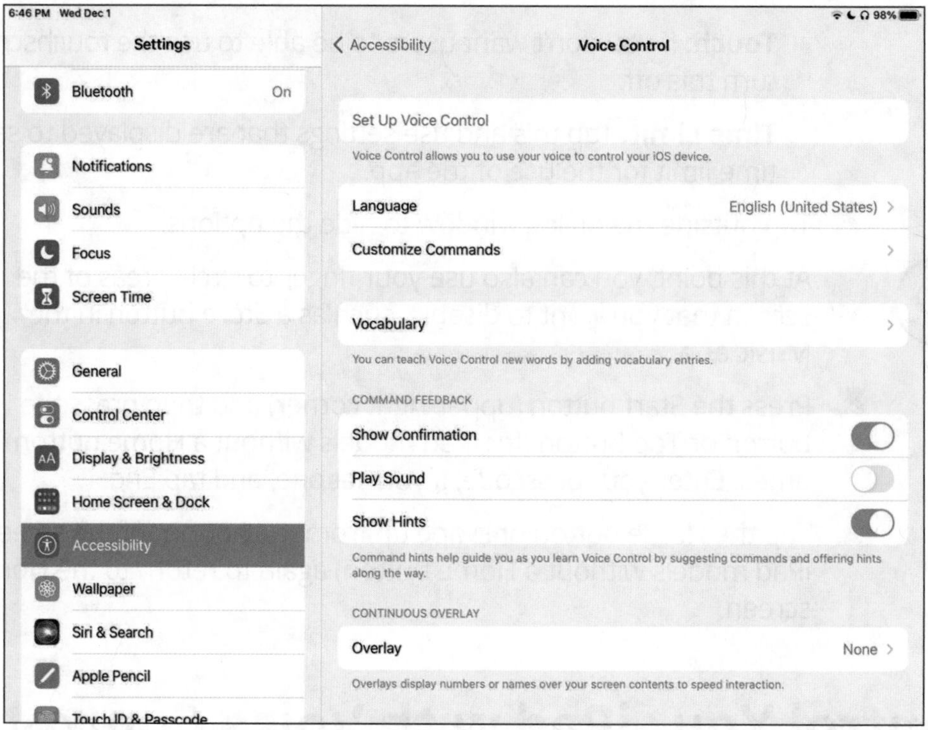
6:46 PM Wed Dec 1
98%
Settings
Bluetooth On
Notifications
Sounds
Focus
Screen Time
General
Control Center
Display & Brightness
Home Screen & Dock
Accessibility
Wallpaper
Siri & Search
Apple Pencil
Touch ID & Passcode
Accessibility
Voice Control
Set Up Voice Control
Voice Control allows you to use your voice to control your iOS device.
Language English (United States)
Customize Commands
Vocabulary
You can teach Voice Control new words by adding vocabulary entries.
COMMAND FEEDBACK
Show Confirmation
Play Sound
Show Hints
Command hints help guide you as you learn Voice Control by suggesting commands and offering hints along the way.
CONTINUOUS OVERLAY
Overlay None
Overlays display numbers or names over your screen contents to speed interaction.

FIGURE 4-15

TIP

You can easily tell when Voice Control is on because there will be a blue circle containing a microphone in the upper-right corner of your iPad's screen.

3. Tap Customize Commands to see what commands are built in to Voice Control (shown in **Figure 4-16**), enable or disable commands, and even create your own custom commands.

   I suggest taking your time in this section of the Voice Control options because you'll be surprised by how much you can do from the start with this amazing tool. Tap the Voice Control button in the upper-middle of the screen to return to the main Voice Control options.

4. You may need or want to use words that Voice Control doesn't know or understand, so Apple has given you the ability to add words. This ability is particularly useful with dictation. In the Voice Control options, tap Vocabulary and then tap the plus sign (+) in the upper right to add your own words. Type the word or phrase you'd like to

add in the Add New Entry window, and then tap the Save button. Tap Voice Control in the upper left to return to the main Voice Control screen.

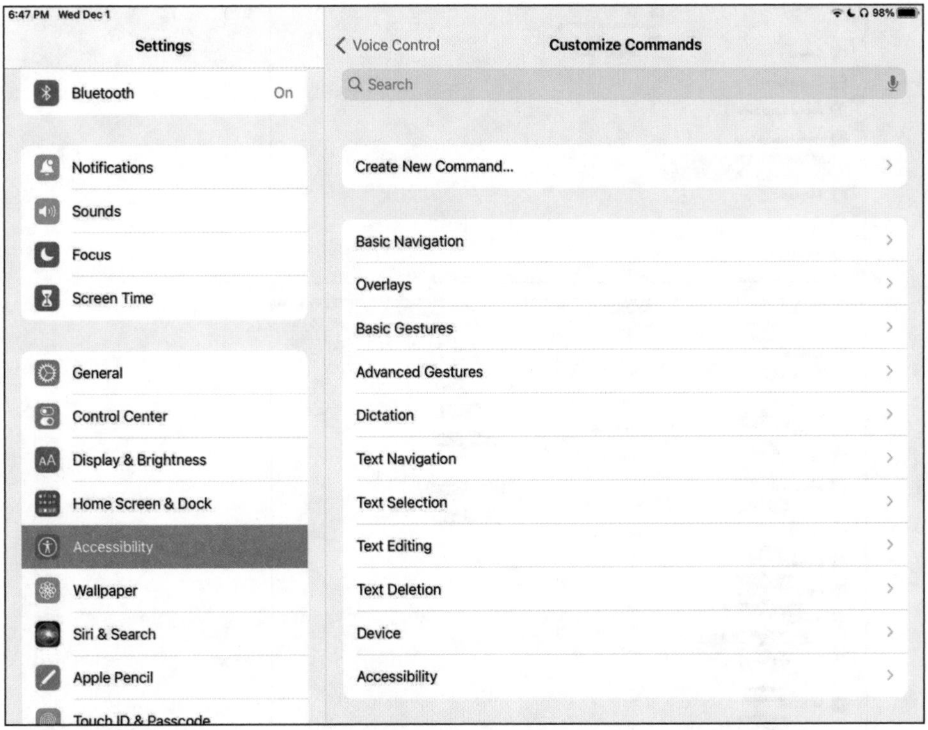

FIGURE 4-16

5. Overlays are a fantastic accessibility feature in iPadOS 15. If you use them, clickable items on the screen are labeled with numbers, names, or a numbered grid. Whenever you want to click an item, simply execute a command such as "tap three" to "tap" the item with your voice. Each of the three overlays is displayed in **Figure 4-17.**

The number and name labels fade to a light gray so that you can more clearly see the screen when not actively using the feature, but they darken again when you do use it.

TIP

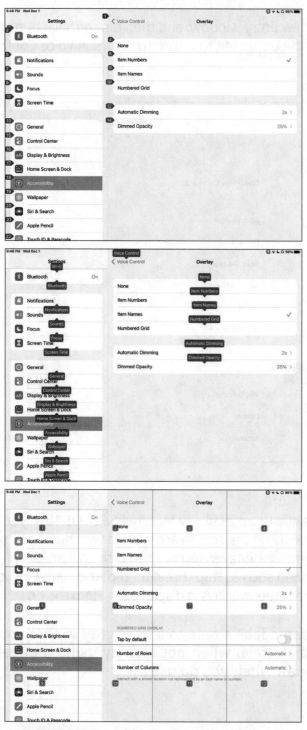

FIGURE 4-17

Chapter **5**

Conversing with Siri

One of the most talked about (pun intended) features on your iPad is Siri, a personal assistant feature that responds to the commands you speak to your iPad. With Siri, you can ask for nearby restaurants, and a list appears. You can dictate your email messages rather than type them. You can open apps or the App Store itself with a voice command. Placing a FaceTime call to your mother is as simple as saying, "Call Mom." Want to know the capital of Rhode Island? Just ask. Siri checks several online sources to answer questions ranging from the result of a mathematical equation to the next scheduled flight to Rome (Italy or Georgia). You can have Siri search photos and videos and locate what you need by date, location, or album name. Ask Siri to remind you about an app you're working in, such as Safari, Mail, or Notes, at a later time so that you can pick up where you left off.

You can also have Siri perform tasks, such as returning calls and controlling Music. Siri can play music at your request and identify tagged songs (songs that contain embedded information that identifies them by categories such as artist or genre) for you. You can also hail a ride with Uber or Lyft, watch live TV just by saying "Watch ESPN" (or, say, another app you might use, such as Netflix), find tagged photos, make payments with some third-party apps, and more.

With iPadOS 15, Siri can offer you curated suggestions for Safari, Maps, and Podcasts. Siri also features new voice technology that allows it to sound more natural and smooth, particularly when speaking long phrases. Another nice update to Siri in iPadOS 15 is that processing for Siri requests is now performed entirely on your iPad, if it has an A12 Bionic chipset or newer. This means that requests you make of Siri are performed much faster than before, which is always a treat.

Activate Siri

When you first turn on your iPad, Apple walks you through the process of registering and setting it up onscreen. Tap Get Started to begin making settings for your location, using iCloud, and so on, and at one point, you will see the option to activate Siri. As you begin to use your device, the iPad reminds you about using Siri by displaying a message.

If you buy a car with the Car Play feature, you can interact with your car using your voice and Siri.

Siri is available on the iPad only when you have Internet access, but remember that cellular data charges may apply when Siri checks online sources. In addition, Apple warns that available features may vary by area.

If you didn't activate Siri during the registration process, you can use Settings to turn Siri on by following these steps:

1. Tap the Settings icon on the Home screen.

2. Tap Siri & Search (see **Figure 5-1**).

Settings		Siri & Search

12:20 PM Fri Dec 3   🛜 🔋 63% ▮

Settings

- 🔤 Display & Brightness
- ▦ Home Screen & Dock
- ♿ Accessibility
- 🖼 Wallpaper
- ◼ **Siri & Search**
- ✏️ Apple Pencil
- 🔲 Touch ID & Passcode
- 🔋 Battery
- ✋ Privacy

- 🅰 App Store
- 💳 Wallet & Apple Pay

- 🔑 Passwords
- ✉️ Mail

Siri & Search

ASK SIRI

Listen for "Hey Siri"   ⬤◯

Press Home for Siri   ⬤◯

Allow Siri When Locked   ⬤◯

Language   English (United States) ›

Siri Voice   Australian (Voice 2) ›

Siri Responses   ›

Announce Calls   ›

Announce Notifications   ›

My Information   Dwight Spivey ›

Siri & Dictation History   ›

Voice input is processed on iPad, but transcripts of your requests are sent to Apple. About Ask Siri & Privacy...

CONTENT FROM APPLE

Show in Look Up   ⬤◯

Show in Spotlight   ⬤◯

FIGURE 5-1

3. In the Siri & Search dialog on the right, toggle the On/Off switch to On (green) to activate any or all of the following features:

- If you want to be able to activate Siri for hands-free use, toggle the Listen for "Hey Siri" switch to turn on the feature. When you first enable "Hey Siri," you'll be prompted to set up the feature. Just walk through the steps to enable it and continue.

  With this feature enabled, just say "Hey, Siri," and Siri opens up, ready for a command. In addition, with streaming voice recognition, Siri displays in text what it's hearing as you speak, so you can verify that it has understood you correctly. This streaming feature makes the whole process of interacting with Siri faster.

  TIP

  Some iPad models must be plugged into a power source to use the "Hey Siri" feature, and others don't. Visit `https://support.apple.com/en-us/HT209014` to find out whether your model supports using "Hey Siri" without needing to be plugged in.

- Press Home/Top Button for Siri requires you to press the Home button or the top button (for iPads without a Home button) to activate Siri.

- Allow Siri When Locked allows you to use Siri even when the iPad is locked.

Be careful with enabling this option. Others with nefarious intentions may be able to use it to access personal and sensitive information.

4. If you want to change the language Siri uses, tap Language and choose a different language in the list that appears.

5. To change the nationality or gender of Siri's voice from American to British or Australian (for example), or from female to male, tap Siri Voice and make your selections. Some nationalities have multiple voices that you can select.

Give several nationalities and genders a shot. Over the years, I've found that the Australian female voice (Voice 2) coupled with the English (United States) Language option was easier for me to understand, for whatever reason.

6. Let Siri know about your contact information by tapping My Information and selecting yourself from your Contacts.

If you want to customize when Siri verbally responds to your requests, tap Siri Responses in the Siri & Search settings and make one of three selections. The Always option causes Siri to verbally respond to your requests all the time — period. The When Silent Mode Is Off option prevents Siri from verbally responding to you when silent mode is enabled on your iPad. The Only with "Hey Siri" option allows Siri to verbally respond to your requests when you make them using the "Hey Siri" command to launch Siri.

Discover All That Siri Can Do

Siri allows you to interact by voice with many apps on your iPad.

TIP

No matter what kind of action you want to perform, first press and hold the Home button or top button (depending on your iPad model) until Siri opens. Or, if you've enabled "Hey Siri," simply say the phrase.

You can pose questions or ask to do something like make a FaceTime call or add an appointment to your calendar, for example. Siri can also search the Internet or use an informational service called Wolfram|Alpha to provide information on just about any topic.

To see examples of what Siri can do for you, engage Siri and say "What kind of questions can I ask you?" A dialog will appear onscreen telling you "Siri's here to help"; tap that dialog to visit www.apple. com/siri in Safari (or whatever your default browser is), as shown in **Figure 5-2**.

Siri also checks with Wikipedia, Bing, and Twitter to get you the information you ask for. In addition, you can use Siri to tell the iPad to return a call, play your voicemail, open and search the App Store, control Music playback, dictate text messages, and much more.

TIP

I find using Siri easier if it shows me the text of what it heard me say and what it says back to me. These features are disabled by default for some reason, so if you want to use them (as I do throughout this chapter), go to Settings ⇨ Siri & Search ⇨ Siri Responses and toggle the switches to On (green) for the Always Show Siri Captions option (to read what Siri says to you) and for the Always Show Speech option (to read what Siri heard you say).

Siri learns your daily habits and will offer suggestions throughout the day when appropriate. For example, say that you usually stop by the local coffee shop around the same time each morning and use the shop's app to order a drink from your iPad. Siri picks up on this activity and eventually begins asking if you'd like to order a drink when you're within proximity of the coffee shop.

Tap here

FIGURE 5-2

With iPadOS 15, Siri is much better at maintaining the context of questions. For example, you can ask something like "Where is the nearest Starbucks location?" and then follow it with "What's the phone number there?" Siri will automatically know you're asking for the phone number of the Starbucks location it finds. It's not always perfect, but this feature does make for a vastly improved Siri experience.

Siri knows what app you're using, though you don't have to have that app open to make a request involving it. However, if you're in the Messages app, you can make a statement like "Tell Sasha I'll be late," and Siri knows that you want to send a message. You can also ask Siri to remind you about what you're working on, and Siri notes what you're working on and which app you're working in, and reminds you about it at a later time that you specify.

TIP

If you want to dictate text in an app like Notes, use the Dictation key on the onscreen keyboard to do so. See the section "Use Dictation," later in this chapter, for more about this feature.

New to iPadOS 15, Siri is now able to announce possibly time-sensitive notifications when you're wearing AirPods (second generation or newer). For example, if you're in the aforementioned coffee shop and it's getting close to time for a meeting, Siri will interrupt whatever you're listening to so that you're aware of the upcoming appointment.

Siri requires no preset structure for your questions; you can phrase things in several ways. For example, you might say, "Where am I?" to see a map of your current location, or you could say, "What is my current location?" or "What address is this?" and get the same results.

If you ask a question about, say, the weather, Siri responds to you both verbally and with text information (see **Figure 5-3;** tap the small arrow next to the temperature when it displays to see a bit more info, as I've done in the figure). Or Siri might open a form, as with email, or provide a graphic display for some items, such as maps. When a result appears, you can tap it to make a choice or open a related app.

FIGURE 5-3

TIP Sometimes Siri's dialogs can get lost among the other items on your screen. To hide everything else and let Siri take center stage, go to Settings ⇨ Accessibility ⇨ Siri and toggle the Show Apps Behind Siri switch to Off (light gray; green is On). I do this for screenshots going forward through this chapter.

Siri works with FaceTime, the App Store, Music, Messages, Reminders, Calendar, Maps, Mail, Weather, Stocks, Clock, Contacts, Notes, social media apps (such as Twitter), and Safari (see **Figure 5-4**). In the following sections, I provide a quick guide to some of the most useful ways you can use Siri.

TIP Siri now supports many different languages, so you can finally show off those language lessons you took in high school. Some languages supported for translation include Chinese, Dutch, English, French, German, Italian, Spanish, Arabic, Danish, Finnish, Hebrew, Japanese, and Korean. However, Siri can speak to you only in English, French, German, Swedish, Danish, Norwegian, Finnish, Spanish, Mandarin Chinese, and Japanese when providing the results of inquiries.

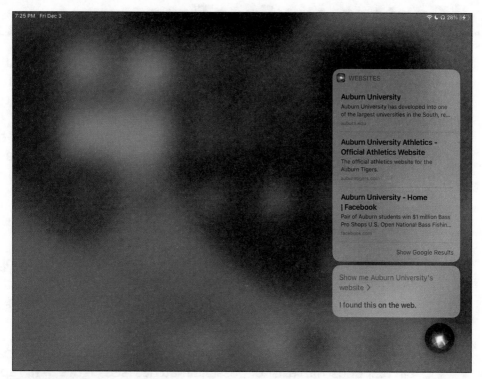

FIGURE 5-4

Get Suggestions

Siri anticipates your needs by making suggestions when you swipe from left to right on the Home screen and tap within the Search field at the top of the screen. Siri lists contacts you've communicated with recently, apps you've used, and nearby businesses, such as restaurants, gas stations, or coffee spots. If you tap an app in the suggestions, it opens displaying the last viewed or listened to item.

Additionally, Siri lists news stories that may be of interest to you based on items you've viewed before.

Call Contacts via FaceTime

First, make sure that the person you want to call is entered in your Contacts app and include that person's phone number in their record. If you want to call somebody by stating your relationship to them, such as "Call sister," be sure to enter that relationship in the Add Related Name field in her contact record. Also make sure that the settings for Siri (refer to Figure 5-1) include your own contact name in the My Information field. (See Chapter 7 for more about creating contact records.)

To call contacts via FaceTime, follow these steps:

1. Press and hold the Home button (or say "Hey, Siri," if you're using that feature) until Siri appears.

2. Speak a command, such as "Make a FaceTime call to Cindy," or say "FaceTime Mom."

3. If you have more than one contact who might match a spoken name, Siri responds with a list of possible matches (see **Figure 5-5**). Tap one in the list or state the correct contact's name to proceed.

4. The call is placed. To end the call before it completes, press the Home button and then tap End.

TIP

To cancel any spoken request, you have three options: Say "Cancel," tap the Siri button on the Siri screen (looks like swirling bands of light), or press the Home or Top button (depending on your iPad model). If you're using a headset or Bluetooth device, tap the End button on the device.

FIGURE 5-5

Create Reminders and Alerts

You can also use Siri with the Reminders app:

1. To create a reminder or alert, press and hold the Home button or Top button (depending on your iPad model) and then speak a command, such as "Remind me to call Dad on Thursday at 10 a.m." or "Wake me up tomorrow at 6:15 a.m."

2. A preview of the reminder or alert is displayed (see **Figure 5-6**). Tell Siri to Cancel or Remove if you change your mind.

3. If you want a reminder ahead of the event that you created, activate Siri and speak a command, such as "Remind me tonight about the play on Thursday at 8 p.m." A second reminder is created, which you can confirm or cancel if you change your mind.

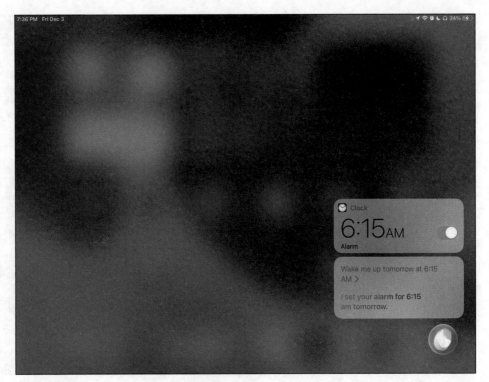

7:36 PM Fri Dec 3   34%

Clock
6:15AM
Alarm

Wake me up tomorrow at 6:15
AM >

I set your alarm for 6:15
am tomorrow.

FIGURE 5-6

Add Tasks to Your Calendar

You can also set up events on your Calendar using Siri:

1. Press and hold the Home or Top button and then speak a phrase, such as "Set up a meeting at 3 p.m. tomorrow."

2. Siri sets up the appointment (see **Figure 5-7**) and may ask you to let it know if you want to make changes.

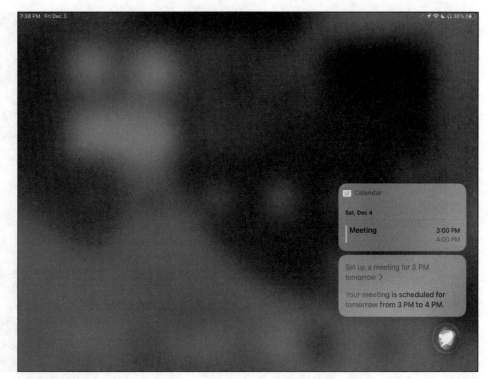

FIGURE 5-7

Play Music

You can use Siri to play music from the Music app:

1. Press and hold the Home or Top button until Siri appears.

2. To play music, speak a command, such as "Play music" or "Play Jazz radio station" to play a specific song, album, or radio station, as shown in **Figure 5-8**.

Apple has integrated Siri into Shazam, a music identifier app, to identify music. To use this integration:

1. When you're near an audio source playing music, press and hold the Home button or Top button to activate Siri.

2. Ask Siri a question, such as "What music is playing?" or "What's this song?"

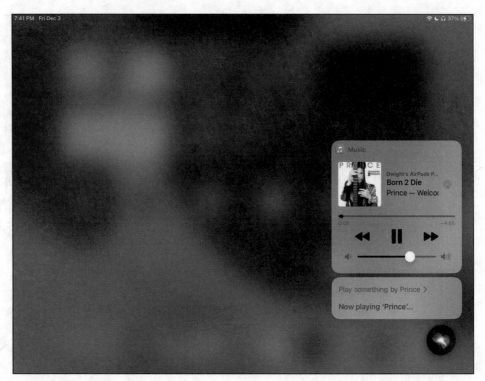

7:41 PM Fri Dec 3   37%

♫ Music

Dwight's AirPods P...
Born 2 Die
Prince — Welco

0:08   -4:55

◀◀   ❚❚   ▶▶

Play something by Prince >

Now playing 'Prince'...

FIGURE 5-8

3. Siri listens for a bit. If Siri recognizes the song, it shows you the song name, artist, any other available information, and the ability to purchase the music in the iTunes Store.

TIP

If you're listening to music or a podcast with earphones plugged in and stop midstream, the next time you plug in earphones, Siri recognizes that you may want to continue with the same item.

Get Directions

You can use the Maps app and Siri to find your current location, get directions, find nearby businesses (such as restaurants or a bank), or get a map of another location. Be sure to turn on Location Services to allow Siri to know your current location (go to Settings and tap Privacy ⇨ Location Services; make sure Location Services is on and that Siri & Dictation is turned on further down in these settings).

Here are some of the commands that you can try to get directions or a list of nearby businesses:

- » **"Where am I?"** Displays a map of your current location.

- » **"Where is Big Potato Company?"** Displays a map of the city where that restaurant is located, as shown in **Figure 5-9.**

- » **"Find pizza restaurants."** Displays a list of restaurants near your current location. Tap one to display a map of its location.

- » **"Find PNC Bank."** Displays a map with the location of the indicated business (or in some cases, several nearby locations, such as a bank branch and all ATMs).

- » **"Get directions to Auburn Arena."** Loads a map with a route drawn and provides a narration of directions to the site from your current location.

FIGURE 5-9

TIP

After a location is displayed on a map, tap the Information button on the location's label to view its address, phone number, and website address, if available.

Ask for Facts

Siri uses numerous information sources, such as Wolfram|Alpha, Wikipedia, and Bing, to look up facts in response to questions. You can ask "What is the capital of Kansas?" or "What is the square root of 2,300?" or "How large is Mars?" Just press and hold the Home button or Top button and ask your question; Siri consults its resources and returns a set of relevant facts.

You can also get information about other things, such as the weather, stocks, or a scientific fact. Just say a phrase like one of these to get what you need:

» **"What is the weather?"** displays the weather report for your current location. If you want weather in another location, just specify the location in your question.

» **"What is the price of Apple stock?"** gets you the current price of the stock or the price of the stock when the stock market last closed.

» **"How hot is the sun?"** results in Siri's telling you the temperature of the sun, in various unit conversions.

Search the Web

Although Siri can use its resources to respond to specific requests such as, "Who is the Queen of England?", more general requests for information will cause Siri to search further on the web. Siri can also search Twitter for comments related to your search.

For example, if you speak a phrase, such as "Find a website about birds" or "Find information about the World Series," Siri can respond in a couple of ways. The app can simply display a list of search results by using the default search engine specified in your settings for Safari, or Siri can suggest, "If you like, I can search the web for such and such." In the first instance, just tap a result to go to that website. In the second instance, you can confirm that you want to search the web or cancel.

Send Email, Messages, or Tweets

You can create an email or an instant message using Siri and existing contacts. For example, if you say "Email Fr. Stephen Campbell," a form opens that is already addressed to that stored contact. Siri asks for a subject and then a message. Speak your message contents and then say "Send" to speed your message on its way.

Siri also works with messaging apps, such as Messages. If you have the Messages app open and you say "Tell Reid I'll call soon," Siri creates a message for you to approve and send.

Use Dictation

Text entry isn't Siri's strong point, but it's definitely improving. Instead, you can use the Dictation key that appears with a microphone symbol on the onscreen keyboard (see **Figure 5-10**) to speak text rather than type it. This feature is called Dictation.

To use dictation:

1. Go to any app where you enter text, such as Notes or Mail, and tap in the document or form. The onscreen keyboard appears.

2. Tap the Dictation key on the keyboard and speak your text.

3. To end the dictation, tap Done.

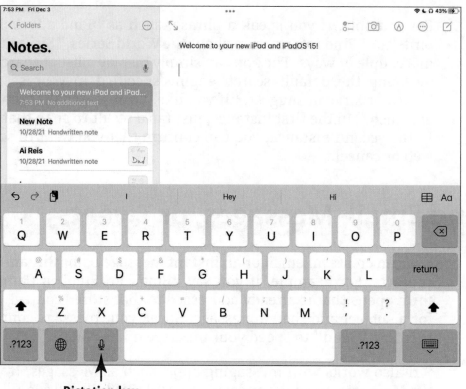

Dictation key

FIGURE 5-10

TIP

When you finish speaking text, you can use the keyboard to make edits to the text Siri entered, although as voice recognition programs go, Dictation is pretty darn accurate. If a word sports a blue underline, which means there may be an error, you can tap to select the word and edit it.

Translate Words and Phrases

One of Siri's coolest features is the ability to translate English into multiple languages (including Mandarin, French, German, Italian, Spanish, and more), with support for more than 40 language pairs, according to Apple. That's great if you're on a road trip and don't speak the local language.

To try Siri's translation feature:

1. Activate Siri.

2. Say "translate" followed by your phrase and the language of your choice, as shown in **Figure 5-11.**

3. Siri displays the translation on your screen and speaks it while also providing a phonetic translation to help with pronunciation.

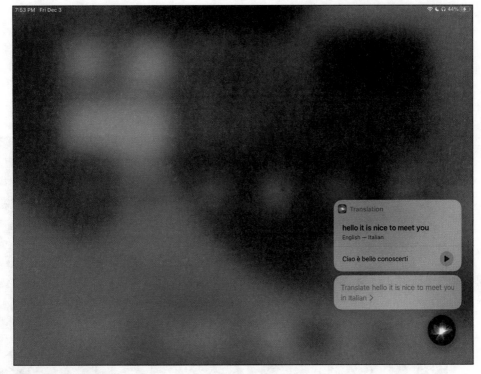

FIGURE 5-11

Tap the Play button to the right of the translation to hear Siri speak it again.

TIP

Type Your Commands or Questions

Type to Siri is another great feature. It allows you to type commands or inquiries instead of verbalizing them.

TIP

This feature is wonderful if you have difficulty speaking or if you're in a situation where you're not able to speak.

To enable this feature:

1. Go to Settings ⇨ Accessibility.

2. Tap Siri and then toggle the switch for Type to Siri to On (green).

3. Now, when you activate Siri, a keyboard appears for you to enter your commands or questions (see **Figure 5-12**).

FIGURE 5-12

Chapter 6

Expanding Your iPad Horizons with Apps

S ome apps (short for *applications*), such as News and Music, come preinstalled on your iPad with iPadOS. But you can choose from a world of other apps out there for your iPad — some for free (such as USA Today) and some for a price (typically, ranging from 99 cents to about $10, though some can top out at much steeper prices).

Apps range from games to financial tools (such as loan calculators) to apps that help you when you're planning an exercise regimen or taking a trip. Still more apps are developed for use by private entities, such as hospitals and government agencies.

In this chapter, I suggest some apps that you may want to check out; explain how to use the App Store feature of your iPad to find, purchase, and download apps; and detail how to organize your apps. You also find out a bit about having fun with games on your iPad.

Search the App Store

Access the App Store by tapping the App Store icon on the Home screen. You can start by exploring the Today tab (which features special apps and articles), by Categories, or by the Top Charts (see the buttons along the bottom of the screen). Or you can tap Search and find apps on your own. Tap an app to see more information about it.

If you've got the time, you can find lots of happy surprises by simply browsing the App Store, but if you're in a hurry or already know what you're looking for, a search is the best way to go.

To search the App Store:

1. Tap the App Store icon on the Home screen; by default, the first time you use App Store, it will open to the Today tab, as shown in **Figure 6-1.**

2. At this point, you have several options for finding apps:

   - Scroll downward to view various featured apps and articles, such as The Daily List, Developer Spotlight, and Our Favorites.

     Tap a category to see more apps in it.

   - Tap the Apps tab at the bottom of the screen to browse by the type of app you're looking for or search by categories (tap the See All button in the Top Categories section), such as Lifestyle or Medical, as shown in **Figure 6-2.**

   - Tap the Games tab at the bottom of the screen to see the newest releases and bestselling games. Explore by paid apps, free apps, by categories, and even by special subjects such as The Most Beautiful Games and What We're Playing Today.

   - Tap the Search button at the bottom of the screen, tap in the Search field, enter a search term, and then tap the result you want to view.

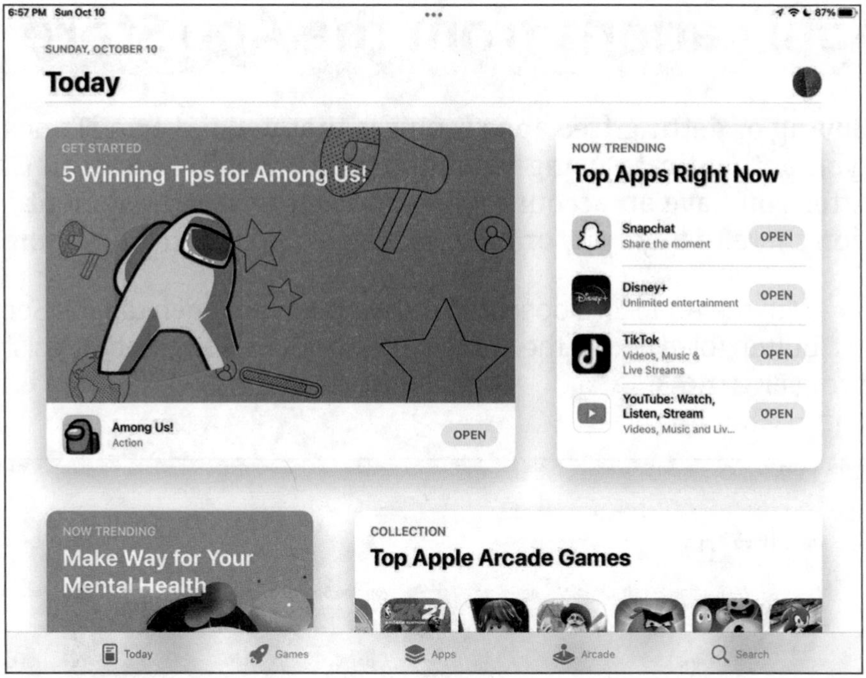

FIGURE 6-1

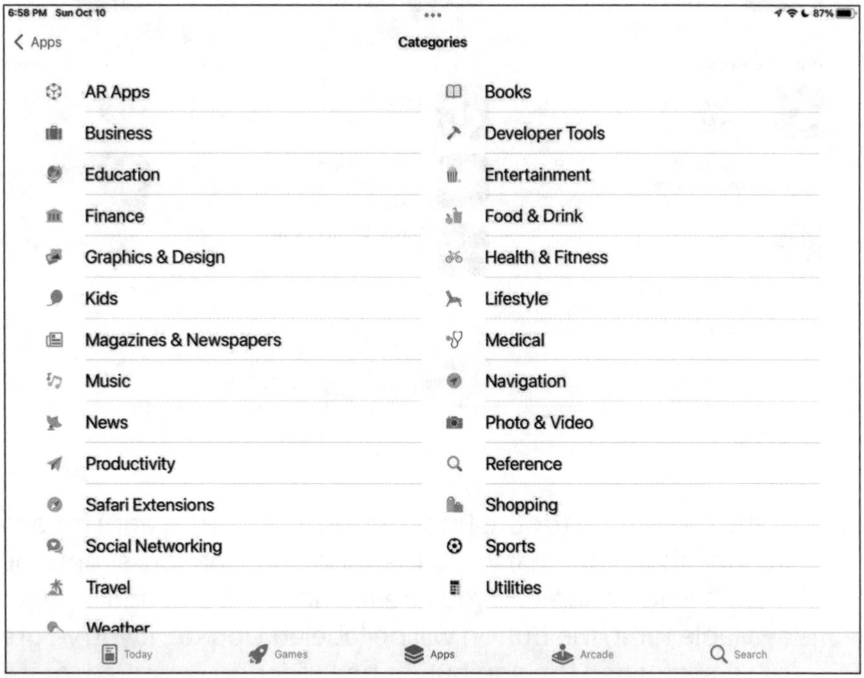

FIGURE 6-2

Get Applications from the App Store

Buying or getting free apps requires that you have an iTunes account (you authenticate using your Apple ID), which I cover in Chapter 3. After you have an account, you can use the saved payment information there to buy apps or download free apps with a few simple steps:

1. With the App Store open, tap the Apps tab and then tap the See All button (blue text to the right) in the Top Free Apps section, as shown in **Figure 6-3.**

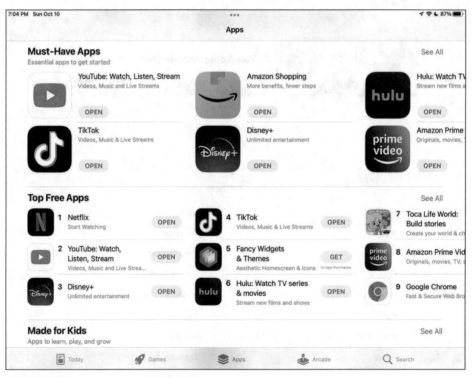

FIGURE 6-3

2. Tap the Get button (or the Price button, if it's a Paid app) for an app that appeals to you or, if you'd like more information, simply tap the app's icon or name. If you already have the app and an update is available for it, the button will be labeled Update. If you've previously downloaded the app but it's no longer on your iPad, or if you've downloaded the app on another device that's signed in to the same Apple ID, the icon looks like a cloud with a downward arrow. Tap to download it again.

TIP

If you've opened an iCloud account, you can set it up so that anything you purchase on your iPad is automatically pushed to other Apple iPadOS or iOS devices (such as an iPhone or another iPad) and your iTunes library, and vice versa. See Chapter 3 for more about iCloud.

3. A dialog window opens onscreen, listing the app and the iTunes account being used to get or purchase the app. Tap Enter Password at the bottom of the sheet, tap the Password field, and then enter the password. Alternatively, you may simply need only to use Touch ID or Face ID (whichever your iPad model supports) to approve the download/purchase. The Get (or Price) button changes to the Installing button, which looks like a circle; the thick blue line on the circle represents the progress of the installation.

4. The app downloads, and you can find it on one of the Home screens. If you purchase an app that isn't free, your credit card or gift card balance is charged at this point for the purchase price.

Organize Your Applications on Home Screens

As explained in Chapter 2, your iPad has multiple Home screens. The first two contain preinstalled apps, and after those initial screens are full of app icons, other screens are created to contain any further apps you download or sync to your iPad. At the bottom of any iPad Home screen (just above the Dock), dots indicate the number of Home screens you've filled with apps; a solid white dot specifies which Home screen you're on now, as shown in **Figure 6-4.**

1. Press the Home button to open the last displayed Home screen.

2. Flick your finger from right to left to move to the next Home screen. To move back, flick from left to right.

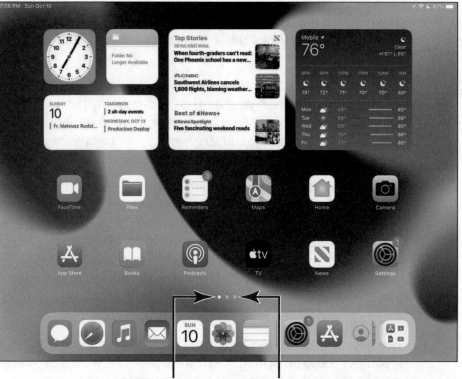

Screen you're on   Dots indicating the number of home screens

FIGURE 6-4

3. To reorganize apps on a Home screen, press and hold any app on that page to open a contextual menu; tap Edit Home Screen, as shown in **Figure 6-5.** Alternatively, press and hold the app icon just a bit longer to skip the menu, if you prefer.

4. The app icons begin to jiggle (see **Figure 6-6**), and many (not all) apps will sport a Delete button, which looks like a gray circle with a black minus sign (–) on it.

5. Press, hold, and drag an app icon to another location on the screen to move it.

TIP

To move an app from one page to another, while the apps are jiggling, you can press, hold, and drag an app to the left or right to move it to the next Home screen. You can also manage which app resides on which Home screen and change the order of the Home screens from iTunes when you've connected your iPad to iTunes on your computer via a cable or wireless sync. If you have a Mac that uses the Apple Music app instead of iTunes, you can download another app called Apple Configurator 2 from your Mac's App Store; this app allows you to organize your iPad's Home screens from your Mac, too.

6. Tap an empty area of the screen, or press the Home button (you can swipe up from the bottom if your iPad doesn't have a Home button) to stop all those icons from jiggling!

Tap here to rearrange apps

FIGURE 6-5

A Delete button

FIGURE 6-6

Organize Apps in Folders

The iPad lets you organize apps in folders so that you can find them more easily. The process is simple:

1. Press and hold an app until all apps start jiggling.

2. Drag one app on top of another app.

The two apps appear in a box with a placeholder name in a box above them (see **Figure 6-7**).

3. To change the name, tap in the field at the end of the placeholder name, and the keyboard appears.

4. Tap the Delete key to delete the placeholder name and type one of your own.

5. Tap Done and then tap anywhere outside the box to close it.

6. Press the Home button to stop the icons from dancing around. You see your folder on the Home screen where you began this process.

Here's a neat trick that allows you to move multiple apps together at the same time (you'll probably want to place your iPad on a flat surface or support it in a case to pull this off more smoothly):

1. Press and hold the first app you'd like to move until the apps are jiggling.

2. Move the app just a bit so that it's no longer in its original place.

3. With your free hand, tap the other app(s) you'd like to move along with the first app. As you tap additional apps, their icons "move under" or "attach themselves" to the first app.

4. After you've selected all your apps, move them to their new location; they'll all move together in a little app caravan.

Delete Apps You No Longer Need

When you no longer need an app you've installed, it's time to get rid of it. You can also remove most of the preinstalled apps that are native to iPadOS.

If you use iCloud to push content (that is, install things you buy or download on one device on others you own) across all Apple iPadOS or iOS devices, deleting an app on your iPad won't affect that app on other devices. Follow these steps to delete an app:

1. Display the Home screen that contains the app you want to delete.

2. Press and hold the app until all apps begin to jiggle.

3. Tap the Delete button, which is the gray circle containing the black minus sign (–), for the app you want to delete. A confirmation like the one shown in **Figure 6-8** appears.

4. Tap Delete App to proceed with the deletion.

FIGURE 6-7

FIGURE 6-8

TIP

If you want the app to remain in the App Library, tap the Remove from Home Screen button instead.

Update Apps

App developers update their apps all the time, so you might want to check for those updates. The App Store icon on the Home screen displays the number of available updates in a red badge. To update apps, follow these steps:

1. Tap the App Store icon on the Home screen.

2. Tap the Account button (an icon in the upper-right on the Apps screen, similar to the one shown in **Figure 6-9**); it will display a red badge with a number in it if updates are available. If you don't see a badge with a number, no updates are available.

3. In the Account window that opens, scroll down to the Available Updates section and tap the Update button for any item you want to update. To update all at one time, tap the blue Update All button to the left.

TIP

Note that if you have Family Sharing turned on, there will be a folder titled Family Purchases that you can tap to display apps that are shared across your family's devices.

4. You may be asked to confirm that you want to update, or to enter your Apple ID; after you do, tap OK to proceed. You may also be asked to confirm that you are over a certain age or agree to terms and conditions. If so, scroll down the terms dialog and, at the bottom, tap Agree. The download progress is displayed.

Account button

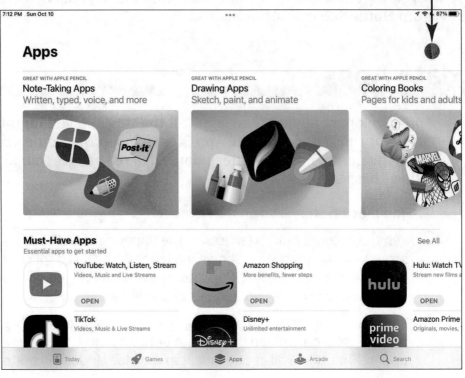

FIGURE 6-9

Purchase and Download Games

Time to get your game on!

The iPad is super for playing games, with its bright screen, porta-
ble size, and ability to rotate the screen as you play and track your
motions. You can download game apps from the App Store and play
them on your device.

1. Open the App Store.

2. Tap the Games button at the bottom of the screen to view the Games
   screen.

3. Navigating the Games screen is simple:

- Swipe from right to left to see featured apps in such categories as "What We're Playing Today" and "Editors' Choice."

- Swipe down to find the Top Paid and Free games or to shop by categories (tap See All to view all the available categories).

4. Explore the list of games in the type you selected until you find something you like; tap the game to see its information screen (see **Figure 6-10** for an example).

FIGURE 6-10

5. To buy a game, tap the button labeled with either the word *Get* or the price (such as $2.99).

6. When the dialog appears at the bottom of the screen, tap Purchase (if it's a Paid game) or Install (if it's a Free game), type your password in the Password field on the next screen, and then tap Sign In to download the game. Alternatively, use Touch ID or Face ID (for iPad models that support them) if it's enabled for iTunes and App Store purchases.

The dialog will display "Pay with Touch ID," or you'll be prompted to double-click the Side button to initiate Face ID authentication (iPad models without a Home button only).

TIP

Beware of using Touch ID or Face ID for iTunes and App Store purchases. I know it's simpler than entering a password, but it can also make it easier for others to make purchases. In case you're wondering how that could be so, my children have actually tried holding my iPad in front of my face while I was asleep in a clandestine attempt at purchasing the latest game craze with Face ID. Imagine your grandkids trying to do the same and I believe you'll see where I'm coming from.

7. The game downloads. Tap the Open button to go to the downloaded game or find the games icon on your Home screen and tap to open it.

8. Have fun!

Chapter **7**

Managing Contacts

The Contacts app is the iPad equivalent of the dog-eared address book that used to sit by your phone. This app is simple to set up and use, and it has some powerful features beyond simply storing names, addresses, and phone numbers.

For example, you can pinpoint a contact's address in the iPad's Maps app. You can use your contacts to address email, Facebook messages, and Twitter tweets quickly. If you store a contact record that includes a website, you can use a link in Contacts to view that website instantly. In addition, of course, you can easily search for a contact by a variety of criteria, including how people are related to you, such as family or mutual friends, or by groups you create.

In this chapter, you discover the various features of Contacts, including how to save yourself time spent entering contact information by syncing contacts with such services as iCloud.

Add a Contact

To add a contact to Contacts:

1. Tap the Contacts icon on one of the Home screens. An alphabetical list of contacts appears, like the one shown in **Figure 7-1**.

![Contacts screen showing an alphabetical list on the left with names including Skyline Family Dental Care PC, Harry Snipes, Spire, Christine Spivey, Debbie Spivey, and others. On the right is the Apple Inc. contact with phone, email, homepage, and address details.]

3:07 PM   Sun Oct 10

‹ Groups   **Contacts**   +   Edit

Q Search

S
Skyline Family Dental Care PC

Harry Snipes

Spire

Christine **Spivey**

Debbie **Spivey**

Debbie **Spivey**

Dwight **Spivey**   me

Faye **Spivey**

Frank **Spivey**

Kenneth **Spivey**

Preston **Spivey**

Trisha **Spivey**

Winston **Spivey**

St. Dominic Catholic Church

St. Dominic Catholic School

Apple Inc.

message   main   video   mail   pay

main
1 (800) MYAPPLE

work
tcook@apple.com

homepage
http://www.apple.com

work
1 Apple Park Way
Cupertino CA 95014
United States

Notes

FIGURE 7-1

2. Tap the Add button, the button with the small plus sign (+) on it in the upper-right corner of the Contacts list. A blank New Contact page opens (see **Figure 7-2**). Tap in any field, and the onscreen keyboard displays.

3. Enter any contact information you want.

TIP

Only one of the First name, Last name, or Company fields is required, but do feel free to add as much information as you like.

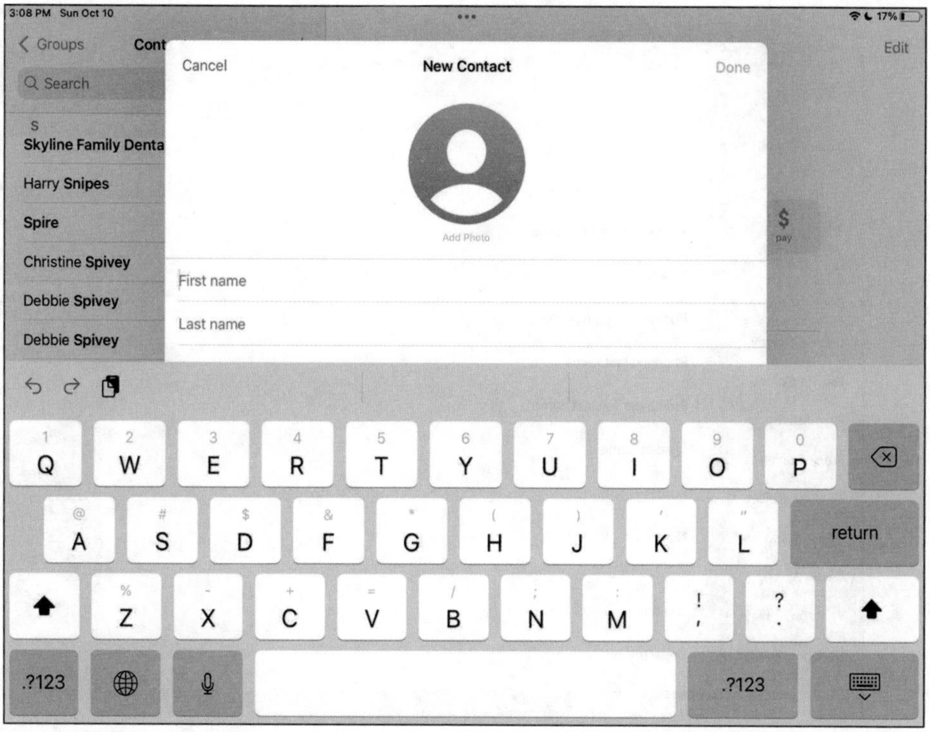

FIGURE 7-2

4. To scroll down the contact's page and see more fields, flick up on the screen with your finger.

5. If you want to add information (such as a mailing or street address), you can tap the relevant Add field, which opens additional entry fields.

6. To add an information field, such as Nickname or Job Title, tap the blue Add Field button at the bottom of the page. In the Add Field dialog that appears (see **Figure 7-3**), choose a field to add, then populate it with the relevant info.

> **TIP** You may have to flick up or down the screen with your finger to view all the fields.

> **TIP** If your contact has a name that's difficult for you to pronounce, consider adding the Phonetic First Name or Phonetic Last Name field, or both, to that person's record (refer to Step 6).

‹ Groups   Cont   Edit

🔍 Search

S
Skyline Family Denta | Cancel   **Add Field**

Harry **Snipes**   Prefix

Spire   Phonetic first name $
                                                                         pay
Christine **Spivey**   Pronunciation first name

Debbie **Spivey**   Middle name

Debbie **Spivey**   Phonetic middle name

Dwight **Spivey**   Phonetic last name

Faye **Spivey**   Pronunciation last name

Frank **Spivey**   Maiden name

Kenneth **Spivey**   Suffix

Preston **Spivey**   Nickname

Trisha **Spivey**

Winston **Spivey**   Job title

St. Dominic Catholic   Department

St. Dominic Catholic School

FIGURE 7-3

7. Tap the Done button in the upper-right corner when you finish making entries. The new contact appears in your address book. Tap it to see details (see **Figure 7-4**).

TIP

You can choose a distinct ringtone or text tone for a new contact. Just tap the Ringtone or Text Tone field in the New Contact form or when editing a contact to see a list of options. When that person calls either on the phone or via FaceTime, or texts you via SMS, MMS, or iMessage, you will recognize them from the tone that plays.

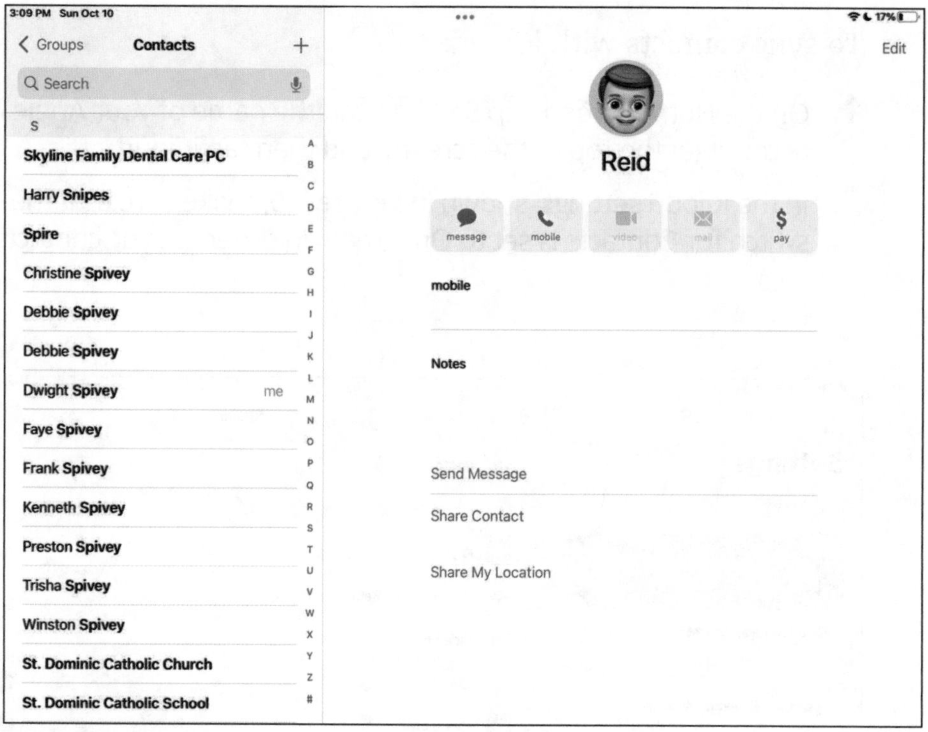

FIGURE 7-4

Sync Contacts with iCloud

You can use your iCloud account to sync contacts from your iPad to iCloud to back them up. These also become available to your email account, if you set one up.

TIP Mac users can also use iTunes or Finder (if your Mac is running macOS Catalina) to sync contacts among all your Apple devices. Windows PC users also use iTunes. See Chapter 3 for more about adjusting iTunes settings.

To sync contacts with iCloud:

1. On the Home screen, tap Settings, tap the name of your Apple ID account (at the top of the screen), and then tap iCloud.

2. In the iCloud settings, shown in **Figure 7-5,** make sure that the On/Off switch for Contacts is set to On (green) in order to sync contacts.

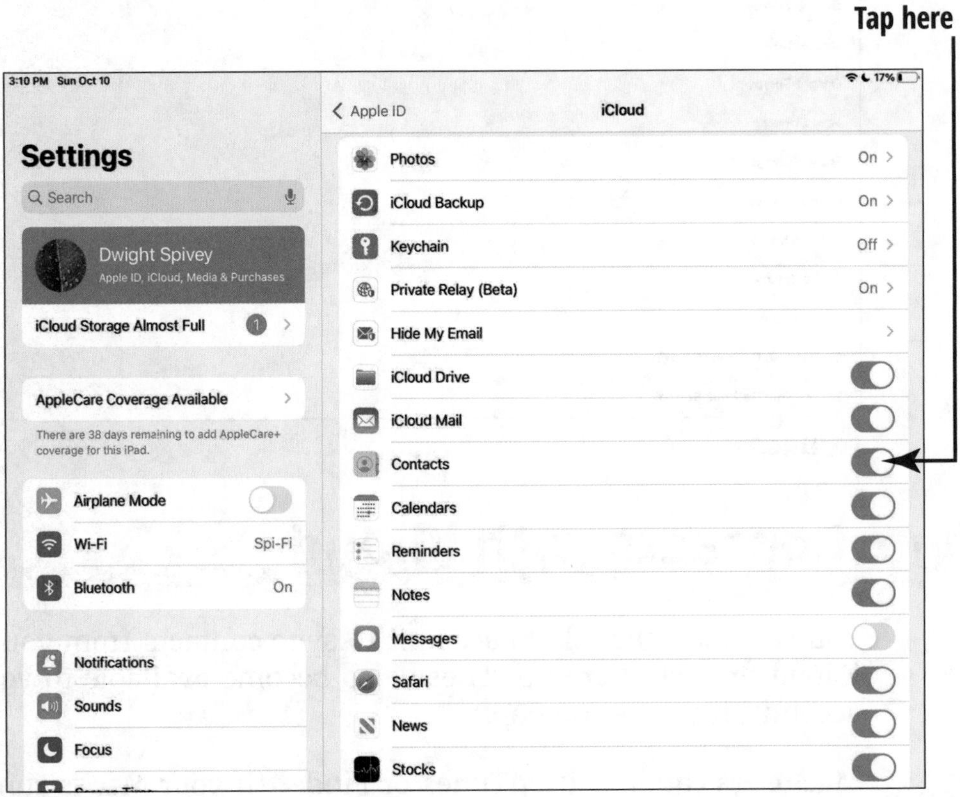

Tap here

3:10 PM Sun Oct 10		🤍 🔋 17%
	‹ Apple ID iCloud	
Settings	🌼 Photos	On ›
🔍 Search 🎤	🔄 iCloud Backup	On ›
Dwight Spivey	🔑 Keychain	Off ›
Apple ID, iCloud, Media & Purchases	🌐 Private Relay (Beta)	On ›
iCloud Storage Almost Full ① ›	✉️ Hide My Email	›
	📁 iCloud Drive	⬤
AppleCare Coverage Available ›	✉️ iCloud Mail	⬤
There are 38 days remaining to add AppleCare+ coverage for this iPad.	👤 Contacts	⬤
✈️ Airplane Mode ⬤	📅 Calendars	⬤
📶 Wi-Fi Spi-Fi	📋 Reminders	⬤
🔵 Bluetooth On	🗒️ Notes	⬤
	⬜ Messages	◯
🔔 Notifications	🧭 Safari	⬤
🔊 Sounds	📰 News	⬤
🌙 Focus	Stocks	⬤

FIGURE 7-5

3. To choose which email account to sync with (if you have more than one account set up), tap Mail in the Settings list on the left, and in the Accounts section, tap the email account you want to use (it's usually listed as iCloud).

4. In the following screen (see **Figure 7-6**), toggle the Contacts switch to On to merge contacts from that account via iCloud.

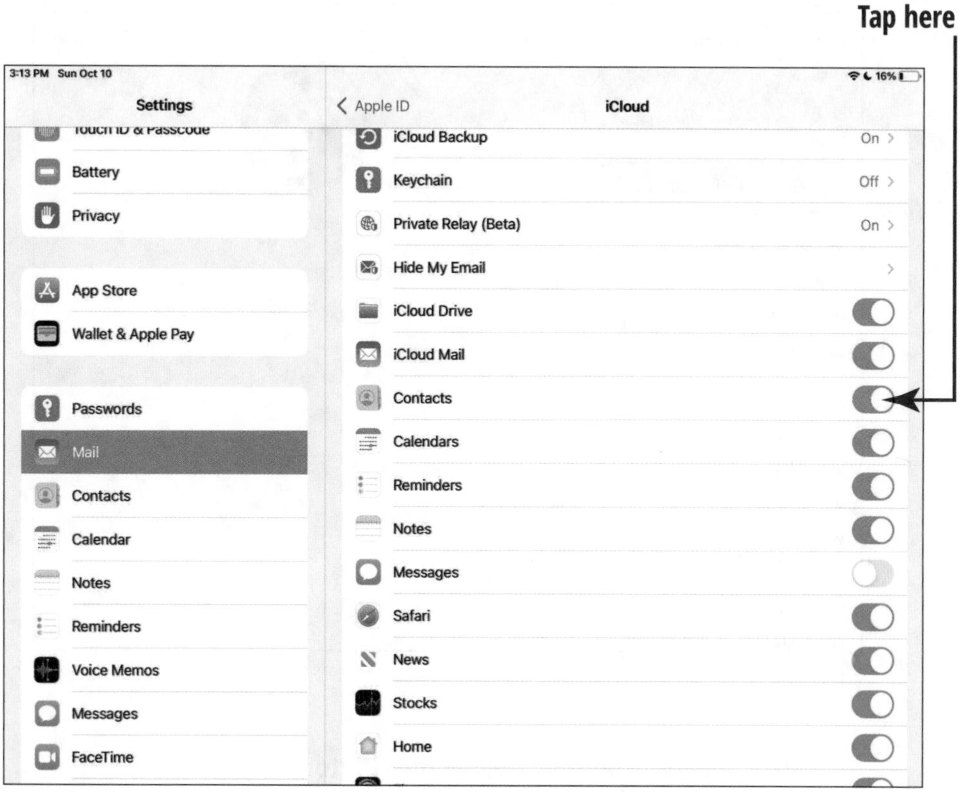

Tap here

FIGURE 7-6

Assign an Image to a Contact

Assigning images to a contact can be both functional and aesthetic. To assign an image to a contact:

1. With Contacts open, tap a contact to whose record you want to add an image.

2. Tap the Edit button.

3. On the Info page that appears (see **Figure 7-7**), tap Add Photo.

4. In the menu that appears, tap a suggested photo, a Memoji, or the All Photos icon (two stacked photos, shown in **Figure 7-8**) to choose an existing photo.

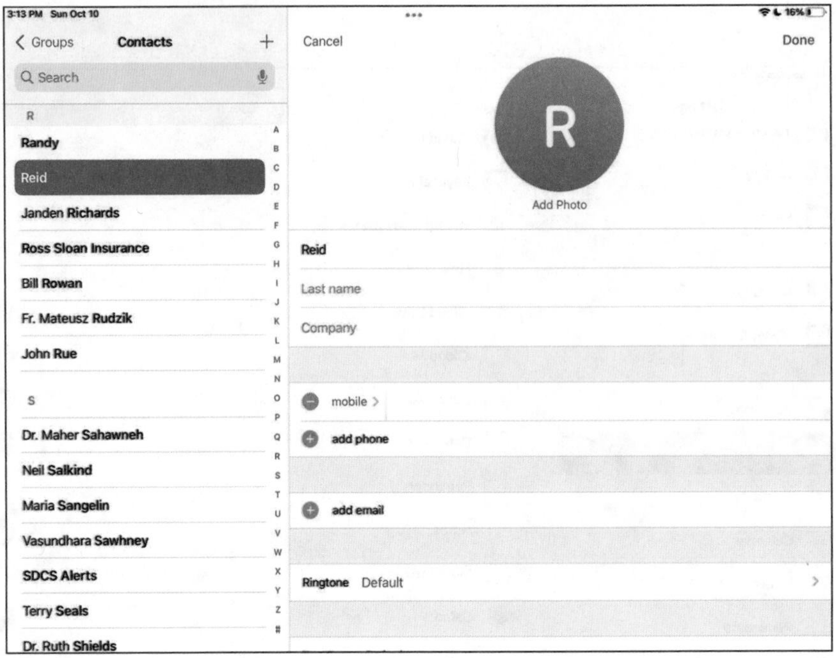

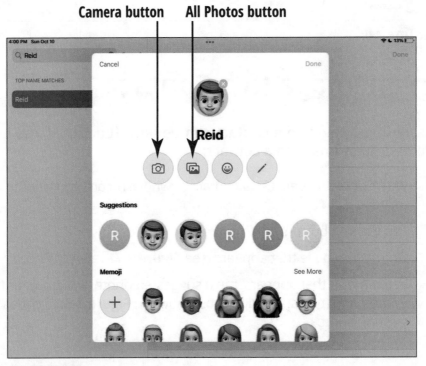

FIGURE 7-7

Camera button   All Photos button

FIGURE 7-8

TIP

You can also tap the Camera icon to take that contact's photo on the spot.

5. After you've selected an image, the Move and Scale dialog, shown in **Figure 7-9,** appears. Center the image the way you want it by dragging it with your finger. You can also pinch and unpinch your fingers on the iPad screen to shrink or expand the image.

FIGURE 7-9

6. Tap the Choose button to use the image for this contact. If prompted, you may also select a filter to use with the image.

7. Tap Done in the upper-right corner to save changes to the contact. The image appears on the contact's Info page (see **Figure 7-10**).

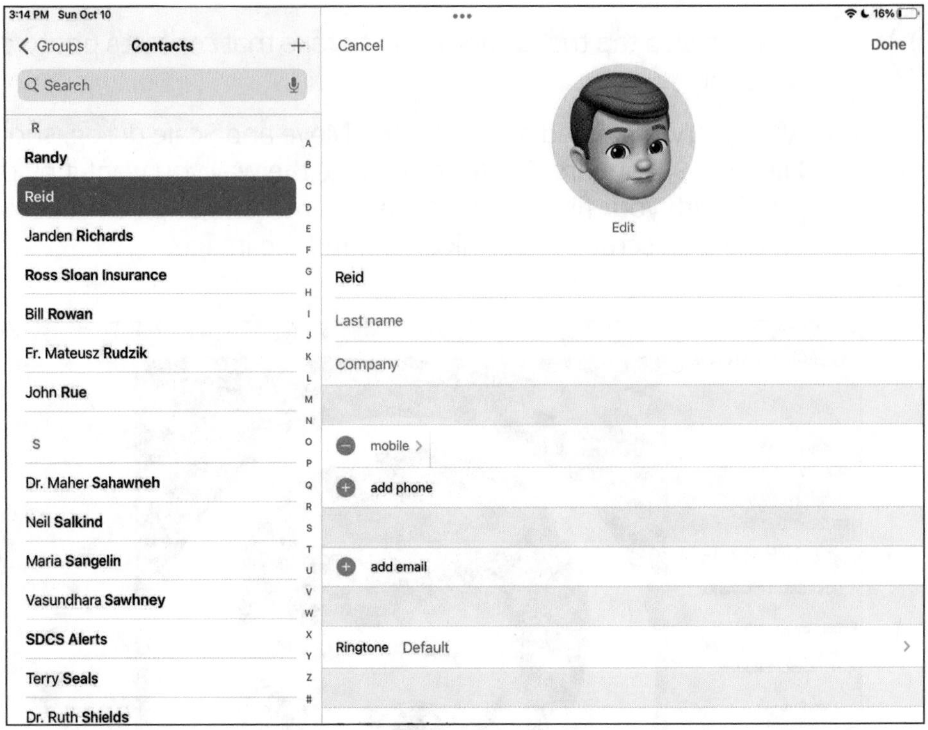

FIGURE 7-10

Add Social Media Information

iPad users can add social media information to their Contacts so that they can quickly tweet (send a short message to) others using Twitter, comment to a contact on Facebook, and more. Some of the social media platforms available in Contacts are Twitter, Facebook, Flickr, LinkedIn, Myspace, and Sina Weibo.

To add social media information to contacts:

1. Open the Contacts app.

2. Tap the Edit button in the upper-right corner of the screen.

3. Scroll down and tap Add Social Profile.

   You may add multiple social profiles if you like.

TIP

4. Twitter is the default service that pops up, but you can easily change it to a different service by tapping "Twitter" and selecting from the list of services (which may differ, depending on the apps you have installed on your iPad), as shown in **Figure 7-11.** Tap Done after you've selected the service you'd like to use.

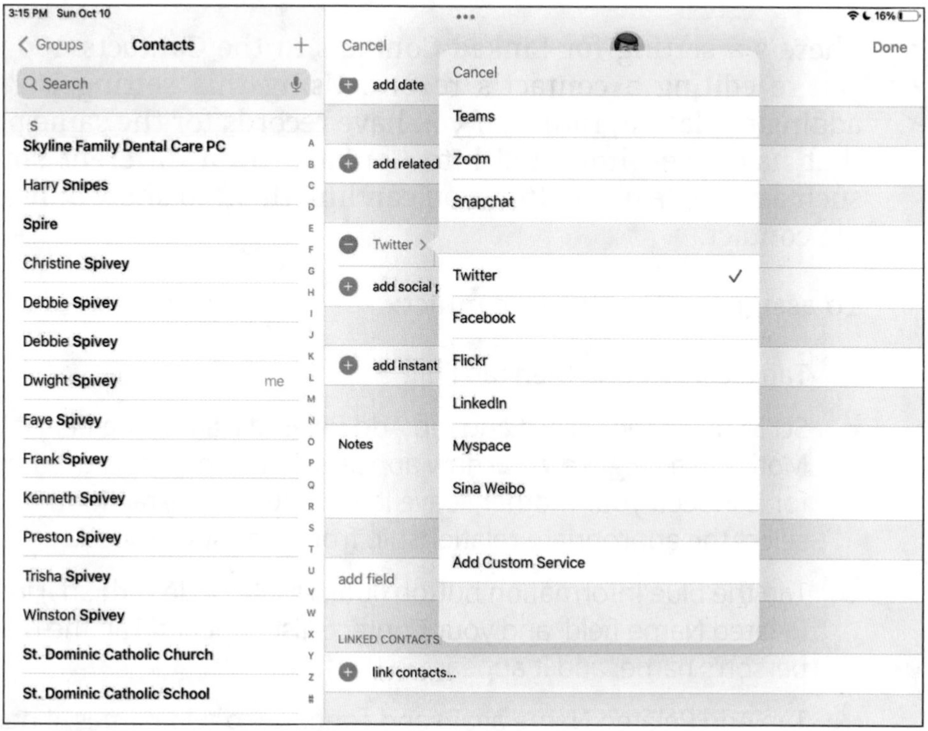

FIGURE 7-11

5. Enter the information for the social profile as needed.

6. Tap Done, and the information is saved.

The social profile account is now displayed when you select the contact, and you can send tweets, Facebook messages, or what-have-you by simply tapping the username, tapping the service you want to use to contact the person, and then tapping the appropriate command (such as for Facebook posting).

Assign a Relationship Label to a Contact

You can quickly designate relationships in a contact record if those people are saved to Contacts. One great use for this feature is using Siri to simply say "FaceTime daughter" to FaceTime someone who is designated in your contact information as your daughter.

TIP

There's a setting for Linked Contacts in the Contacts app when you're editing a contact's record. Using this setting isn't like adding a relation; rather, if you have records for the same person that have been imported into Contacts from different sources, such as Google or Twitter, you can link them to show only a single contact.

To assign a relation to a contact:

1. Tap a contact and then tap Edit.

2. Scroll down the record and tap Add Related Name. The field labeled Mother (see **Figure 7-12**) now appears. If the contact you're looking for is indeed your mother, leave it as is; otherwise, tap Mother and select the appropriate relationship from the list provided.

3. Tap the blue Information button (looks like a circle with an *i*) in Related Name field, and your Contacts list appears. Tap the related person's name, and it appears in the field.

4. Tap Add Related Name again and continue to add names, if needed.

5. Tap Done to complete the edits.

TIP

After you add relations to a contact record, when you select the person in the Contacts main screen, all the related people for that contact are listed there.

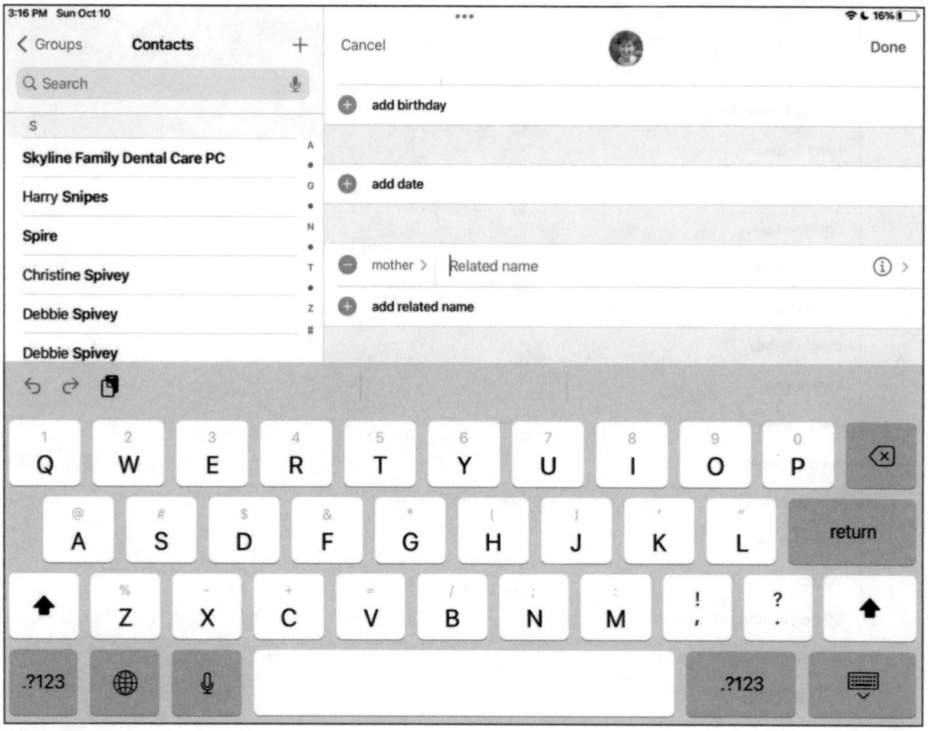

FIGURE 7-12

Delete a Contact

When it's time to remove a name or two from your Contacts, it's easy to do:

1. With Contacts open, tap the contact you want to delete.

2. On the Information page (refer to **Figure 7-4**), tap the Edit button.

3. On the Info page that displays, scroll down to the bottom of the page and then tap the Delete Contact button.

4. The confirmation dialog, shown in **Figure 7-13,** appears; tap the Delete Contact button to confirm the deletion.

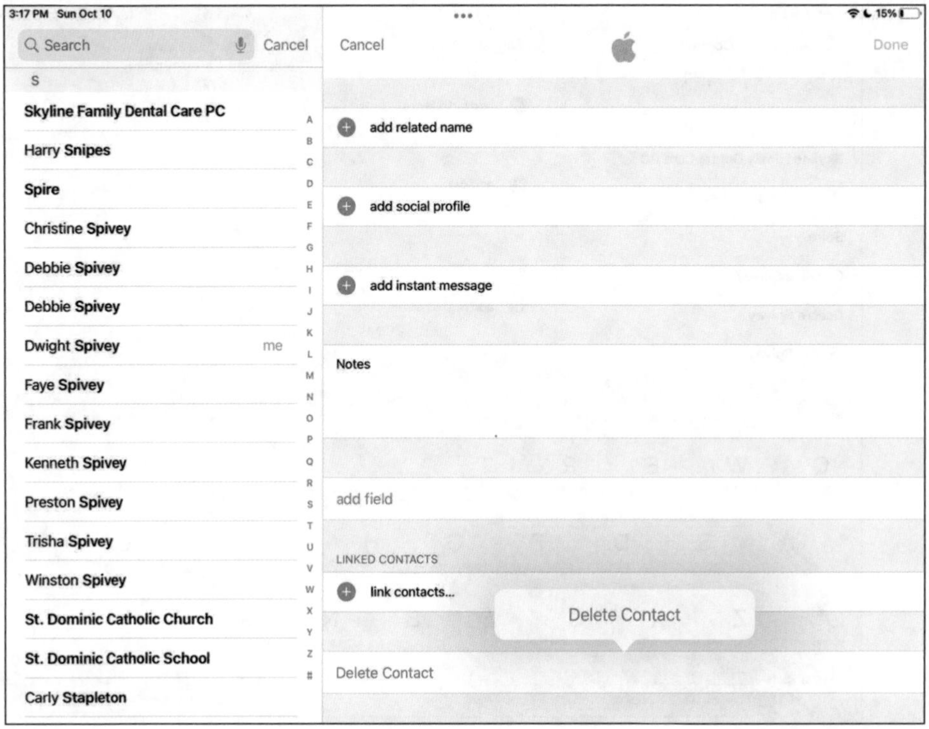

Q Search   🎤   Cancel   Cancel   ⬤   Done

S

Skyline Family Dental Care PC

Harry **Snipes**

Spire

Christine **Spivey**

Debbie **Spivey**

Debbie **Spivey**

Dwight **Spivey**   me

Faye **Spivey**

Frank **Spivey**

Kenneth **Spivey**

Preston **Spivey**

Trisha **Spivey**

Winston **Spivey**

St. Dominic Catholic Church

St. Dominic Catholic School

Carly **Stapleton**

⊕ add related name

⊕ add social profile

⊕ add instant message

Notes

add field

LINKED CONTACTS

⊕ link contacts...

Delete Contact

Delete Contact

FIGURE 7-13

TIP

During this process, if you change your mind before you tap Delete, tap anywhere on the screen outside the confirmation dialog, and then tap the Cancel button in Step 4. Be careful: After you tap Delete, there's no going back! Your contact is deleted from your iPad as well as from any other device that syncs to your iPad via iCloud, Google, or other means.

Chapter 8

Getting Social with Your iPad

Your iPad offers many ways to communicate with friends, family, and others. For example, FaceTime is an excellent video-calling app that lets you call people who have FaceTime on their devices using either a phone number or an email address. You and your friend, colleague, or family member can see each other as you talk, which makes for a much more personal calling experience.

iPadOS 15 puts a new face (user interface) on FaceTime, and adds some other tweaks and techs. Among my favorites are audio upgrades. One of those upgrades is spatial audio, which helps make people you're speaking with sound like they're right in the room; their voice is cast in whatever direction they face in the call. Another audio upgrade is voice isolation mode, which isolates your voice from other noises around you, allowing others to hear you and not your neighbor's lawn mower. I also like portrait mode, which causes your iPad's cameras to focus on you while blurring everything behind you.

Another communication tool on your iPad is iMessage, which allows instant messaging (IM) and is available through the preinstalled Messages app. IM involves sending a text message to somebody's iPad, iPod touch, Mac running macOS 10.9 or later, or iPhone (using the person's phone number or email address to carry on an instant conversation). You can even send audio and video via Messages.

More ways for you to keep in close digital contact with friends, family, and the rest of the world are social media apps, which have become as important a digital staple as email, if not more so for some folks. Facebook, Twitter, and Instagram are some of the most popular social media apps.

Facebook is a platform for sharing posts about your life, with or without photos and video, and it allows you to be as detailed as you please in your posts. Twitter, on the other hand, is meant to share information in quick bursts, allowing users only 280 characters in which to alert you to their latest comings and goings. Instagram is basically a photo-sharing app, allowing you to add captions to personalize your pictures.

In this chapter, I introduce you to FaceTime and the Messages app and review their simple controls. You also take a look at finding, installing, and customizing Facebook, Twitter, and Instagram. In no time, you'll be socializing with all and sundry.

What You Need to Use FaceTime

Here's a quick rundown of the device and information you need for using FaceTime's various features:

» You can use FaceTime to call people over a Wi-Fi connection who have an iPhone 4 or later, an iPad 2 or a third-generation iPad or later, all iPad mini and iPad Pro models, a fourth-generation iPod touch or later, or a Mac (running macOS 10.6.6 or later). If you want to connect over a cellular connection, you must have an iPhone 4s or later and iPad third generation or later (as long as the iPad supports cellular data).

» You can use a phone number or an email address to connect with anyone with an iPhone, an iPad, or a Mac and an iCloud account.

» The person you're contacting must have enabled FaceTime in the Settings app.

An Overview of FaceTime

FaceTime works with the iPad's built-in cameras so that you can call other folks who have a device that supports FaceTime. You can use FaceTime to chat while sharing video images with another person. This preinstalled app is useful for seniors who want to keep up with distant family members and friends and see (as well as hear) the latest and greatest news.

When connected, you can show the person on the other end what's going on around you. Just remember that you can't adjust audio volume from within the app or record a video call. Nevertheless, on the positive side, even though its features are limited, this app is straightforward to use.

You can use your Apple ID and iCloud account to access FaceTime, so it works pretty much right away. See Chapter 3 for more about getting an Apple ID.

TIP If you're having trouble using FaceTime, make sure that the FaceTime feature is turned on. You can do so quickly: Tap Settings on the Home screen, tap FaceTime, and then tap the FaceTime switch to turn it to On (green), if it isn't already. On the same screen, you can also select the phone number, email addresses, or both that others can use to make FaceTime calls to you, as well as which one of those is displayed as your caller ID.

To view information for recent calls, open the FaceTime app and then tap the information icon (the letter *i* in a circle) on a recent call, and your iPad displays that person's information. You can tap the contact to call the person back.

TIP

FaceTime is very secure, meaning that your conversations remain private. Apple encrypts (digitally protects) all your FaceTime calls, both one-on-one and group calls, with industry-leading technology to make sure that snoops are kept at bay.

Make a FaceTime Call with Wi-Fi or Cellular

If you know that someone you're calling has FaceTime available on their device, adding that person to your iPad's Contacts is a good idea so that you can initiate FaceTime calls from within the Contacts app, if you like, or from the Contacts list that you can access through the FaceTime app.

When you call somebody using an email address, the person must be signed in to their Apple iCloud account and have verified that the address can be used for FaceTime calls. You can access this setting by tapping Settings and then FaceTime ⇨ You Can Be Reached by FaceTime At.

To make a FaceTime call:

1. Tap the FaceTime icon to launch the app.

If you've made or received FaceTime calls already, you will see a list of recent calls in the FaceTime menu on the left side of the screen. You can simply tap one of those to initiate a new call, or continue to learn how to start a new call from scratch.

2. Tap the green New FaceTime button in the upper-left corner to open the New FaceTime screen. Enter a contact's name (shown in **Figure 8-1**) by tapping the To field, or find a contact in your Contacts list by tapping the green plus (+) button to the right of the To field.

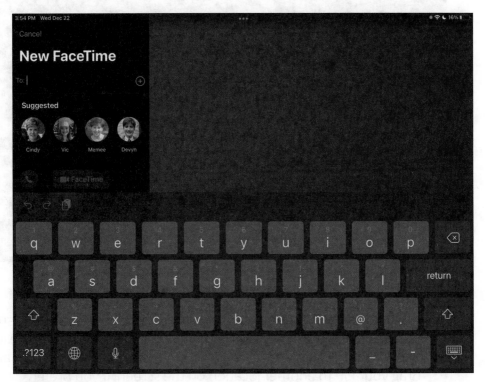

FIGURE 8-1

3. Tap one of the green buttons below the To field and Suggested section (but above the keyboard, shown in **Figure 8-2**) to choose a video call (large, green FaceTime button) or an audio call (small, green phone button).

   Video includes your voice and image; audio includes only your voice.

TIP

   You see a Video button if that contact's device supports FaceTime video, and an Audio button if the contact's device supports FaceTime audio. (If you haven't saved this person in your contacts and you know the phone number to call or email, you can just enter that information in the Enter Name, Email, or Number field.)

FIGURE 8-2

4. When the person accepts the call, you see a large screen that displays the recipient's image and a small screen, referred to as a Picture in Picture (PiP), containing your image superimposed. You can tap and drag your PiP to another location on the screen, if you prefer.

Use a Memoji with FaceTime

Want to have a little fun? Use memoji characters during your call! Memoji characters are digital illustrations that you can superimpose over your face, if your iPad supports Face ID. During your FaceTime call, tap the effects icon, which looks a bit like a star (if you don't see it, just tap the screen), tap the memoji icon (smiling illustrated character), and then select a memoji character from the list. You can create your own memoji characters, as can the people you're speaking with (again, if their iPad, iPhone, or Mac supports Face ID).

iOS 6 and later versions allow you to use FaceTime over a Wi-Fi network or your iPad's cellular connection (only if your iPad supports cellular, of course). However, if you use FaceTime over a cellular connection, you may incur costly data usage fees. To avoid the extra cost, in Settings under Cellular, toggle the FaceTime switch to Off (white).

Accept and End a FaceTime Call

If you're on the receiving end of a FaceTime call, accepting the call is about as easy as it gets. To accept and end a FaceTime call, follow these steps:

1. When the call comes in, tap the Accept button to take the call (see **Figure 8-3**).

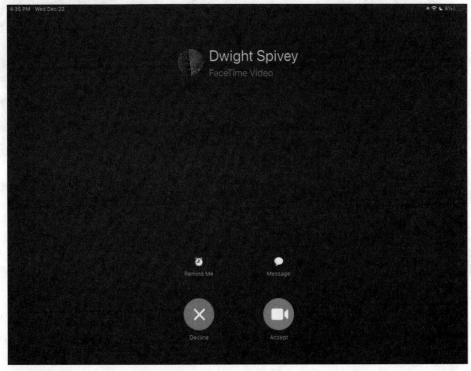

FIGURE 8-3

To reject the call, tap the Decline button.

2. Chat away with your friend, swapping video images.

3. To end the call, tap the red End button in the call controls window, as shown in **Figure 8-4.**

Call controls window   **Switch Cameras**

FIGURE 8-4

TIP

To mute sound during a call, tap the Mute button in the call controls window, which looks like a microphone with a line through it (refer to **Figure 8-4**). Tap the button again to unmute your iPad.

FaceTime in iPadOS 15 allows group calls for up to 32 people! You can have a family reunion without leaving your front porch. To add more folks to a current call:

1. Tap the screen to open the call controls window in the lower-left corner (refer to **Figure 8-4**) if it's not already open.

2. Tap the call controls window to expand it.

3. Tap the Add People button.

4. Tap the To field, enter or find a contact, tap a contact to add them to the To field, and finally, tap the green Add Person to FaceTime button to place them in the call.

Switch Views

When you're on a FaceTime call, you might want to use the iPad's built-in, rear-facing camera to show the person you're talking to what's going on around you.

1. Tap the Switch Camera button (refer to **Figure 8-4**) in your tile (the window with your image in it) to switch from the front-facing camera that's displaying your image to the back-facing camera that captures whatever you're looking at.

2. Tap the Switch Camera button again to switch back to the front camera displaying your image.

Set Up an iMessage Account

iMessage is a feature available through the preinstalled Messages app that allows you to send and receive instant messages (IMs) to others using an Apple iOS device, iPadOS device, or a suitably configured Mac. iMessage is a way of sending instant messages through a Wi-Fi network, but you can send messages through your cellular connection without having iMessage activated, assuming that your iPad supports cellular data.

TIP

Instant messaging differs from email or tweeting in an important way. Whereas you might email somebody and wait for days or weeks before that person responds, or you might post a tweet on Twitter that could sit there awhile before anybody views it, with instant messaging, communication happens almost immediately. You send an IM, and it appears on somebody's Apple device right away.

Assuming that the person wants to participate in a live conversation, the chat begins immediately, allowing a back-and-forth dialogue in real time.

1. To set up Messages, tap Settings on the Home screen.

2. Tap Messages. The settings shown in **Figure 8-5** appear.

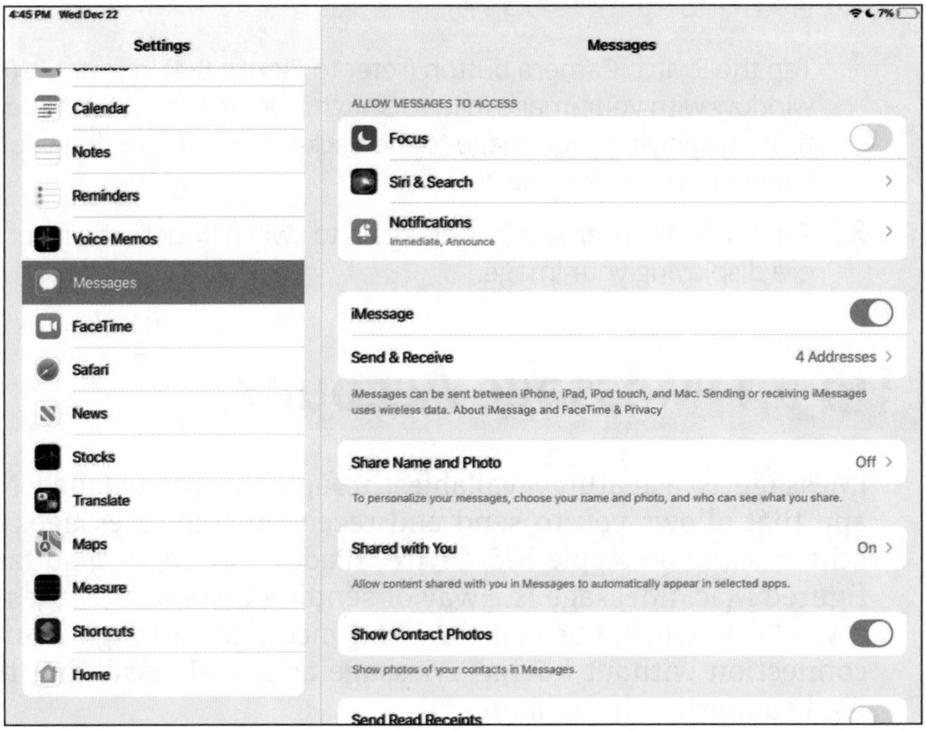

4:45 PM Wed Dec 22	🔋 7%
Settings	**Messages**

Calendar	ALLOW MESSAGES TO ACCESS
Notes	🌙 Focus
Reminders	📱 Siri & Search >
Voice Memos	🔔 Notifications
Messages	Immediate, Announce >
FaceTime	iMessage ⬤
Safari	Send & Receive 4 Addresses >
News	iMessages can be sent between iPhone, iPad, iPod touch, and Mac. Sending or receiving iMessages uses wireless data. About iMessage and FaceTime & Privacy
Stocks	
Translate	Share Name and Photo Off >
Maps	To personalize your messages, choose your name and photo, and who can see what you share.
Measure	Shared with You On >
Shortcuts	Allow content shared with you in Messages to automatically appear in selected apps.
Home	Show Contact Photos ⬤
	Show photos of your contacts in Messages.
	Send Read Receipts

FIGURE 8-5

3. If iMessage isn't set to On (refer to **Figure 8-5**), tap the On/Off switch to toggle it to On (green).

Be sure that the phone number or email account (or both) associated with your iPad under the Send & Receive setting is correct. (It should be set up automatically based on your iCloud settings.) If it isn't, tap the Send & Receive field, add an email or phone, and then tap Messages to return to the previous screen.

4. To allow a notice to be sent to the sender when you've read a message, tap the On/Off switch for Send Read Receipts. You can also choose to show a subject field in your messages.

5. Press the Home button or swipe up from the bottom of the screen (depending on your iPad model) to leave Settings.

To enable or disable email accounts used by Messages, tap Send & Receive and then tap an email address to enable (check mark appears to the left) or disable it (no check mark appears to the left).

Use Messages to Address, Create, and Send Messages

After you set your iMessage account, you're ready to use Messages:

1. From the Home screen, tap the Messages button.

2. Tap the New Message button (blue square containing a pen-and-paper icon) in the top-right corner of the Messages list (on the left of the screen) to begin a conversation.

3. In the form that appears (see **Figure 8-6**), you can address a message in a few ways:

- Begin to type a name in the To field, and a list of matching contacts appears.

- Tap the Dictation key (looks like a microphone) on the onscreen keyboard and speak the address.

- Tap the plus (+) button on the right side of the To field, and the Contacts list is displayed.

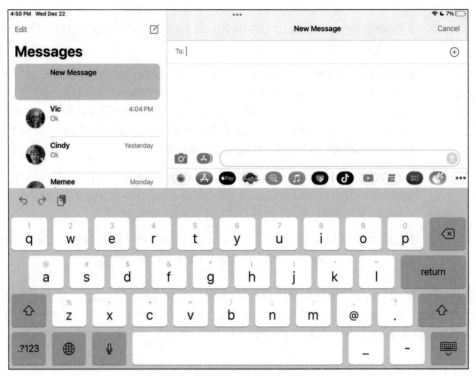

FIGURE 8-6

4. Tap a contact on the list you chose from in Step 3. If the contact has both an email address and a phone number stored, the Info dialog appears, allowing you to tap one or the other, which addresses the message.

5. To create a message, simply tap in the message field (near the bottom of the screen if the onscreen keyboard is collapsed), shown in **Figure 8-6,** and type your message.

6. To send the message, tap the Send button (the round blue button with the white arrow in **Figure 8-6**). When your recipient (or recipients) responds, you see the conversation displayed on the screen. Tap in the message field again to respond to the last comment.

TIP

You can address a message to more than one person by simply choosing more recipients in Step 2 of the preceding list.

Read Messages

When you receive a message, it's as easy to read as email — easier, to be honest!

1. Tap Messages on the Home screen.

2. When the app opens, you see a list of text conversations you've engaged in.

3. Tap a conversation to see the message string, including all attachments, as shown in **Figure 8-7.**

FIGURE 8-7

Clear a Conversation

When you're done chatting, you might want to delete a conversation to remove the clutter before you start a new chat.

1. With Messages open and your conversations displayed, swipe to the left on the conversation you want to delete.

2. Tap the red Delete button (looks like a trash can) next to the conversation you want to get rid of (see **Figure 8-8**).

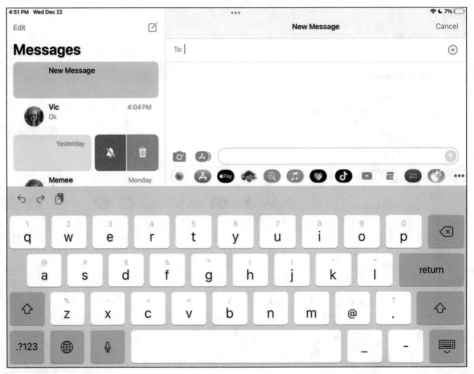

FIGURE 8-8

TIP

Tap the blue Hide Alerts button (looks like a bell with a slash through it) to keep from being alerted to new messages in the conversation. Swipe again and tap the Show Alerts button to reactivate alerts for the conversation.

Send Emojis in Place of Text

Emojis are small pictures that can help convey a feeling or idea — for example, smiley faces and sad faces to show emotions, thumbs-up to convey approval, and the like.

To send an emoji in place of text:

1. From within a conversation, tap the Emoji key on the onscreen keyboard. If you can't see the keyboard, tap in the Message field to display it.

2. When the emojis appear (see **Figure 8-9**), swipe left and right to find the right emoji for the moment and tap to select it. You can add as many as you like to the conversation.

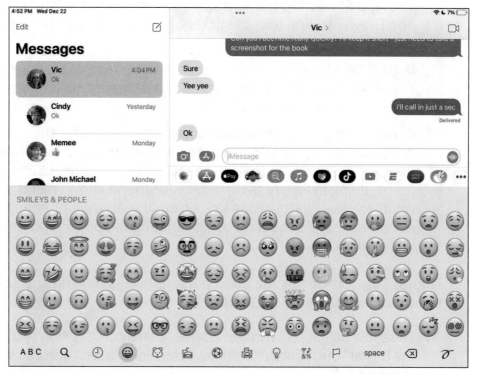

FIGURE 8-9

Use the App Drawer

The App Drawer allows you to add items that spice up your messages with information from other apps that are installed on your iPad, as well as drawings and other images from the web.

To use the App Drawer:

1. Tap the App Drawer icon (looks like an *A*) to the left of the iMessage field in your conversation. The App Drawer displays at the bottom of the screen.

2. Tap an item in the App Drawer to see what it offers your messaging.

The App Drawer is populated by

» **The App Store:** Tap the App Store all the way to the left of the App Drawer to find tons of stickers, games, and apps for your messages.

» **Digital Touch:** Allows you to send special effects in Messages. These can range from sending your heartbeat to sketching a quick picture to sending a kiss.

» **Other apps you have installed may also appear if they have the ability to add functions and information to your messages.** For example, send the latest scores using ESPN (as I'm doing in **Figure 8-10**) or let your friend know what the weather's like nearby using icons from the AccuWeather app. Another example could be using Fandango's app to send movie information.

Digital Touch is one of the most personal ways to send special effects to others, so take a closer look at it:

1. To send a Digital Touch in a message, open a conversation and tap the Digital Touch button (black oval containing a red heart), as shown in **Figure 8-11.**

FIGURE 8-10

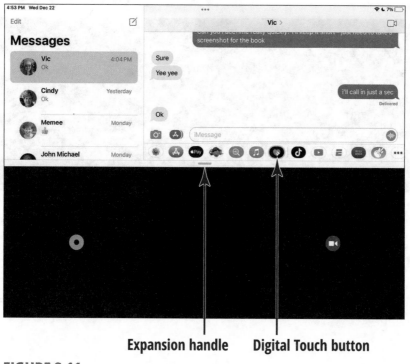

Expansion handle   Digital Touch button

FIGURE 8-11

2. In the Digital Touch window, tap the gray expansion handle (shown in **Figure 8-11** in the very middle of the screen immediately under the message field) to open the full window. Tap the Information button in the lower right (a gray circle with a white letter *i*), and you see a list of the gestures and what they do.

3. Perform a gesture in the Digital Touch window, and it will go to your recipient. If you've created a drawing, tap the blue Send button (see **Figure 8-12**) to send it.

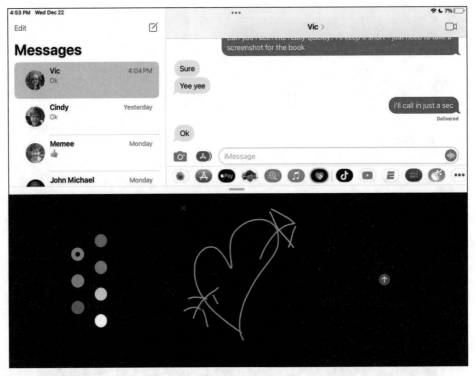

FIGURE 8-12

Send and Receive Audio

When you're creating a message, you can also create an audio message:

1. With Messages open, tap the New Message button.

2. Enter an addressee's name in the To field.

3. Press and hold the Audio button (the microphone symbol to the right of the screen in the message field).

4. Speak your message or record a sound or music near you as you continue to hold down the Audio button.

5. Release the Audio button when you're finished recording.

6. Tap the Send button (an upward-pointing arrow at the top of the recording circle). The message appears as an audio track in the recipient's Messages inbox (see **Figure 8-13**). To play the track, the recipient just taps the Play button.

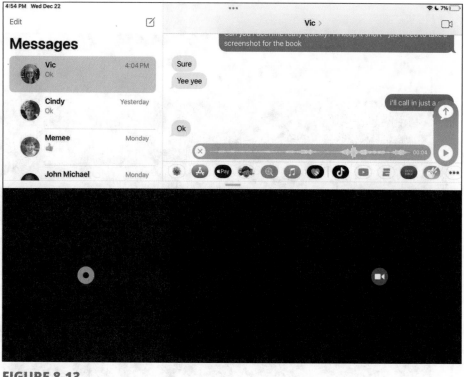

FIGURE 8-13

Send a Photo or Video

When you're creating a message, you can also send a picture or create a short video message:

1. With Messages open, tap the New Message button.

2. Tap the Camera button to the left of the message field to open the Camera app; then take a picture.

3. After you take the picture, the tools shown in **Figure 8-14** appear, and you can work with the picture before sending it along to your recipient:

- Tap Retake in the upper-left corner to take a different picture.

- Tap Edit (icon of circle containing three lines) to edit the picture.

FIGURE 8-14

- Tap Markup (the marker tip icon) to add notes or other text to your picture.

- Tap Effects (the star icon) to add effects to your picture. When you tap it, a row of buttons appears in the lower-left of your screen. Tap one to see how it adds neat effects to your call.

- Tap Done to place the picture in your message but not send it yet.

- Tap the Send button (the blue circle containing the white arrow in the lower-right) to send the picture immediately.

Send a Map of Your Location

When responding to a message, you can also send a map showing your current location:

1. Tap a message, tap the picture of the recipient in the upper-center of the screen, and then tap the Info button underneath.

2. Tap Send My Current Location (see **Figure 8-15**), and a map will be inserted as a message attachment.

TIP

You can also share your location in the middle of a conversation rather than send a map attachment with your message. In the screen shown in **Figure 8-15,** tap Share My Location and then tap Share for One Hour, Share Until End of Day, or Share Indefinitely. A map showing your location appears above your conversation until you stop sharing.

FIGURE 8-15

Understand Group Messaging

If you want to start a conversation with a group of people, you can use group messaging. Group messaging is great for keeping several people in the conversational loop.

Group messaging functionality includes the following features:

» When you participate in a group message, you see all participants in the Info for the message (see **Figure 8-16**). You can drop people whom you don't want to include any longer and leave the conversation yourself when you want to by simply tapping Info and then tapping Leave This Conversation.

» When you turn on Hide Alerts in the Details in a message (see **Figure 8-16**), you won't get notifications of messages from this group, but you can still read the group's messages at a later time (this also works for individuals).

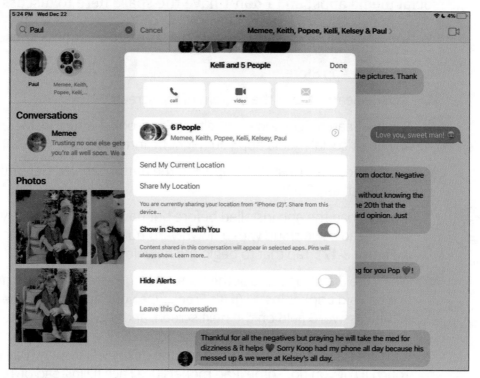

FIGURE 8-16

Taking you further into the workings of group messages is beyond the scope of this book, but if you're intrigued, go to `https://support.apple.com/en-us/HT202724` for more information.

Find and Install Social Media Apps

To begin using social media apps, you first need to find and install them on your iPad. I focus on Facebook, Twitter, and Instagram in this chapter because they're currently three of the most popular social media apps, and I don't have the space here to discuss more.

To find and install the apps using the App Store, follow these steps:

1. Open the App Store.

2. Tap the Search tab at the bottom of the screen.

3. Tap the Search field and enter either Facebook, Twitter, Instagram, or any other social media app you might be interested in.

4. To download and install the app, tap the button labeled Get or the price (such as $2.99).

TIP

If you've had the app installed before but have since deleted it, you will instead see a cloud with a downward-pointing arrow (as shown in **Figure 8-17**). Tap that to begin the download.

5. When the dialog appears at the bottom of the screen, tap Purchase (if it's a Paid app) or Install (if it's Free), type your Apple ID password in the Password field on the next screen, and then tap Sign In to download the app. Alternatively, use Touch ID if you have it enabled for iTunes and App Store purchases; the dialog will display "Pay with Touch ID" if you do. Some iPad models use Face ID instead of Touch ID. When you're prompted to pay (with Face ID enabled), double-click the top button and glance at your iPhone to initiate payment.

The app will download and install on one of your Home screens.

TIP

The deluge of false news on social media is beginning to take its toll on society, and social media developers are taking steps to combat the misuse of their platforms. For example, Facebook tries to flag demonstrably false articles and posts while still giving you the option to view them, as is your right. They also provide a page in their Help Center called "Tips to Spot False News" (www.facebook.com/help/188118808357379) to help you differentiate false information from the real thing.

A FEW SOCIAL MEDIA DOS AND DON'TS

Social media, like most things, has its upsides and downsides. Although you can connect with old friends, swap stories with others, and share vacation pics of the family, you're also in danger of being preyed upon by cyber thugs and other ne'er-do-wells prowling the Internet. This short list (it's by no means exhaustive) of do's and don'ts will help keep you safe on social media:

- Do connect with family and friends, but keep your social media circle close. It's great to reconnect with people you've not seen for a while, but branching out too far can lead to mischief by some who don't know you.

- Do use strong and unique passwords for your accounts. This safeguard makes it tougher for folks with bad intentions to access your account and potentially post things in your name that you wouldn't condone.

- Do set up privacy controls for each social media account you use. You may want some people to see everything you post, but you may also want to keep certain things (such as birthdays and other personal information) closer to the vest.

- Don't ever share your social security number, credit card numbers, banking accounts, or any other financial information of any kind!

- Don't type in ALL CAPS. It's considered the Internet equivalent of yelling. You may mean nothing by it, but because there's no way for your interlocutor to hear or see the context of your text, they could misconstrue your intent. That's how all sorts of social media dust-ups get started.

- Don't accept a friend request from someone you are already friends with on a social media platform. If you're already friends with them on the platform, it's a good indication that something fishy is going on. Send a private message to the friend to confirm that they've sent the friend request.

- Don't believe everything you read! If something sounds too crazy to be true, it probably is. It's always best — and I do mean always — to research the topic via multiple trustworthy and varied sources before commenting on it in social media environs.

- Don't advertise that you're on vacation. Wait until you return to post pictures of your dream trip. If someone with ill intent knows that you're away, they might take advantage of the opportunity to pay your home an unannounced and unwanted visit.

FIGURE 8-17

Create a Facebook Account

You can create a Facebook account from within the app.

If you already have a Facebook account, you can simply use that account information to log in.

TIP

To create an account in the Facebook app, follow these steps:

1. Launch the newly downloaded Facebook app.

2. Tap the Sign Up for Facebook option at the bottom of the screen, as shown in **Figure 8-18** (you almost need binoculars to see it).

3. Tap Get Started and walk through the steps to complete the registration of your account.

4. When finished, you'll be logged into your account in the Facebook app.

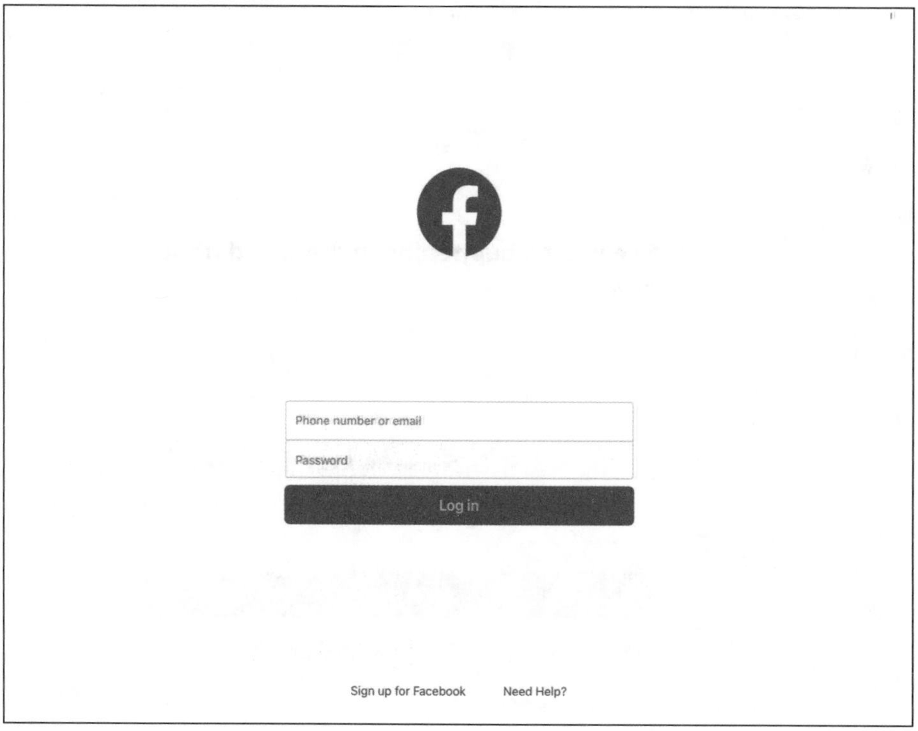

FIGURE 8-18

You may also create a Facebook account by visiting its website at
www.facebook.com.

TIP

Create a Twitter Account

To create an account in the Twitter app, follow these steps:

1. Open the Twitter app by tapping its icon.

2. Tap the blue Create account button near the bottom of the screen, as shown in **Figure 8-19.**

If you already have a Twitter account, tap the tiny Log In button at the very bottom of the screen to log in.

TIP

3. The app asks you some questions to help you create your account.

4. When you're done, the app logs you into your new account.

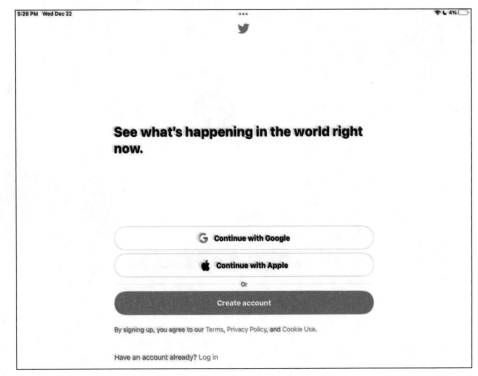

FIGURE 8-19

TIP

As with Facebook, you can create an account on the Twitter website at `www.twitter.com`.

Create an Instagram Account

To create an account in the Instagram app:

1. Open the Instagram app by tapping its icon.

2. Tap the near-microscopic Sign Up button at the bottom of the screen, shown in **Figure 8-20,** to walk through the steps of creating a new Instagram account.

TIP

If you already have an Instagram account, tap the really small Log In button to access it.

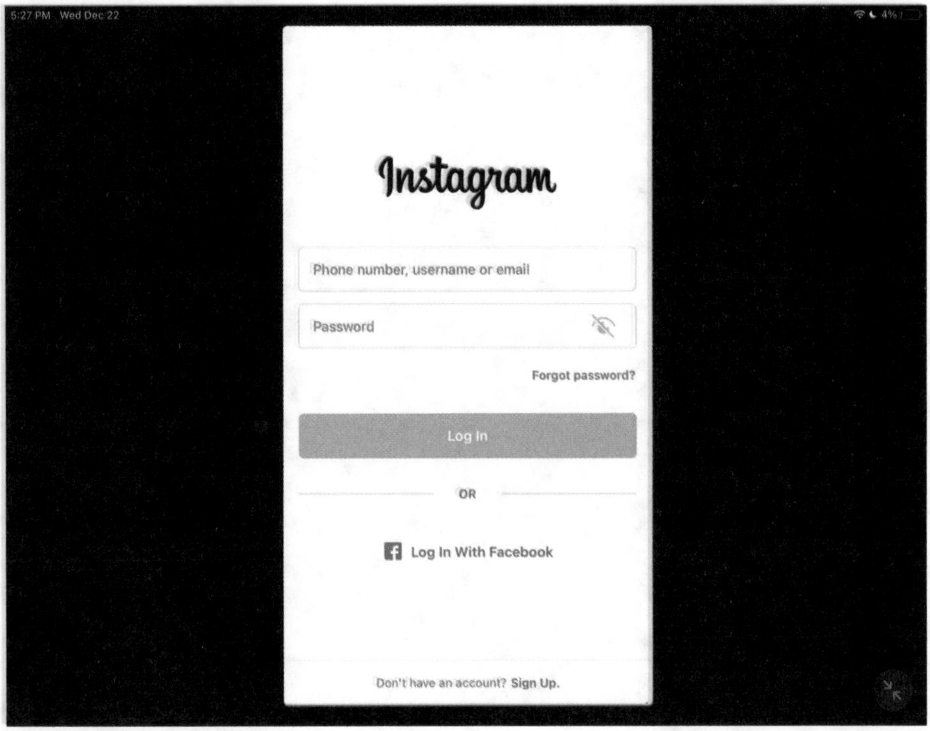

FIGURE 8-20

3. The app asks you several questions to help you create your account.

4. When completed, the app logs you into your new account.

TIP

You can also create an account on the Instagram website at `www.instagram.com`.

Chapter **9**

Browsing with Safari

You can get on the Internet with your iPad by using its Wi-Fi or cellular capabilities. After you're online, the built-in browser (software that helps you navigate the Internet's contents), Safari, is your ticket to a wide world of information, entertainment, education, and more. Safari will look familiar to you if you've used a web browser on a PC or Mac computer, though the way you move around by using the iPad touchscreen may be new to you. If you've never used Safari, don't worry because I take you by the hand and show you all the basics of making it work for you.

In this chapter, you see how to go online with your iPad, navigate among web pages, and use iCloud tabs to share your browsing experience between devices. Along the way, you see how to place a bookmark for a favorite site and create a tab group, a feature new to iPadOS 15. You can also view your browsing history, save online images to the Photos app, search the web, or email or tweet a link to a friend. Finally, you explore how to translate web pages so that you can read what's going on around the world, even if you may not speak the language.

Connect to the Internet

How you connect to the Internet depends on which types of connections are available:

>> You can connect to the Internet via a Wi-Fi network. You can set up this type of network in your own home using your computer and some equipment from your Internet provider. You can also connect over public Wi-Fi networks, referred to as hotspots.

TIP

You might be surprised to discover how many hotspots your town or city has. Look for Internet cafes, coffee shops, hotels, libraries, and transportation centers (such as airports or bus stations). Many of these businesses display signs alerting you to their free Wi-Fi.

>> You can use the paid data network provided by AT&T, Sprint, T-Mobile, Verizon, or almost any other cellular provider to connect from just about anywhere you can get coverage through a cellular network. Of course, you have to have an iPad model that supports cellular connections to hop on the Internet this way.

To enable cellular data (if your iPad supports it), tap Settings and then tap Cellular. Tap to toggle the Cellular Data switch On (green).

TIP

Browsing the Internet using a cellular connection can eat up your data plan allotment quickly if your plan doesn't include unlimited data access. If you think you'll often use the Internet with your iPad away from a Wi-Fi connection, double-check your data allotment with your cellular provider or consider getting an unlimited data plan.

To connect to a Wi-Fi network, you have to complete a few steps:

1. Tap Settings on the Home screen and then tap Wi-Fi.

2. Be sure that the Wi-Fi toggle switch is set to On (green) and choose a network to connect to by tapping it.

Network names should appear automatically when you're in range of them. When you're in range of a public hotspot, if access to several nearby networks is available, you may see a message asking you to tap a network name to select it. After you select a network, you may see a message asking for your password. Ask the owner of the hotspot (for example, a hotel desk clerk or business owner) for this password or enter your own network password if you're connecting to your home network.

Free public Wi-Fi networks usually don't require passwords, or the password is posted prominently for all to see. (If you can't find the password, don't be shy about asking someone.)

3. Tap the Join button when prompted. Once done, you're connected! Your iPad will now recognize the network and connect without repeatedly entering the password.

After you connect to public Wi-Fi, someone else can possibly track your online activities because these are unsecured networks. Avoid accessing financial accounts, making online purchases, or sending emails with sensitive information in them when connected to a public hotspot.

Explore Safari

Safari is your iPad's default web browsing app.

This is not the Safari of old. If you're familiar with versions of Safari prior to this one, enough has changed in iPadOS 15 to warrant your time perusing this chapter.

TIP

You can change your iPad's default browser from Safari to another you've downloaded. Go to Settings, find and tap the name of any browser in the left sidebar (for example, Safari, Chrome, or Edge), tap Default Browser App, and then tap the name of the browser you want to use as default.

Here's how to get around in Safari:

1. After you're connected to a network, tap Safari on the Dock at the bottom of the Home screen. Safari opens, possibly displaying the Apple iPad home page the first time you go online (see **Figure 9-1**).

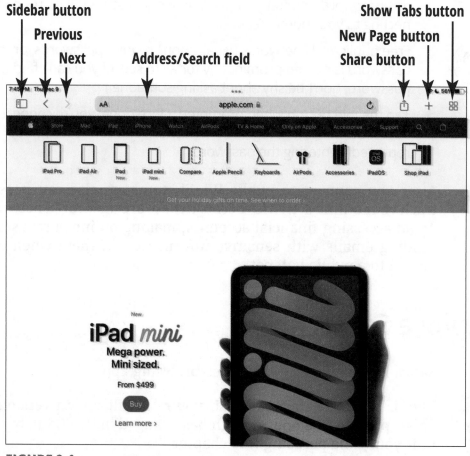

FIGURE 9-1

2. Put two fingers together on the screen and spread them apart to expand the view (also known as zooming in). Place your fingers on the screen about an inch or so apart and quickly bring them together to zoom back out. You can also double-tap the screen with a single finger to restore the default view size. (If you tap a link, though, your gesture will just open that link.)

Using your fingers on the screen to enlarge or reduce the size of a web page allows you to view what's displayed at various sizes, giving you more flexibility than the double-tap method.

3. Put your finger on the screen and flick (or swipe, as some call it) upward to scroll down on the page.

4. To return to the top of the web page, put your finger on the screen and drag downward, or tap the status bar at the very top of the screen twice.

When you zoom in, you have more control by using two fingers to drag from left to right or from top to bottom on the screen. When you zoom out, one finger works fine for making these gestures.

Navigate Web Pages

Web pages are chock-full of information and gateways to other web resources. To navigate the landscape of web pages in Safari:

1. Tap in the Address field at the very top of the screen and the onscreen keyboard appears (see **Figure 9-2**).

2. Enter a web address; for example, you can go to www.dummies.com.

3. Tap the Go key on the keyboard (see **Figure 9-2**). The website appears.

   - If a page doesn't display properly, tap the Reload button at the right end of the Address field.

   - If Safari is loading a web page and you change your mind about viewing the page, you can stop loading the page. To stop loading the page, tap Cancel (looks like an *X*), which appears at the right end of the Address field during this process.

FIGURE 9-2

4. Tap the Previous button (looks like <) in the upper-left corner to go to the last page you displayed.

5. Tap the Next button (looks like >) in the upper-left corner to go forward to the page you just backed up from.

6. To follow a link to another web page (links are typically indicated by colored text or graphics), tap the link with your finger.

TIP

To preview the destination of the link before you tap it, just touch and hold the link. A menu appears next to a preview of the site, as shown in **Figure 9-3**. Choose an option from the menu to proceed, or tap anywhere outside the menu to close it and the preview window.

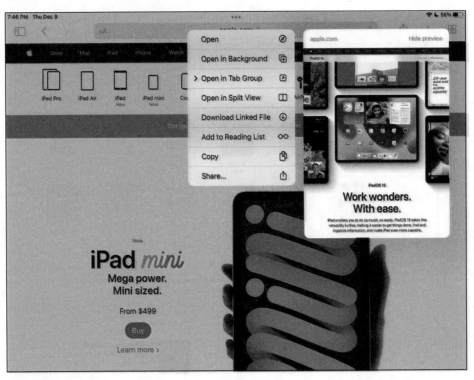

FIGURE 9-3

Use Tabbed Browsing

Tabbed browsing is a feature that allows you to have several websites open at one time so that you can move easily among those sites.

1. With Safari open and a web page already displaying, tap the Show Tabs button in the upper-right corner (refer to **Figure 9-1**). The Tab view appears.

2. To add a new page (meaning that you're opening a new website), tap the New Page button (shaped like a plus sign [+]) in the upper right of the screen (see **Figure 9-4**). A page appears with your favorite or currently open sites and an address bar.

You can get to the same new page by simply tapping in the address bar from any site.

TIP

Tap to open a new page

FIGURE 9-4

3. Tap in the Address field and use the onscreen keyboard to enter the web address for the website you want to open. Tap the Go key. The website opens on the page.

Repeat Steps 1 to 3 to open as many new web pages as you'd like.

TIP

4. You can now switch among open sites by tapping outside the keyboard to close it and tapping the Show Tabs button and scrolling among recent sites. Find the one you want and then tap it.

You can easily rearrange sites in the tabs window. Just press and hold the tab you want to move and then drag it to the right or left in the list until it's in the spot you'd like it to be (the other sites in the window politely move to make room). To drop it in the new location, simply remove your finger from the screen.

TIP

5. To delete a tab, tap the Show Tabs button, scroll to locate the tab, and then tap the Close button in the upper-right corner of the tab (looks like an *X*; it may be difficult to see on some sites, but trust me, it's there). Tap the Done button in the upper-right corner to close the Tabs view.

Organize with Tab Groups

The new tab groups feature in iPadOS 15 enables you to keep similar tabs together so that they're easier to organize and find. This feature is especially helpful if you're someone who likes to keep a million tabs open at one time; tab groups keep you from having to swipe until your fingers bleed to find the site tab you're looking for.

1. With Safari open, tap the Sidebar button in the upper-left corner (refer to **Figure 9-1**).

2. In the sidebar, tap *x* Tabs, where *x* represents the number of open tabs.

   Figure 9-5 shows that I have seven open tabs in Safari.

3. In the sidebar, you can do any of the following:

   - Tap a group to open it (such as my group, Food, in **Figure 9-5**).

   - To create a new group, tap the Tab Groups button in the upper right of the sidebar; then tap New Empty Tab Group (see **Figure 9-5**). You'll be prompted to give it a descriptive name (like Food in **Figure 9-6**). Tap Save to finish.

   - To create a tab group from the tabs you currently have open, tap New Tab Group from *x* Tabs (see **Figure 9-5**). Again, give the new group a descriptive name to help you stay organized; then tap Save.

FIGURE 9-5

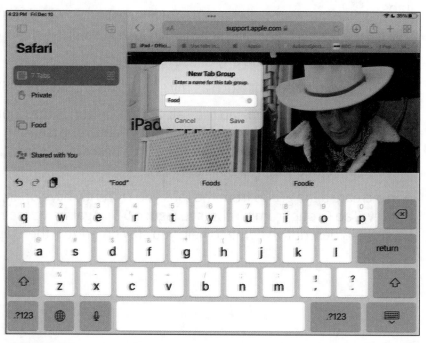

FIGURE 9-6

4. To move a site to a tab group:

    a. Tap the Show Tabs button in the upper right of the Safari window.

    b. Press and hold the tab for the site you want to move until a menu opens.

    c. Tap the Move to Tab Group option.

    d. Tap the name of the group you want to move the site to (see **Figure 9-7**) and it will join that tab group (see **Figure 9-8**).

FIGURE 9-7

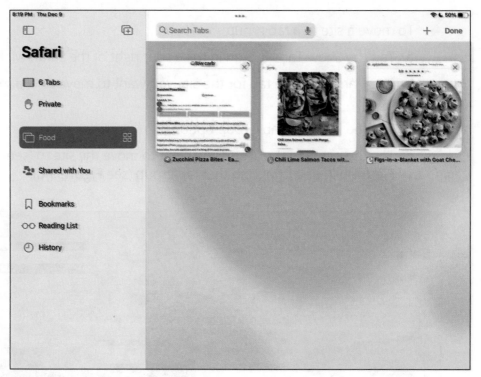

FIGURE 9-8

View Browsing History

As you move around the web, your browser keeps a record of your browsing history. This record can be handy when you want to visit a site that you viewed previously but whose address you've now forgotten.

To view your browsing history:

1. With Safari open, tap the Sidebar button in the upper-left corner, and then tap the History button in the sidebar.

You might prefer a shortcut to view your History list. Tap and hold the Previous button at the upper left on any screen, and your browsing history for the current session appears. You can also tap and hold the Next button to look at sites you backtracked from.

2. In the History list that appears (see **Figure 9-9**), tap a site to navigate to it.

3. Tap the Safari button in the upper-left corner to leave History and return to the sidebar, or tap the Sidebar button to close the sidebar altogether.

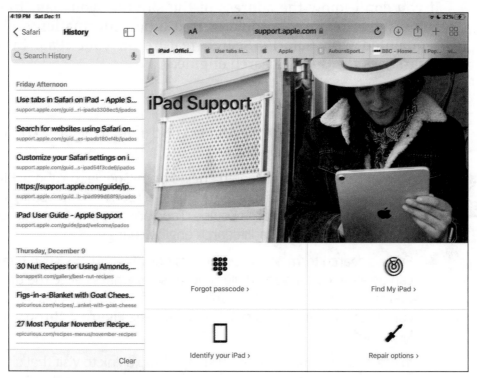

FIGURE 9-9

TIP

To clear the history, tap the Clear button in the bottom of the History list (refer to **Figure 9-9**), and on the screen that appears, tap an option: The Last Hour, Today, Today and Yesterday, or All Time. This button is useful when you don't want your spouse or grandchildren to see where you've been browsing for anniversary, birthday, or holiday gifts!

Search the Web

If you don't know the address of the site that you want to visit (or you want to research a topic or find other information online), get acquainted with Safari's Search feature on your iPad. By default, Safari uses the Google search engine.

To search the web:

1. With Safari open, tap in the Address field (refer to **Figure 9-1**). The onscreen keyboard appears.

TIP

To change your default search engine from Google to Yahoo!, Bing, DuckDuckGo, or Ecosia, go to the Home screen and tap Settings, tap Safari, and then tap Search Engine. Tap Yahoo!, Bing, DuckDuckGo, or Ecosia, and your default search engine changes.

2. Enter a search term. With recent versions of Safari, the search term can be a topic or a web address because of what's called the unified smart search field. You can tap one of the suggested sites or complete your entry and tap the Go key (see **Figure 9-10**) on your keyboard.

3. In the search results that are displayed, tap a link to visit that site.

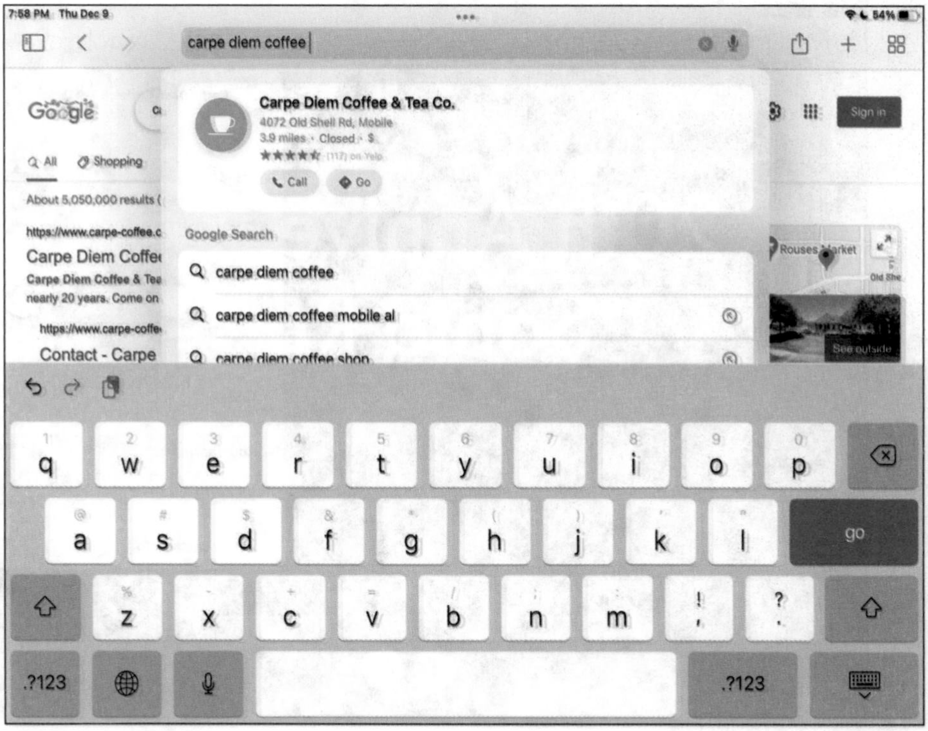

FIGURE 9-10

Add and Use Bookmarks

Bookmarks are a way to save favorite sites so that you can easily visit them again.

To add and use bookmarks:

1. With a site open that you want to bookmark, tap the Share button in the upper-right of the screen (which looks like a box with an upward-pointing arrow).

If you want to sync your bookmarks on your iPad browser, open the Settings app on your iPad and make sure that iCloud is set to sync with Safari.

2. On the menu that appears (see **Figure 9-11**), tap Add Bookmark. (You may need to swipe up the window to see it.)

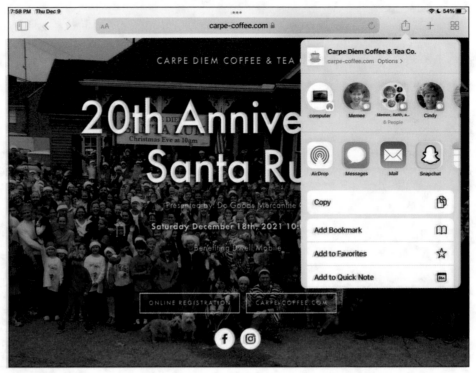

FIGURE 9-11

3. In the Add Bookmark dialog, shown in **Figure 9-12,** edit the name of the bookmark if you want. Tap the name of the site and use the onscreen keyboard to edit its name.

4. Tap the Save button in the upper-right corner of the Add Bookmark dialog. The item is saved to your Favorites by default, but you can select a different location by tapping Favorites and then tapping the preferred location.

5. To go to the bookmark, tap the Sidebar button in the upper left, and then tap the Bookmarks button in the sidebar.

6. In the Bookmarks list that appears, find and tap the bookmarked site that you want to visit. (Use the Search field in the Bookmarks list if you need to.) In **Figure 9-13,** I've searched for and found the site I bookmarked back in Step 3 (it's found under Favorites, which is a sub-section of the Bookmarks list).

FIGURE 9-12

TIP

When you tap the Bookmarks button and the Bookmarks list opens, you can tap Edit in the lower right of the Bookmarks list and then use the New Folder option (in the lower left) to create folders to organize your bookmarks or folders. When you next add a bookmark, you can then choose, from the dialog that appears, any folder to which you want to add the new bookmark.

TIP

You can reorder your bookmarks quite easily. Tap the Bookmarks button to open the Bookmarks list, tap the Edit button (lower right of the list), find the bookmark you'd like to rearrange, press and hold the three parallel lines to the right of the bookmark, and then drag the bookmark up and down the list, releasing it after you get to the place you'd like it to reside. You can also delete bookmarks from the same screen by tapping the red circle to the left of a bookmark and then tapping the red Delete button that appears to the right. Tap Done at the bottom of the Bookmarks list when finished.

FIGURE 9-13

Save Links and Web Pages to Safari Reading List

The Safari Reading List provides a way to save content that you want to read at a later time so that you can easily call up that content again. You essentially save the content rather than a web page address, which allows you to read the content even when you're offline. You can scroll from one item to the next easily.

To save content to the Reading List, follow these steps:

1. Displaying a site that you want to add to your Reading List, tap the Share button.

2. On the menu that appears (refer to **Figure 9-11**), tap the Add to Reading List button (you may need to swipe down to see it). The site is added to your Reading List.

3. To view your Reading List, tap the Sidebar button in the upper-left corner and then tap the Reading List button in the sidebar (the eyeglasses icon).

TIP

If you want to see both the Reading List material you've read and the material you haven't read, tap the Show Unread button in the bottom-left corner of the Reading List. To see all reading material, tap the Show All button.

4. On the Reading List that appears (see **Figure 9-14**), tap the content that you want to revisit and resume reading.

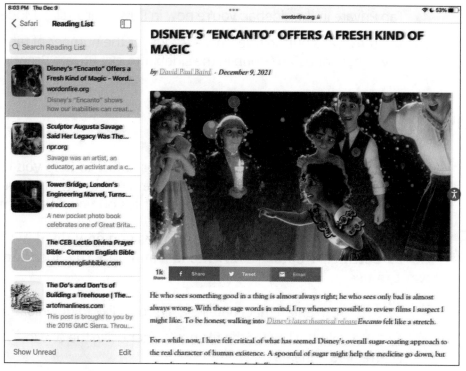

FIGURE 9-14

TIP

To delete an item, with the Reading List displaying, swipe from right to left on an item; a red Delete button appears to the right. Tap this button to delete the item from the Reading List. To save an item for offline (when you're not connected to the Internet) reading, tap the Save Offline button when you swipe. You can also swipe the item from left to right to mark it as read or unread.

Enable Private Browsing

Apple has provided some privacy settings for Safari that you should consider using.

Private Browsing automatically stops Safari from using AutoFill to save information used to complete certain entries as you type, and erases some browsing history information. This feature can keep your online activities more private. To enable Private Browsing:

1. Tap the Sidebar button in the upper-left corner.

2. Tap Private in the sidebar; you're now in Private Browsing Mode.

3. Tap the *x* Tabs button (the *x* here stands for the number of tabs you have open) or a Tab Group in the sidebar to exit Private Browsing.

Download Files

iPadOS 15 includes Download Manager for Safari to help you efficiently download files from websites and store them to a location of your choosing. You can choose to store downloaded files on your iPad or in iCloud.

TIP

Set the default download location for files you download in Safari. Go to Settings ⇨ Safari ⇨ Downloads and tap the location you want to use.

1. Open a site in Safari that contains a file you'd like to download.

2. Tap and hold the link for the file until a menu like the one in **Figure 9-15** appears.

3. Tap Download Linked File to download the file to your iPad, iCloud, or another destination.

4. The Download Manager button (a circle containing a downward-pointing arrow) appears to the right of the address field at the top of the screen (see **Figure 9-16**). Tap it to see the progress of the download. If the download is finished, tap it in the Downloads menu to open it, or tap the magnifying glass button to see where the file is stored.

FIGURE 9-15

FIGURE 9-16

Translate Web Pages

iPadOS 14 introduced a great new trick: web page translation! Visit a compatible web page, and Safari can translate it into several languages (with more sure to come): English, Spanish, Brazilian Portuguese, Simplified Chinese, German, Russian, and French.

1. Open a site in Safari that's in a language you'd like to translate.

2. Tap AA in the URL field (see **Figure 9-17**), and then tap the Translate To option. If you don't see this option, Safari is unable to translate the site.

The page is translated into the language you selected.

Tap to translate

FIGURE 9-17

Chapter **10**

Working with Email in Mail

S taying in touch with others by email is a great way to use your iPad. You can access an existing account using the handy Mail app supplied with your iPad via iPadOS 15, or sign in to your email account using the Safari browser. In this chapter, you take a look at using Mail, which involves adding an existing email account. Then you can use Mail to write, format, retrieve, and forward messages from that account.

Mail offers the capability to mark the messages you've read, delete messages, and organize your messages in a small set of folders, as well as use a handy search feature. You can also create a VIP list so that you're notified when that special person sends you an email.

In this chapter, you find out about the Mail app and its various features.

Add an Email Account

You can add one or more email accounts, including the email account associated with your iCloud account, using iPad Settings. If you have an iCloud, Microsoft Exchange (often used for business accounts), Gmail, Yahoo!, AOL, or Outlook.com (this includes Microsoft accounts from Live, Hotmail, and so on) account, the iPad pretty much automates the setup.

TIP If you have an iCloud account and have signed in to it already, your iCloud email account will already be set up for you in Mail.

TIP If this is the first time you're adding an account, and if you need to add only one, save yourself a few taps: Just open Mail and begin from Step 4 in the following steps.

Follow these steps to set up your iPad to retrieve messages from your email account at one of these popular providers:

1. Tap the Settings icon on the Home screen.

2. In Settings, tap Mail and then Accounts. The screen shown in **Figure 10-1** appears.

3. Tap Add Account, found in the Accounts section. The options shown in **Figure 10-2** appear.

4. Tap iCloud, Microsoft Exchange, Google, Yahoo!, AOL, or Outlook.com. Enter your account information in the form that appears and follow any instructions to complete the process. (Each service is slightly different, but none are complicated.) If you have a different email service than these, skip to the next section, "Manually Set Up an Email Account."

5. After your iPad takes a moment to verify the account information, on the next screen (shown in **Figure 10-3**), you can tap any On/Off switch to have services from that account synced with your iPad.

6. When you're done, tap Save in the upper-right corner. The account is saved, and you can now open it using Mail.

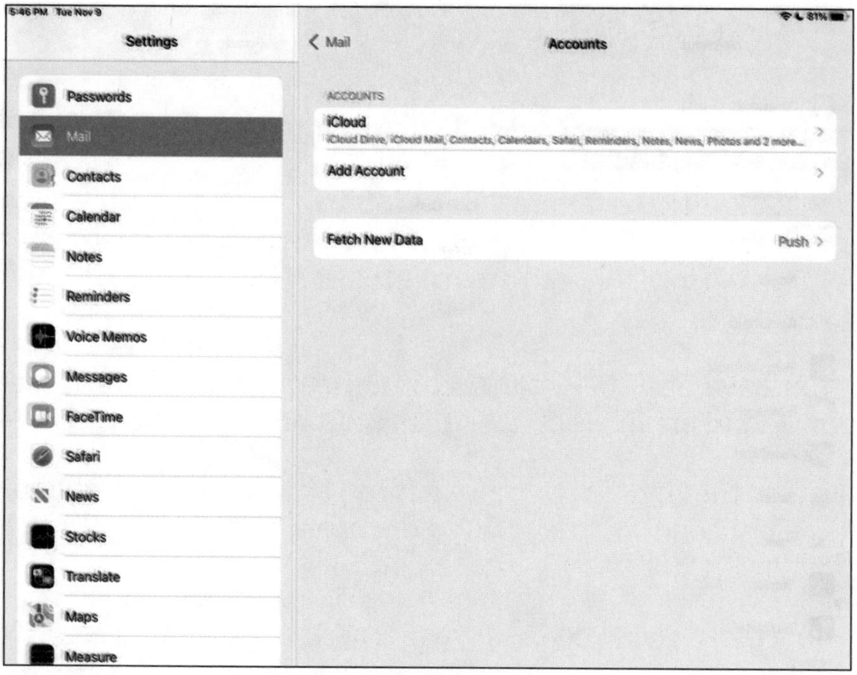

FIGURE 10-1

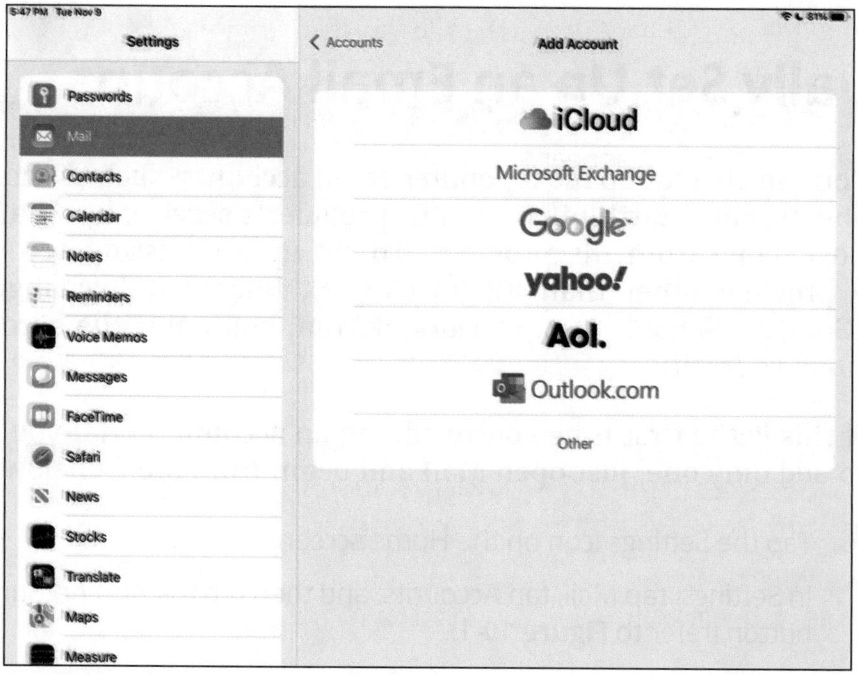

FIGURE 10-2

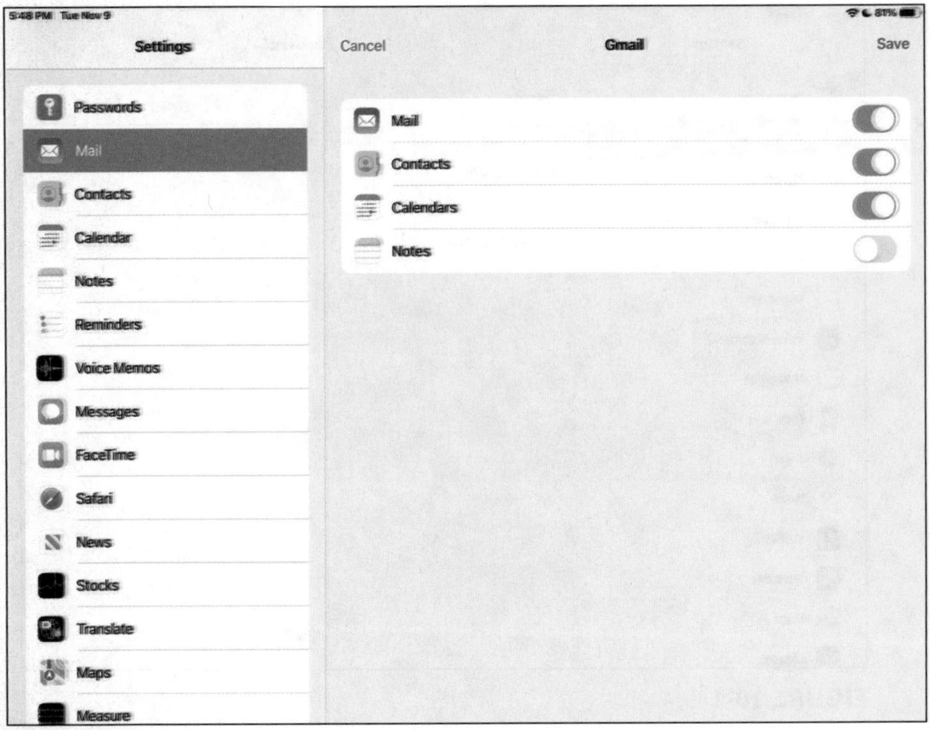

![Gmail settings screen showing toggles for Mail, Contacts, Calendars, and Notes](figure image)

FIGURE 10-3

Manually Set Up an Email Account

You can also set up most popular email accounts, such as those available through Earthlink or a cable provider's service, by obtaining the host name from the provider. To set up an existing account with a provider other than iCloud (Apple), Microsoft Exchange, Gmail (Google), Yahoo!, AOL, or Outlook.com, you enter the account settings yourself:

TIP

If this is the first time you're adding an account, and if you need to add only one, just open Mail and begin from Step 3 below.

1. Tap the Settings icon on the Home screen.

2. In Settings, tap Mail, tap Accounts, and then tap the Add Account button (refer to **Figure 10-1**).

3. On the screen that appears (refer to **Figure 10-2**), tap Other.

4. On the screen, shown in **Figure 10-4,** tap Add Mail Account.

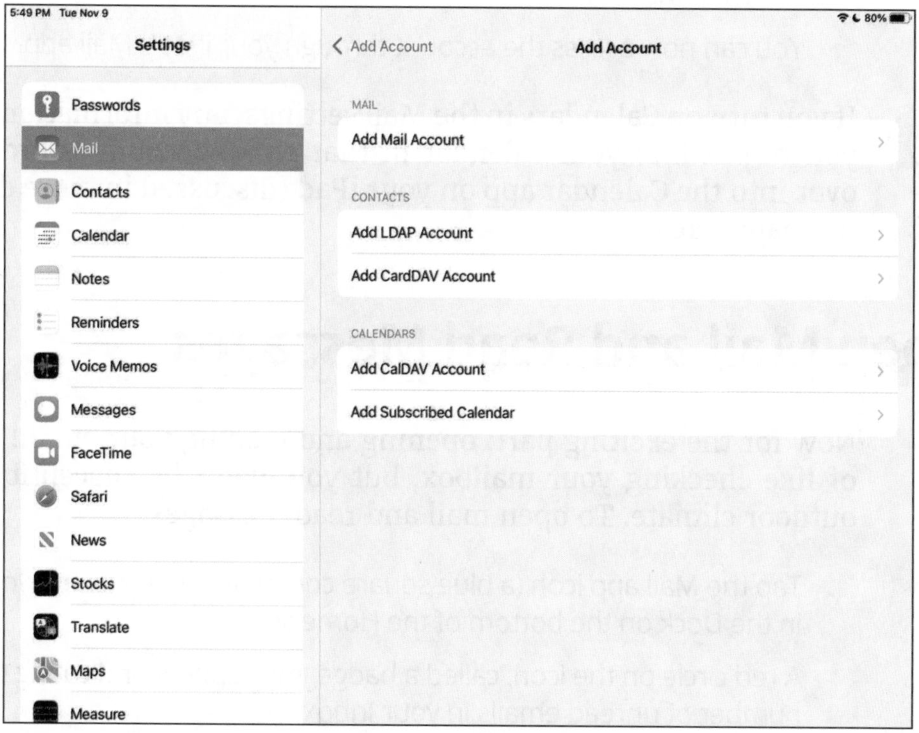

5:49 PM Tue Nov 9	🛜 🔋 80% ⬛
Settings	‹ Add Account **Add Account**
🔑 Passwords	MAIL
✉️ Mail	Add Mail Account ›
👤 Contacts	CONTACTS
📅 Calendar	Add LDAP Account ›
📝 Notes	Add CardDAV Account ›
≔ Reminders	
🎙️ Voice Memos	CALENDARS
💬 Messages	Add CalDAV Account ›
📷 FaceTime	Add Subscribed Calendar ›
🧭 Safari	
📰 News	
📈 Stocks	
🌐 Translate	
📍 Maps	
📏 Measure	

FIGURE 10-4

5. In the form that appears, enter your name and an account email address, password, and description, and then tap Next.

The iPad takes a moment to verify your account and then returns you to the Passwords & Accounts page, with your new account displayed.

TIP

Your iPad will probably add the outgoing mail server (SMTP) information for you. If it doesn't, you may have to enter it yourself. If you have a less mainstream email service, you may have to enter the mail server protocol (POP3 or IMAP — ask your provider for this information) and your password.

6. To make sure that the account is set to receive email, tap the account name. In the dialog that appears, toggle the On/Off switch for the Mail field to On (green) and then tap the Accounts button to return to Mail settings.

You can now access the account through your iPad's Mail app.

If you turn on Calendars in the Mail settings, any information that you've put into your calendar in that email account is brought over into the Calendar app on your iPad (discussed in more detail in Chapter 16).

Open Mail and Read Messages

Now for the exciting part: opening and reading your email! It's kind of like checking your mailbox, but you won't be susceptible to the outdoor climate. To open mail and read messages:

1. Tap the Mail app icon (a blue square containing an envelope) located in the Dock on the bottom of the Home screen.

A red circle on the icon, called a badge, may appear, indicating the number of unread emails in your Inbox.

2. In the Mail app (see **Figure 10-5**), tap an Inbox (possibly named after one of your account names) on the left to see your emails. If you have more than one account listed, tap the Inbox whose contents you want to display.

3. Tap a message to read it. It opens on the right side (see **Figure 10-6**).

You can preview an email before you open it. Simply press lightly and hold down on an email in the Inbox to open a preview of the message. From the preview, you can elect to perform several functions, such as Reply, Forward, Mark as Read or Unread, or send to Trash. If you want to view the entire message, release the hold and tap the message again.

4. If you need to scroll to see the entire message, just place your finger on the screen and flick upward to scroll down.

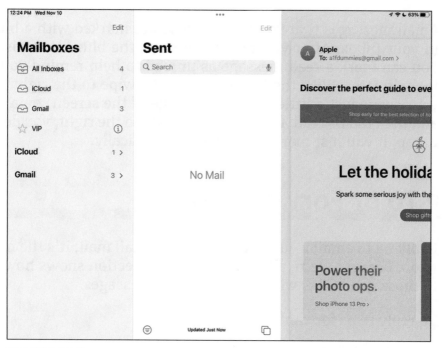

FIGURE 10-5

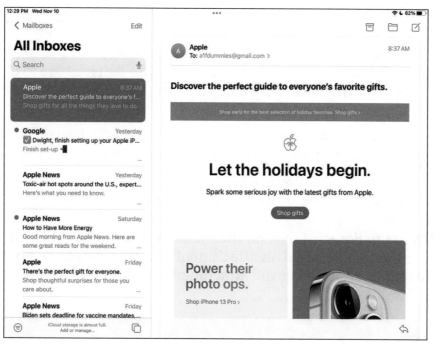

FIGURE 10-6

Email messages that you haven't read are marked with a blue circle in your Inbox. After you read a message, the blue circle disappears. You can mark a read message as unread to help remind you to read it again later. With the Inbox displayed, swipe to the right (starting your swipe just a little in from the edge of the screen) on a message and then tap Unread. If you swipe quickly to the right, you don't need to tap; it will just mark as unread automatically.

Reply To or Forward Email

Replying to email is just like replying to snail mail; it's the nice thing to do. Because we're all nice people, this section shows how to reply to those good folks who are sending us messages.

To reply to or forward email:

1. With an email message open, tap the Reply/Forward button in the lower-right corner, which looks like a left-facing arrow (refer to **Figure 10-6**). Then tap Reply, Reply All (available if there are multiple recipients), or Forward in the menu that appears (see **Figure 10-7**).

2. In the new email message that appears (see **Figure 10-8**), tap in the To field and enter another addressee if you like (you have to do this if you're forwarding). Next, tap in the message body and enter a message (see **Figure 10-9**).

TIP

If you want to move an email address from the To field to the Cc or Bcc field, press and hold the address and drag it to the other field.

3. Tap the Send button in the upper-right corner (blue circle with an upward-pointing arrow) and the email goes on its way.

TIP

If you tap Forward to send the message to somebody else and the original message had an attachment, you're offered the option of including or omitting the attachment.

FIGURE 10-7

FIGURE 10-8

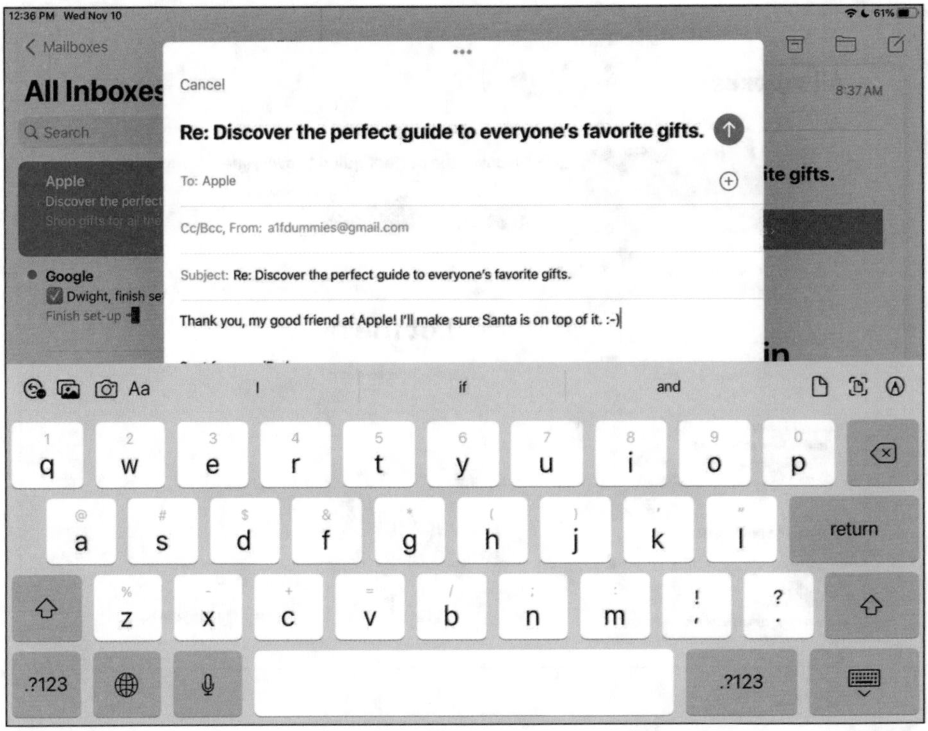

FIGURE 10-9

Create and Send a New Message

To create and send a new message:

1. With Mail open, tap the New Message button in the upper-right corner (this looks like a page with a pencil on it). A blank email appears (see **Figure 10-10**).

2. Enter a recipient's address in the To field by tapping in the field and typing the address. If you have addresses in Contacts, tap the plus sign (+) in the To field to choose an addressee from the Contacts list that appears.

3. If you want to send a copy of the message to other people, tap the Cc/Bcc field. When the Cc and Bcc fields open, enter addresses in either or both. Use the Bcc field to specify recipients of blind carbon copies, which means that no other recipients are aware that that person received this reply (being sneaky, are we?).

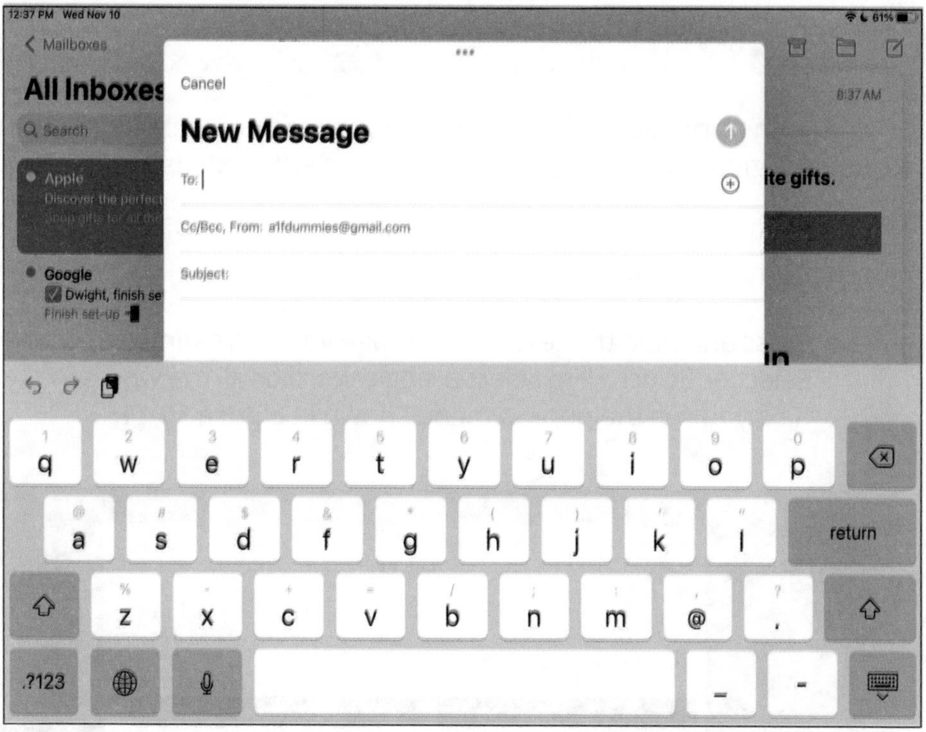

FIGURE 10-10

4. Enter the subject of the message in the Subject field.

5. Tap in the message body and type your message.

6. If you want to check a fact or copy and paste some part of another message into your draft message, tap anywhere outside the email message to minimize it (you can see it in a small window near the bottom of the screen) and display your Inbox and other folders. Locate the message you want to check or copy from, and when you're ready to return to your draft, tap the minimized window of your draft email near the bottom of the screen.

7. When you've finished creating your message, tap Send.

Format Email

You can apply some basic formatting to email text. You can use bold, underline, and italic formats, and indent text using the Quote Level feature.

To format an email:

1. Press and hold the text in a message you're creating and choose Select or Select All to select a single word or all the words in the email; next you see the pop-up menu shown in **Figure 10-11.**

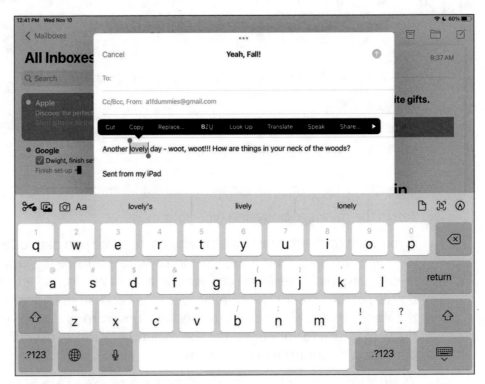

FIGURE 10-11

When you make a selection, blue handles appear that you can drag to add adjacent words to your selection. If the menu disappears after you select the text, just tap one of the selection handles, and it will reappear.

TIP

2. To apply bold, italic, or underline formatting, tap the BIU button.

To see more tools (such as adding documents or inserting drawings), tap the arrow on the toolbar that appears to the right.

3. In the toolbar that appears (see **Figure 10-12**), tap Bold, Italic, or Underline to apply formatting.

FIGURE 10-12

4. To change the indent level, press and hold at the beginning of a line and then tap Quote Level.

5. Tap Increase to indent the text or Decrease to move indented text farther toward the left margin.

To use the Quote Level feature, make sure that it's on. From the Home screen, tap Settings ⇨ Mail ⇨ Increase Quote Level and then toggle (tap) the Increase Quote Level On/Off switch to turn it On (green).

Mail in iPadOS 15 allows you to go beyond the basics, though. It introduces much-improved text formatting and font support, freeing you to create some really great-looking emails. However, it doesn't stop there: The format bar (which appears above the keyboard, shown in **Figure 10-13**) allows you to easily jazz up your email with a variety of options. There are four buttons on the left of the format bar (Undo/Redo, Photos, Camera, and Format) and three on the right (Attachment, Scan Document, and Insert Drawing).

FIGURE 10-13

If you see words above the keyboard and not the format bar, tap the arrow to the right of the words to bring the format bar back into view.

TIP

The format bar enables you to format text. Just tap the Aa button to see a bevy of formatting options (shown in **Figure 10-14**), such as

» Choose Bold, Italic, Underline, and Strikethrough.

» Change the font by tapping Default Font and browsing a surprisingly extensive list of fonts to choose from.

» Decrease or increase text size by tapping the small A or the large A, respectively.

» Tap the color wheel to select a color for your text.

» Insert numbered or bulleted lists.

» Select left, center, or right justification.

» Increase or decrease the quote level.

» Indent or outdent paragraphs.

FIGURE 10-14

The format bar also offers these tools:

» **Undo/Redo:** Tap to undo or redo your previous action.

» **Photos:** Tap to insert a photo or video from the Photos app.

» **Camera:** Tap to insert a new photo or video directly from the Camera app.

» **Attachment:** Tap to add an attachment to the email from the Files app. (See Chapter 3 for more info about Files.)

» **Scan Document:** Tap to scan a paper document and add it to your email.

» **Insert Drawing:** Tap to create a new drawing and insert it into your email.

Search Email

What do you do if you want to find all messages from a certain person or containing a certain word? You can use Mail's handy Search feature to find these emails.

To search email:

1. With Mail open, tap an account to display its Inbox.

2. In the Inbox, tap in the Search field to make the onscreen keyboard appear. If you don't see the Search field, just swipe down on the Inbox's email list and it should appear at the top.

You can also use the Search feature covered in Chapter 2 to search for terms in the To, From, or Subject lines of email messages.

3. Tap the All Mailboxes tab to view messages that contain the search term in any mailbox, or tap the Current Mailbox tab to see only matches within the current mailbox. (These options may vary slightly depending on which email service you use.)

4. Enter a search term or name, as shown in **Figure 10-15.** If multiple types of information are found, such as People or Subjects, tap the one you're looking for.

Matching emails are listed in the results.

FIGURE 10-15

Mark Email as Unread or Flag for Follow-Up

You can use a simple swipe to access tools that either mark an email as unread after you've read it (placing a blue dot before the message) or flag an email (which by default places an orange flag to the right of it, although you can choose an alternative color). If the email is both marked as unread and flagged, both a blue dot and an orange flag will appear on the message. These methods help you remember to reread an email that you've already read or to follow up on a message at a later time.

To mark email as unread or to flag it for follow-up:

1. With Mail open and an Inbox displayed, swipe to the left on an email in the Inbox list to display three options: More, Flag, and Trash/Archive. Whether Trash or Archive appears is dependent on the settings for each account.

2. Tap More. On the menu shown in **Figure 10-16,** you're given several options, including Mark as Read or Mark as Unread (depending on the current state of the email) and Flag.

You can also get to the Mark As Read/Unread command by swiping to the right on a message displayed in your Inbox.

3. To mark a message as read or unread, tap the appropriate command.

You return to your Inbox.

4. To assign a flag to the email, tap Flag and choose a color for the flag (again, the default is orange). To remove the flag, just tap More and then tap Unflag.

There's another way to get to the Flag command. Swipe to the left on an email and then tap Flag. An orange flag appears to the right of the email. Perform the same action to unflag it, if you like.

On the menu shown in **Figure 10-16,** you can also select Mute or Notify Me, among a few other options. Mute allows you to mute a thread of emails that just won't stop bugging you. Notify Me causes Mail to notify you when someone replies to this email thread.

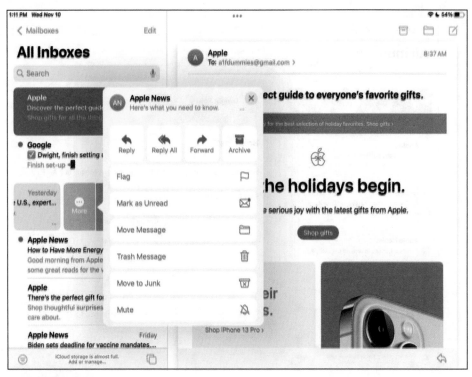

FIGURE 10-16

Create an Event from Email Contents

A neat feature in Mail is the ability to create a Calendar event from within an email. To test this, follow these steps:

1. Create an email to yourself, mentioning a reservation on a specific airline on a specific date and time.

   You could also mention another type of reservation, such as for dinner, or mention a phone number.

2. Send the message to yourself and then open Mail.

3. In your Inbox, open the email. (The pertinent information is displayed in underlined text.)

4. Tap the underlined text, and the menu shown in **Figure 10-17** appears.

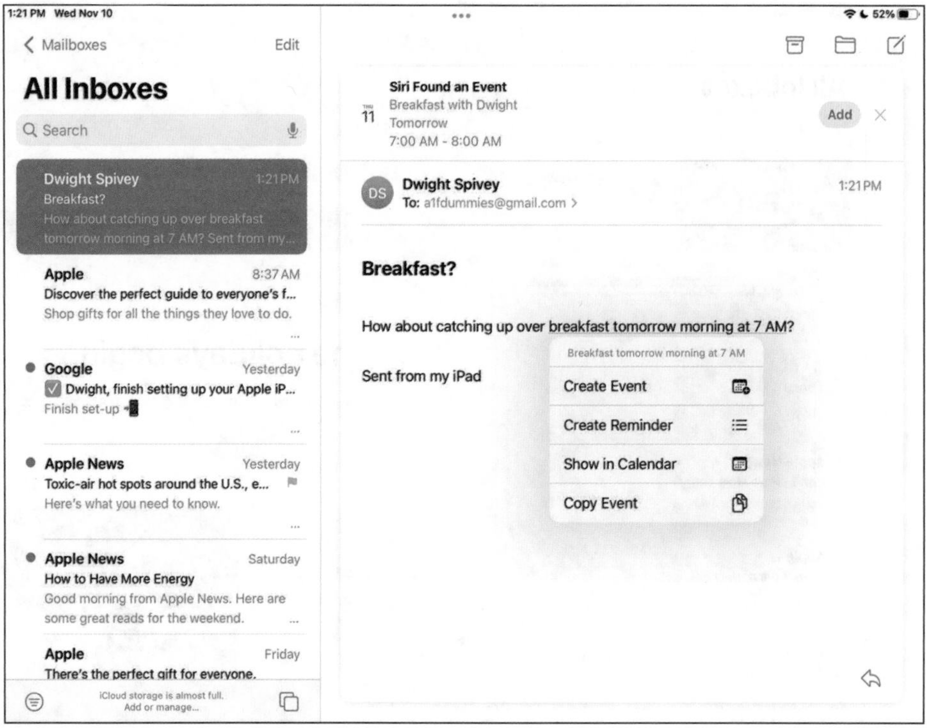

FIGURE 10-17

5. Tap Create Event to display the New Event form from Calendar.

6. Enter additional information about the event and then tap Done.

ALTERNATIVE EMAIL APPS

You can choose from lots of great email apps for your iPad if Mail isn't what you're used to (or if you simply don't like it). Here are a few of the better options: Gmail (the official app for Google Mail), Outlook (Microsoft's official app for Outlook), Edison Mail, Airmail, Spark, and Yahoo! Mail (Yahoo!'s official app).

iPadOS 15 offers a way for you to replace Mail with a third-party email app as your default. Just go to Settings, scroll down until you see the name of your favorite email app, and tap it. Then tap the Default Mail App option, and tap the name of the email app to set it as default.

Siri may also detect an event in your email (as is the case in **Figure 10-17**). If so, you see a notification at the top of the email that Siri did indeed find an event. Tap the small Add button to quickly create the event with little to no muss or fuss.

TIP

Delete Email

When you no longer want an email cluttering your Inbox, you can delete it.

1. With the Inbox displayed, tap the Edit button (found just to the left of center screen). Circular check buttons are displayed to the left of each message (see **Figure 10-18**).

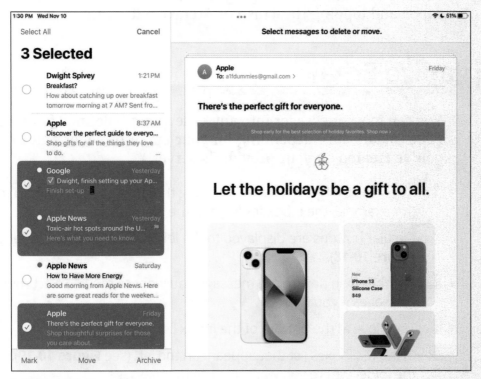

FIGURE 10-18

2. Tap the circle next to the message that you want to delete. A message marked for deletion shows a check mark in the circular check button, and it's highlighted in blue.

TIP

You can tap multiple items if you have several emails to delete.

3. Tap the Trash or Archive button at the bottom of the Inbox list. The selected messages are moved to the Trash or Archive folder.

TIP

What's the difference between Trash and Archive? Basically, email sent to a Trash folder typically is deleted forever after a certain amount of time (usually 30 days); email sent to an Archive folder is removed from the Inbox but kept indefinitely for future use.

TIP

You can also delete an open email by tapping the Reply button in the bottom-right corner of the screen and tapping the Trash/Archive button, or by swiping left on a message displayed in an Inbox and tapping the Trash or Archive button that appears.

Organize Email

You can move messages into any of several predefined folders in Mail. (The folders vary depending on your email provider and the folders you've created on your provider's server.)

1. After displaying the folder containing the message you want to move (for example, the Inbox folder), tap the Edit button.

Circular buttons are displayed to the left of each message (refer to **Figure 10-18**).

2. Tap the circle next to the message you want to move. Select multiple messages if you like.

3. Tap Move at the bottom of the Inbox list.

4. In the Mailboxes list that appears on the left (see **Figure 10-19**), tap the folder where you want to store the message.

The message is moved.

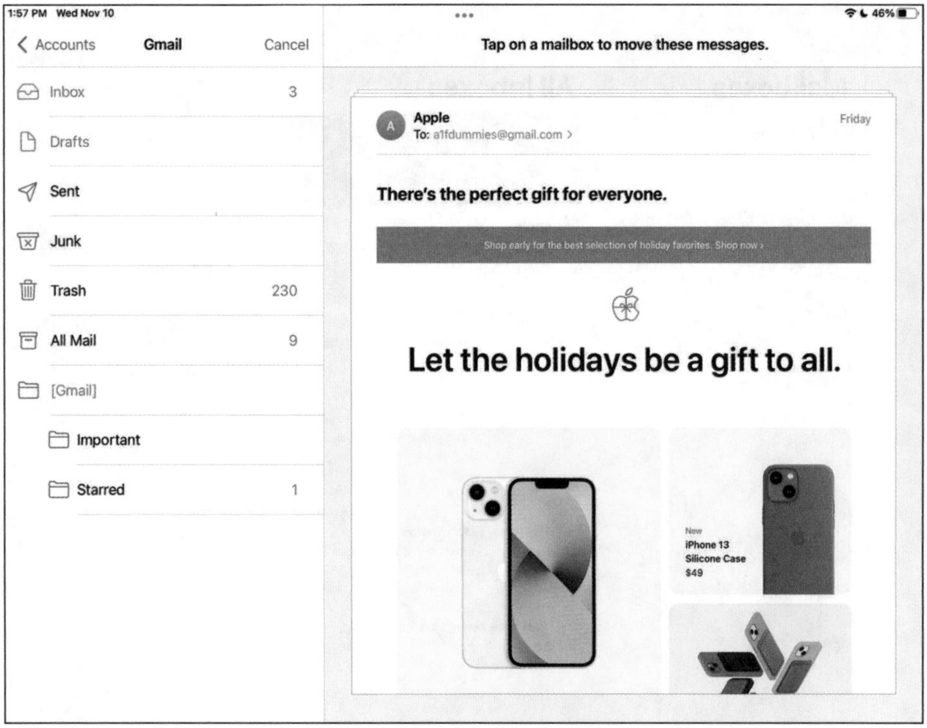

FIGURE 10-19

Create a VIP List

A VIP list is a way to create a list of senders that you deem more important than others. When any of these senders sends you an email, you'll be notified of it through the Notifications feature of iPadOS.

1. In the main list of Mailboxes, tap the info icon (the circled *i*) next to the VIP option (refer to **Figure 10-5**).

2. Tap Add VIP (see **Figure 10-20**), and your Contacts list appears.

3. Tap a contact to make that person a VIP.

4. To make settings for whether VIP mail is flagged in Notification Center, press the Home button or swipe up from the bottom of the screen (if your iPad uses FaceID), and then tap Settings.

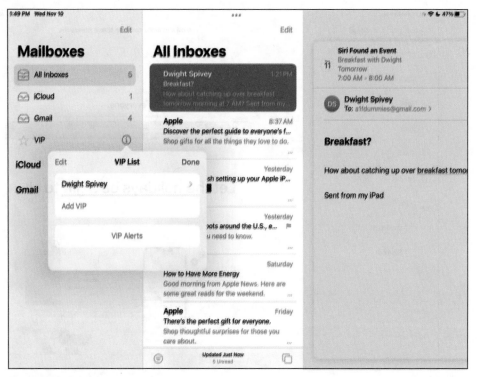

FIGURE 10-20

5. Tap Notifications and then tap Mail. In the settings that appear, shown in **Figure 10-21,** tap Customize Notifications at the bottom of the list.

6. Tap VIP and then toggle the Alerts switch to On (green).

7. To close Settings, press the Home button or swipe up from the bottom of the screen (on iPad models without a Home button).

   New mail from your VIPs should now appear in Notification Center. And, depending on the settings you chose, new mail may cause a sound to play, a badge icon to appear on your lock screen, or a blue star icon to appear to the left of the message in the Inbox in Mail. Definitely VIP treatment.

1:51 PM Wed Nov 10
Settings
Airplane Mode
Wi-Fi
Spi-Fi
Bluetooth
On
Notifications
Sounds
Focus
Screen Time
General
Control Center
Display & Brightness
Home Screen & Dock
Accessibility
Wallpaper
Notifications
Mail
ALERTS
9:41
Lock Screen
Notification Center
Banners
Banner Style
Temporary
Sounds
None
Badges
ANNOUNCE
Announce Notifications
Off
LOCK SCREEN APPEARANCE
Show Previews
Always (Default)
Notification Grouping
Automatic
Customize Notifications

FIGURE 10-21

3
Enjoying Media

IN THIS PART . . .

Shopping for movies, music, and more

Finding, buying, and reading books

Listening to audio and video

Taking and sharing photos and videos

> » **Preview music, videos, and audiobooks**
>
> » **Find and buy selections**
>
> » **Rent movies**
>
> » **Use Apple Pay, Wallet, and Family Sharing**

Chapter **11**

Shopping the iTunes Store

The iTunes Store app lets you easily shop for music, movies, and TV shows. As Chapter 12 explains, you can also get electronic and audiobooks via the Apple Books app.

In this chapter, you discover how to find content in the iTunes Store. You can download the content directly to your iPad or to another device and then sync it to your iPad. With the Family Sharing feature, which I cover in this chapter, as many as six people in a family can share purchases using the same credit card. Finally, I cover using Apple Pay to make real-world purchases using a stored payment method.

TIP

Chapter 3 tells you how to sign in to iTunes, or, if you don't have an iTunes (Apple ID) account, how to find Apple support for opening one. You might need to read Chapter 3 before digging into this chapter.

Explore the iTunes Store

Visiting the iTunes Store from your iPad is easy with the iTunes Store app.

If you're in search of other kinds of content, the Podcasts app and iTunes U app allow you to find and then download podcasts and online courses, respectively, to your iPad.

To check out the iTunes Store, follow these steps:

1. Go to your Home screen and tap the iTunes Store icon (you might find it on the second Home screen).

2. Tap the Music button (if it isn't already selected) in the row of buttons at the bottom of the screen. Swipe up and down the screen, and you'll find several categories of selections, such as New Music, Pre-Orders, and Recent Releases (these category names change from time to time).

3. Flick your finger up to scroll through the featured selections, or tap the See All button to see more selections in any category, as shown in **Figure 11-1.**

The navigation techniques in these steps work essentially the same in any of the content categories (the buttons at the bottom of the screen), which are Music, Movies, and TV Shows.

4. Tap the Top Charts tab at the bottom of the screen and then tap the Music tab at the top of the screen. Doing so displays lists of bestselling songs, albums, and music videos in the iTunes Store.

5. Tap any listed item to see more detail about it, as shown in **Figure 11-2,** and hear a brief preview when you tap the title of a song. Tap anywhere on the screen outside the information window to close it.

A See All button

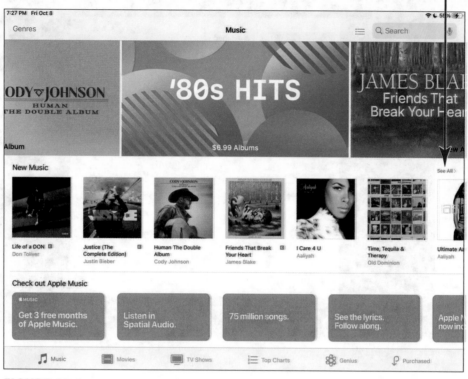

FIGURE 11-1

TIP

If you want to use the Genius playlist feature, which recommends additional purchases based on the contents of your library in the iTunes app on your iPad, tap the Genius button at the bottom of the screen. If you've made enough purchases in iTunes, song and album recommendations appear based on those purchases as well as the content in your iTunes Match library (a fee-based service), if you have one.

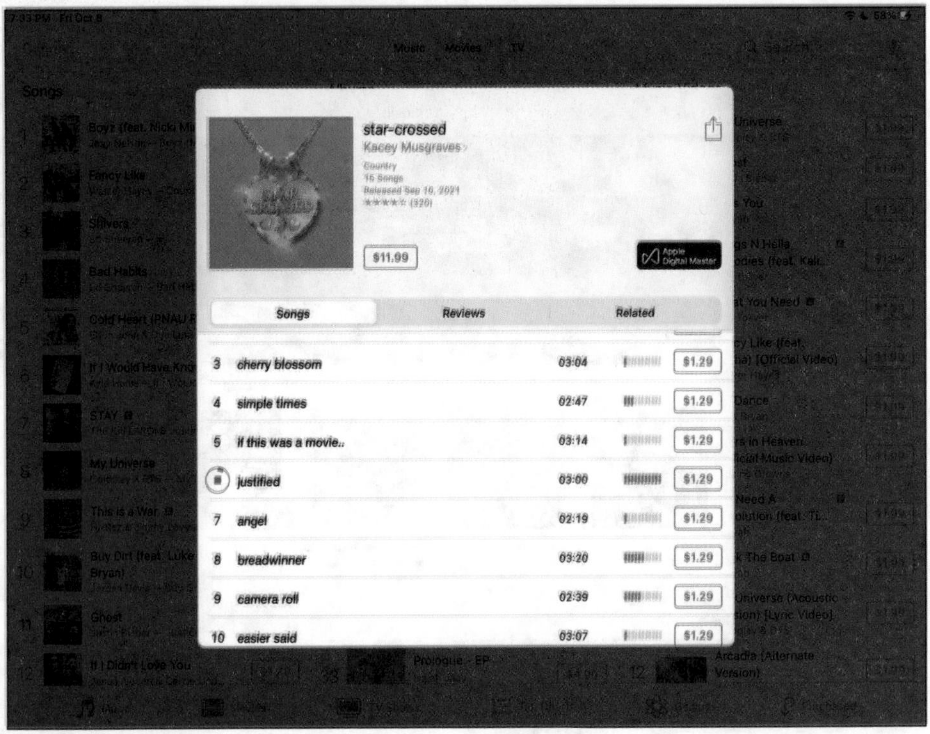

FIGURE 11-2

Find a Selection

You can look for a selection in the iTunes Store in several ways. You can use the Search feature, search by genre or category, or view artists' pages. Here's how these work:

» Tap the Search field in the upper-right corner of the screen, and the Search field shown in **Figure 11-3** appears. Tap in the field and enter a search term using the onscreen keyboard. Tap the Search button on the keyboard or, if a suggestion in the list of search results appeals to you, just tap that suggestion.

» Tap an item at the bottom of the screen (such as Music) and then tap the blue Genres button in the upper left of the screen.

A list of genres like the one shown in **Figure 11-4** appears.

FIGURE 11-3

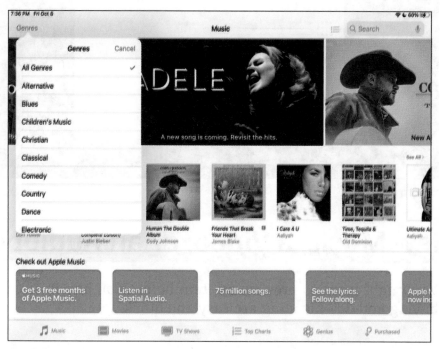

FIGURE 11-4

» On a description page that appears when you tap a selection, you can find more offerings by the people involved with that particular work. For example, for a music selection, tap to display details about it and then tap the Reviews tab at the middle of the page to see all reviews of the album (see **Figure 11-5**). For a movie (tap Movies at the bottom of the iTunes Store screen), tap to open details and then tap Reviews, or tap the Related tab to see more movies starring any of the lead actors.

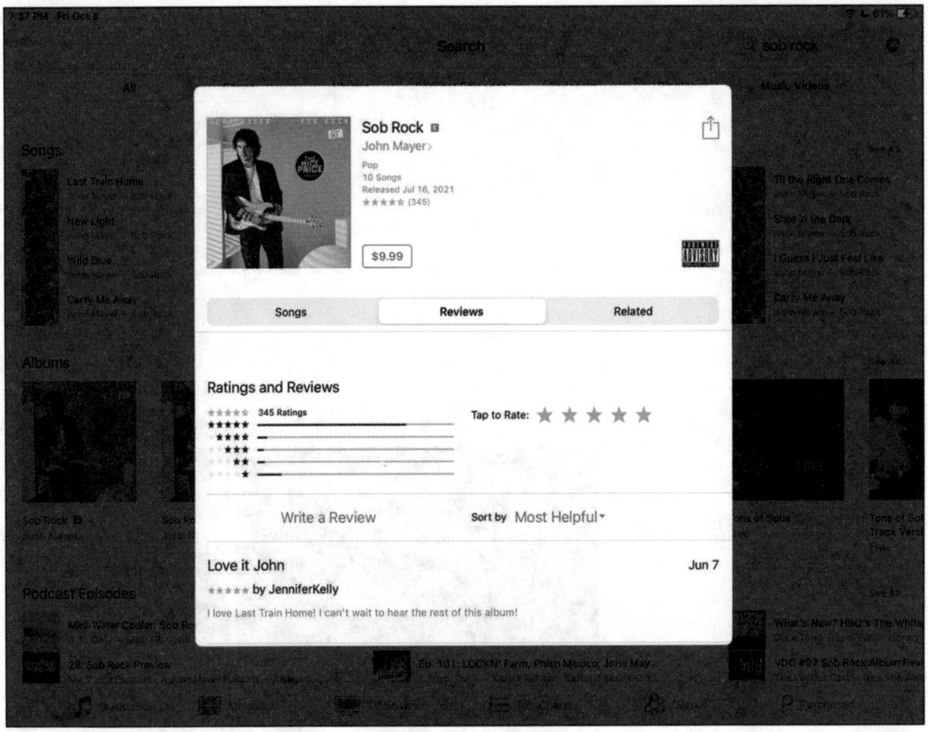

FIGURE 11-5

Preview Music, a Video, or an Audiobook

You might want to preview an item before you buy it. If you like it, buying and downloading are easy and quick.

To preview items in the iTunes Store, follow these steps:

1. Open the iTunes Store app and use any method outlined in earlier tasks to locate a selection that you might want to buy.

2. Tap the item to see detailed information about it, as shown in **Figure 11-6.**

FIGURE 11-6

3. For a TV show, tap an episode to get further information (refer to **Figure 11-6**). If you're looking at a music selection, tap the track number or name of a selection to play a preview. For a movie or audiobook selection, tap the Trailers Play button (movies), shown in **Figure 11-7.**

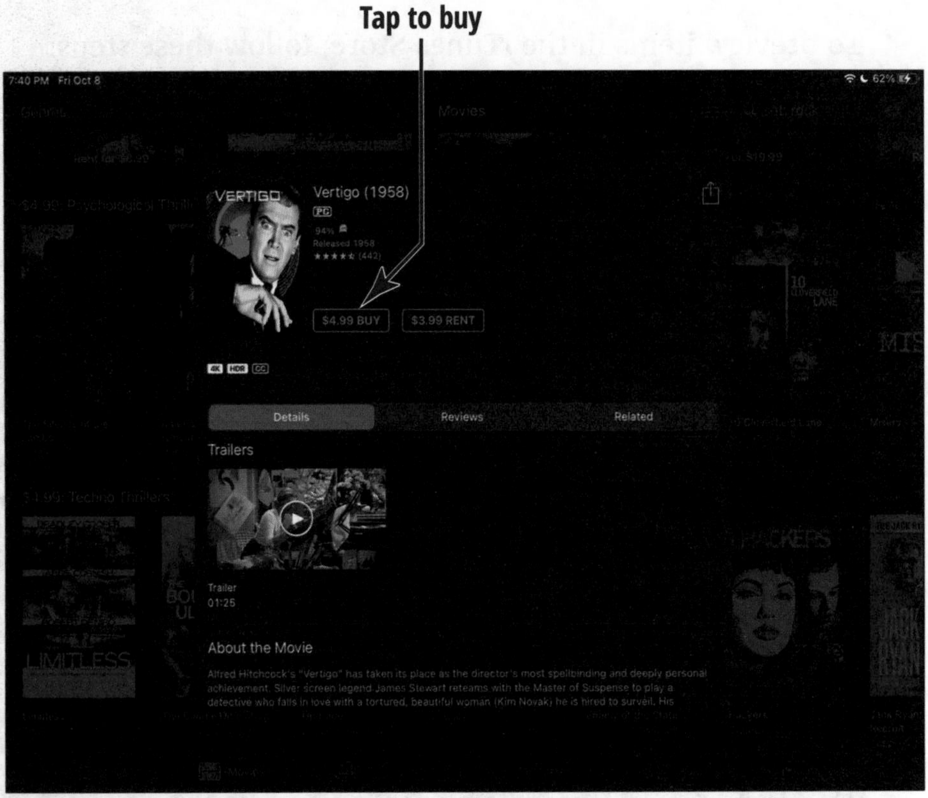

Tap to buy

FIGURE 11-7

Buy a Selection

To buy a selection:

1. When you find an item that you want to buy, tap the button that shows either the price (if it's a selection available for purchase; refer to **Figure 11-7**) or the button labeled "Get" (if it's a selection available for free).

If you want to buy music, you can open the description page for an album and tap the album price, or buy individual songs rather than the entire album. Tap the price for a song and then proceed to purchase it.

2. When the dialog appears at the bottom of the screen, tap Purchase, type your password in the Password field on the next screen, and then tap Sign In to buy the item. Alternatively, use Touch ID or Face ID (depending on your iPad model) if you have it enabled for iTunes and App Store purchases.

3. The item begins downloading, and the cost, if any, is automatically charged to your account. When the download finishes, tap OK in the Purchase Complete message, and you can then view the content using the Music or TV app, depending on the type of content it is.

Rent Movies

In the case of movies, you can either rent or buy content. If you rent, which is less expensive but only a one-time deal, you have 30 days from the time you rent the item to begin watching it. After you have begun to watch it, you have 48 hours from that time left to watch it on the same device, as many times as you like.

To rent movies:

1. With the iTunes Store open, tap the Movies button.

2. Locate the movie you want to rent and tap it.

3. In the detailed description of the movie that appears, tap the Rent button (if it's available for rental); see **Figure 11-8.**

4. When the dialog appears at the bottom of the screen, tap Rent, type your password in the Password field on the next screen, and then tap Sign In to rent the item. Alternatively, use Touch ID or Face ID (depending on your iPad model) if you have it enabled for iTunes Store and App Store purchases. After you've been authenticated, the movie begins to download to your iPad immediately, and your account is charged the rental fee.

5. After the download is complete, you can use the TV app to watch it. (See Chapter 15 to read about how this app works.)

Tap to rent

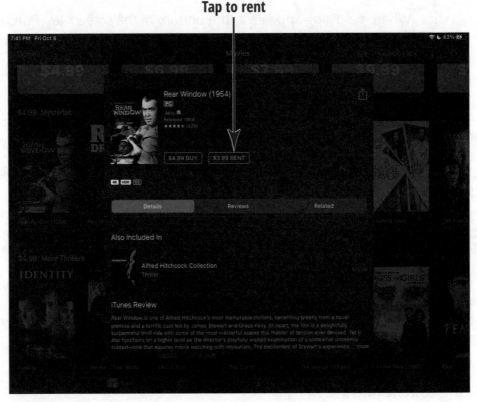

FIGURE 11-8

Use Apple Pay and Wallet

Apple is the creator of an increasingly popular method of paying for items by using your iPad (or other Apple devices). It's called Apple Pay. Fancied as a mobile wallet, this service uses the Touch ID feature in your iPad's Home button (or the Face ID feature if your iPad doesn't have a Home button) to identify you and any credit cards you've stored in the iTunes Store to make payments via a feature called Wallet.

Your credit card information isn't stored on your phone or iPad, and Apple doesn't know a thing about your purchases. In addition, Apple considers Apple Pay safer than paying with a credit card at the store because the store cashier doesn't even have to know your name.

To set up Apple Pay, go to Settings and tap Wallet & Apple Pay. Add information about a credit card. You can also change settings, set your default card, and add and delete cards from within the Wallet app itself.

For more information on Apple Pay, check out `http://www.apple.com/apple-pay`. To learn how to use your iPad with Apple Pay for purchases on websites or within apps, visit `https://support.apple.com/guide/ipad/use-apple-pay-in-apps-app-clips-and-safari-ipad049d8c12/15.0/ipados/15.0`.

Set Up Family Sharing

Family Sharing is a feature that allows as many as six people in your family to share whatever anybody in the group has purchased from the iTunes, Apple Books, and App Stores even though you don't share Apple IDs. Your family must all use the same credit card to purchase items (tied to whichever Apple ID is managing the family), but you can approve purchases by children under 13 years of age. Start by turning on Family Sharing:

1. Tap Settings and then tap the Apple ID at the top of the screen.
2. Tap Set Up Family Sharing.
3. Tap Get Started. On the next screen, you can add a photo of your family. Tap Continue.
4. On the Share Purchases screen, tap Share Purchases from a different account to use another Apple account.
5. Tap Continue and check the payment method that you want to use. Tap Continue.
6. On the next screen, tap Add Family Member. Enter the person's name (assuming that this person is listed in your contacts) or email address. An invitation is sent to the person's email. When the invitation is accepted, the person is added to your family.

TIP

The payment method for this family is displayed under Shared Payment Method in the Family Sharing screen. Go to Settings ⇨ Apple ID ⇨ Media & Purchases, tap the View Account button that pops up and authenticate your Apple ID when prompted, and then tap Manage Payments in the Account Settings window. All those involved in a family have to use a single payment method for family purchases.

There's also an option called Create an Account for a Child. When you click Add Family Member in the Family Sharing window, click Create an Account for a Child and enter information to create the ID. The child's account is automatically added to your Family and retains the child status until the child turns 13. If a child accesses iTunes to buy something, they are prompted to ask permission. You get an Ask to Buy notification on your iPad as well as via email. You can then accept or decline the purchase, giving you control over family spending in the iTunes Store.

Chapter **12**

Reading Books

A traditional e-reader is a device that's used primarily to read the electronic version of books, magazines, and newspapers. Apple has touted the iPad as a great e-reader, and although it isn't a traditional e-reader device like the Kindle Paperwhite, you don't want to miss this cool functionality.

Apple's free app that turns your iPad into an e-reader is Apple Books (formerly known as iBooks), which also enables you to buy and download books (and audiobooks) from the Apple Books Store, which offers millions of books and is growing by the day. You can also use one of several other free e-reader apps — for example, Kindle or Nook. Then you can download books to your iPad from a variety of online sources, such as Amazon and Google, so that you can read to your heart's content.

In this chapter, you discover the options available for reading material and how to buy books. You also learn how to navigate a book or periodical and adjust the brightness and type, as well as how to search books and organize your Apple Books libraries.

Find Books with Apple Books

When you buy a book online, or get one of many free publications, it downloads to your iPad in a few seconds (or minutes, depending on your Internet connection speed and the size of the files) using a Wi-Fi or cellular connection. To shop using Apple Books:

1. Tap the Apple Books application icon to open it. (It's on your first Home screen and looks like a white book against an orange background; it's also simply labeled Books, which is how I refer to it throughout the rest of the chapter.)

2. Tap the Book Store tab at the bottom of the screen.

3. In the Book Store, shown in **Figure 12-1,** featured titles and suggestions (based on your past reading habits and searches) are shown. You can do any of the following to find a book:

   - Swipe left or right to see and read articles and suggestions for the latest books in various categories, such as Trending (*Best sellers you should be reading now*, as shown in **Figure 12-2**), Featured Collection, and the like.

   - Scroll down on the Book Store's main page to see links to popular categories of books, as shown in **Figure 12-3.** Tap a category to view those selections.

   - Scroll down to Top Charts to view both Paid and Free books listed on top bestseller lists. Tap one of the See More . . . buttons under the Top Charts category to focus on books that are the latest hits.

   - Swipe further down to the bottom of the screen to find a list of Genres. Tap All Genres to see everything the Book Store has to offer.

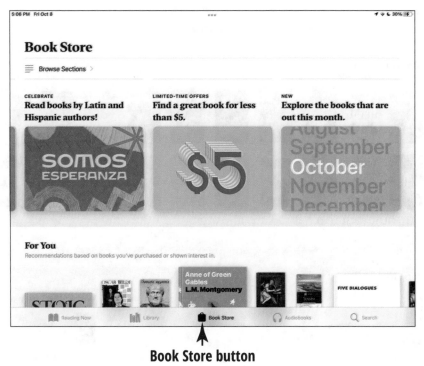

Book Store button

FIGURE 12-1

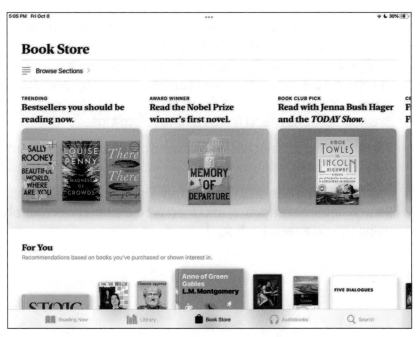

FIGURE 12-2

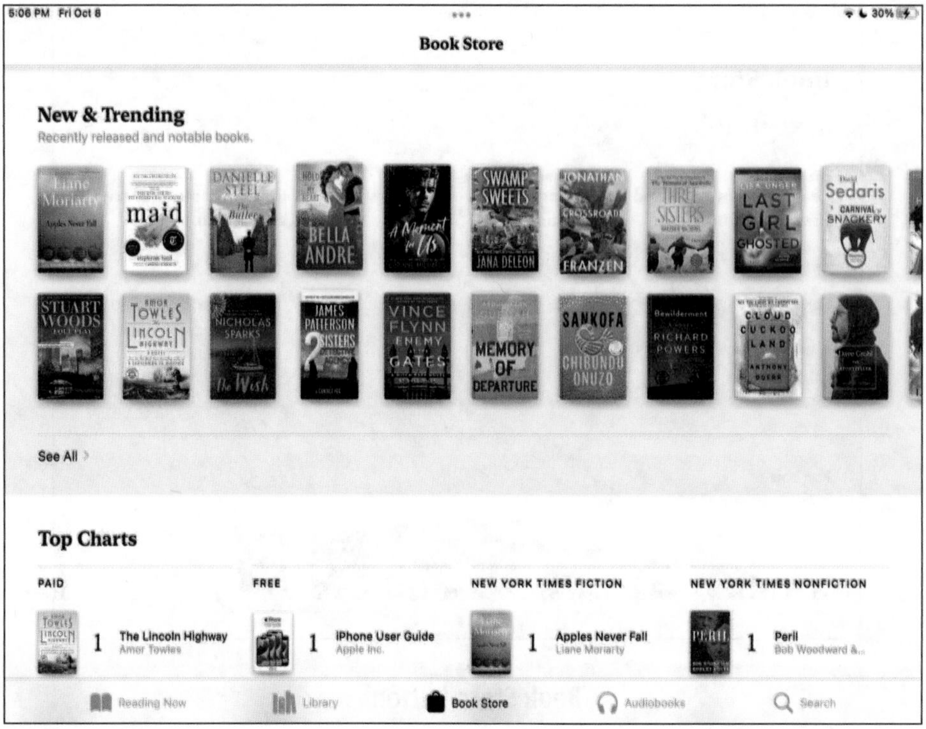

FIGURE 12-3

- On the main screen of the Book Store, tap the Browse Sections button under "Book Store" (at the top of the Book Store screen, if you've scrolled down) to open the Browse Sections menu, shown in **Figure 12-4.** From here, you can easily scroll up and down the screen to browse Book Store sections and genres. Swipe the Browse Sections menu from right to left to close it.

- Tap a suggested selection or featured book to read more information about it.

- Tap the Search button in the bottom-right of the screen, tap in the Search field that appears, and then type a search word or phrase using the onscreen keyboard.

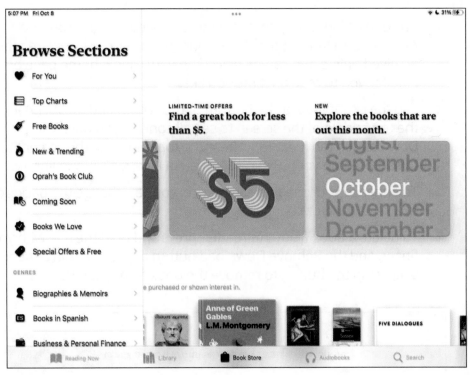

FIGURE 12-4

Explore Other E-Book Sources

Beyond using Apple Books, the iPad is capable of using other e-reader apps to read book content from other bookstores. You first have to download another e-reader application, such as Kindle from Amazon or the Barnes & Noble Nook reader from the App Store (see Chapter 6 for how to download apps). You can also download a non-vendor-specific app such as Bluefire Reader, which handles ePub and PDF formats, as well as the format that most public libraries use (protected PDF). Then use the app's features to search for, purchase, and download content.

Amazon's Kindle e-reader application is shown in **Figure 12-5**. To use the Kindle e-reader:

1. After downloading the free app from the App Store, open the app and enter the email address and password associated with your

Amazon account. Any content you've already bought from the Amazon.com Kindle Store from your computer or Kindle Fire tablet is archived online and can be placed on your Kindle home page on the iPad for you to read anytime you like.

2. Tap the Library tab at the bottom of the screen and tap All near the top middle of the screen to see all content you own. Tap the Downloaded tab (next to All near the top middle of the screen) to see titles stored on your iPad rather than in Amazon's Cloud library.

3. To enhance your reading experience, you can change the background to a sepia tone or change the font.

4. To delete a book from this reader, press and hold the title with your finger, and the Remove Download button appears within a menu; simply tap the button to remove the book from your iPad.

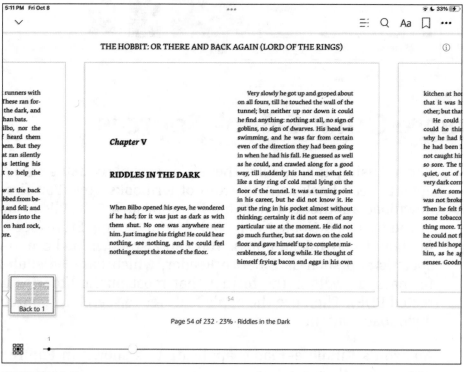

FIGURE 12-5

E-books are everywhere! You can get content from a variety of other sources, such as Project Gutenberg, Google Play, and some publishers like Baen. Download the content using your computer, if you like, and then just add the items to Books in iTunes and sync them to your iPad. You can also open items from a web link or email, and they're copied to Apple Books for you. Another option is to set up iCloud so that books are pushed across your Apple devices, or you can place them in an online storage service (such as Dropbox or Google Drive) and access them from there.

E-books come in different formats, and Apple Books won't work with formats other than ePub or PDF. (For example, it can't use such formats as the Kindle's Mobi and AZW.)

Buy Books

If you've set up an account with iTunes, you can buy books at the Apple Books Store using the Books app. (See Chapter 3 for more about iTunes.)

1. Open the Books app, tap Book Store, and begin looking for a book.

2. When you find a book in the Book Store, you can buy it by tapping it and then tapping the Buy | *Price* button (as shown in **Figure 12-6**) or the Get button (if it's free).

Many books let you download free samples before you buy. You get to read several pages of the book to see whether it appeals to you, and previewing doesn't cost you a dime! Look for the Sample button when you view book details. (The button usually appears below the price of the book.)

You may also tap the Want to Read button if you'd like to keep this book in mind for a future purchase.

Buy/Get button

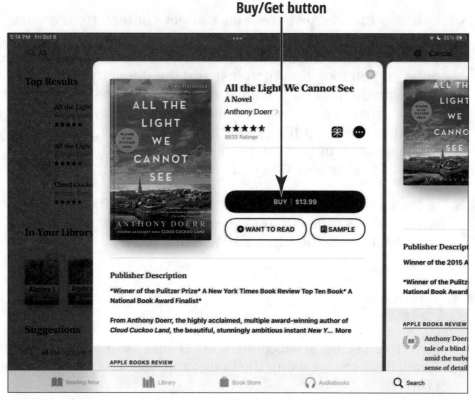

FIGURE 12-6

3. When the dialog appears in the center of the screen, tap Purchase, type your password in the Password field on the next screen, and then tap Sign In to buy the book. Alternatively, use Touch ID or Face ID if you have it enabled for iTunes and App Store purchases (and if your iPad supports it, of course).

4. The book begins downloading, and the cost, if any, is automatically charged to your account. When the download finishes, tap OK in the Purchase Complete message, and you can find your new purchase by tapping the Library button at the bottom of the screen.

TIP

Books that you've downloaded to your computer can be accessed from any Apple device through iCloud. Content can also be synced with your iPad by using the Lightning to USB Cable and your iTunes account, or by using the wireless iTunes Wi-Fi Sync setting on the General Settings menu. See Chapter 3 for more about syncing.

Navigate a Book

Getting around in Apple Books is half the fun!

1. Open Apple Books and, if your Library (which looks a tiny bit like a bookshelf) isn't already displayed, tap the Library button at the bottom of the screen.

2. Tap a book to open it. The book opens to its title page or the last spot you read on any compatible device, as shown in **Figure 12-7.**

Table of Contents button

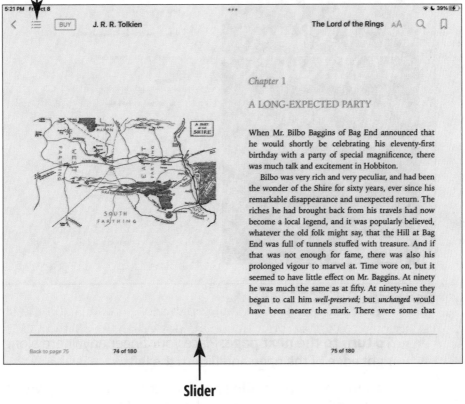

Slider

FIGURE 12-7

3. Take any of these actions to navigate the book:

- **To go to the book's Table of Contents:** Tap the Table of Contents button at the top of the page (refer to **Figure 12-7**) and then tap the name of a chapter to go to it (see **Figure 12-8**).

  TIP

  If you don't see the Table of Contents button, simply tap the screen once to display the navigation controls.

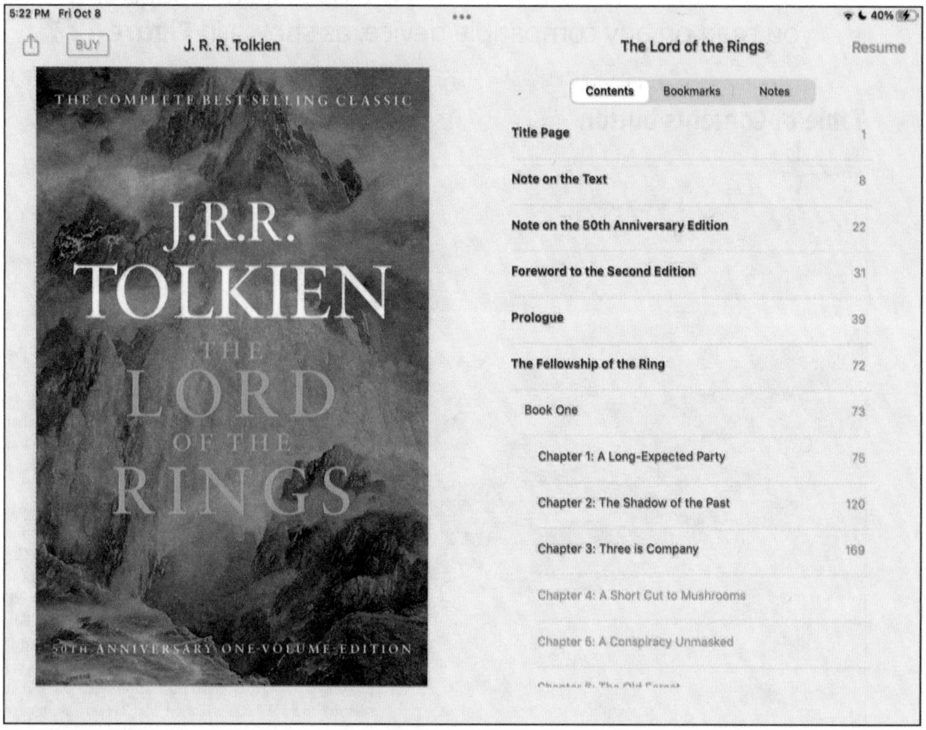

FIGURE 12-8

- **To turn to the next page:** Place your finger anywhere along the right edge of the page and flick to the left.

- **To turn to the preceding page:** Place your finger anywhere on the left edge of a page and flick to the right.

- **To move to another page in the book:** Tap and drag the slider at the bottom of the page (refer to **Figure 12-7**) to the right or left.

TIP

To return to the Library to view another book at any time, tap the Back button, which looks like a left-pointing arrow and is found in the upper-left corner of the screen. If the button isn't visible, tap anywhere on the page, and the button and other onscreen tools appear.

Adjust Brightness in Apple Books

Apple Books offers an adjustable brightness setting that you can use to make your book pages more comfortable to read.

1. With a book open, tap the Display Settings button (looks like aA), shown in **Figure 12-9.**

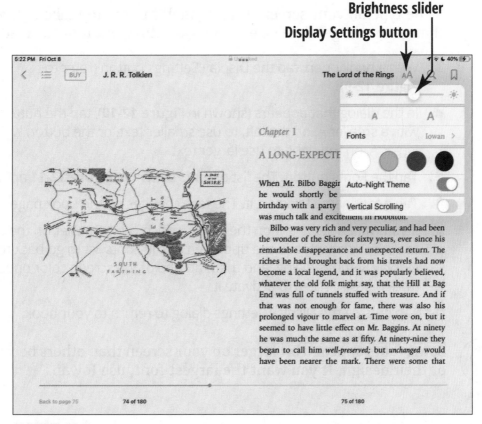

FIGURE 12-9

2. On the Brightness setting that appears at the top (refer to **Figure 12-9**), tap and drag the slider to the right to make the screen brighter, or to the left to dim it.

3. Tap anywhere on the page to close the Display Settings dialog.

TIP

Experiment with the brightness level that works for you, or try the Sepia setting, which you find by tapping the sepia-colored circle in the Display Settings dialog. Bright-white screens are commonly thought to be hard on the eyes, so setting the brightness halfway or less, relative to its default setting, is probably a good idea (and saves on battery life).

Change the Font Size and Type

If the type on your screen is a bit small for you to make out, you can change to a larger font size or choose a different font for readability.

1. With a book open, tap the Display Settings button (refer to **Figure 12-9**).

2. In the dialog that appears (shown in **Figure 12-10**), tap the button with a smaller A, on the left, to use smaller text, or the button with the larger A, on the right, to use larger text.

3. Tap the Fonts button. The list of fonts shown in **Figure 12-11** appears.

4. Tap a font name to select it. The font changes on the book page.

5. If you want a sepia tint on the pages, which can be easier on the eye, tap the Back button in the upper left of the Fonts list to go back to the Display Settings dialog, and then tap one of the screen color options (the colored circles) to activate it.

6. Tap outside the Display Settings dialog to return to your book.

TIP

Some fonts appear a bit larger on your screen than others because of their design. If you want the largest font, use Iowan.

Tap for larger text

Tap for smaller text

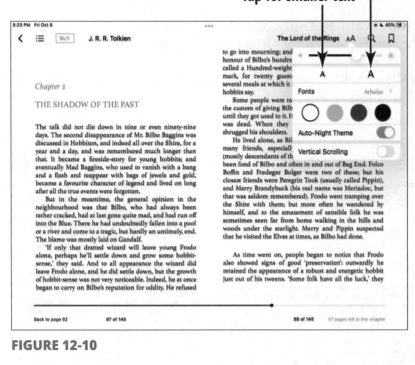

FIGURE 12-10

FIGURE 12-11

Search in Your Book

You may want to find certain sentences or references in your book. Apple Books has a built-in Search feature that makes doing so simple.

1. With a book displayed, tap the Search button, shown in **Figure 12-12**. The onscreen keyboard appears.

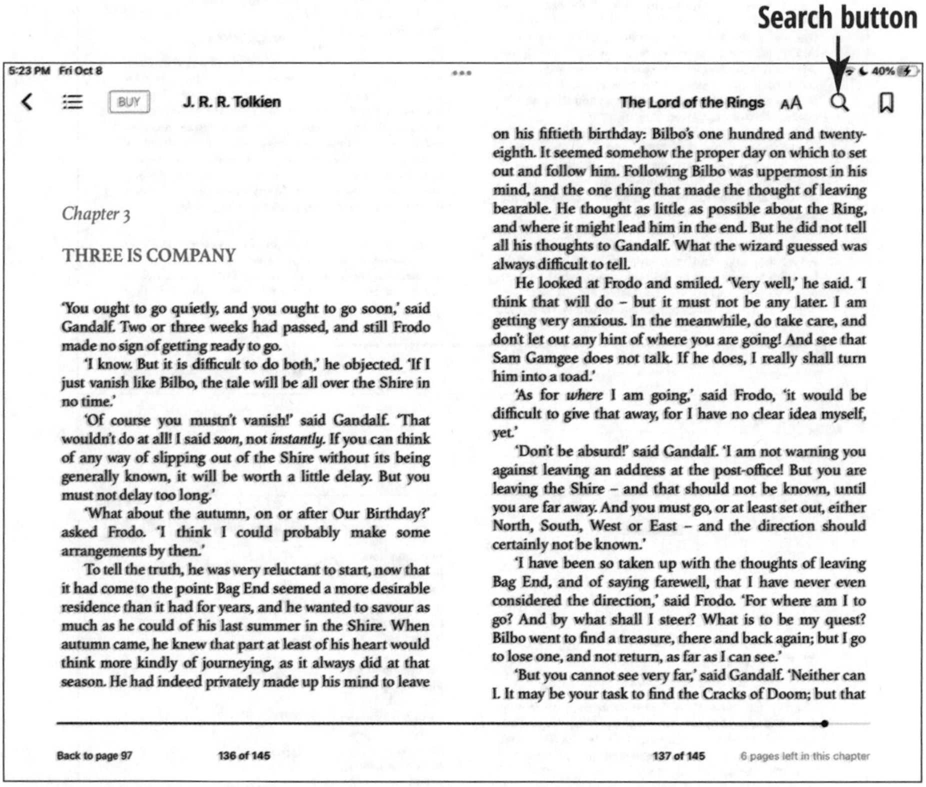

Search button

FIGURE 12-12

2. Enter a search term and then tap the Search key on the keyboard. Apple Books searches for any matching entries.

3. Use your finger to scroll down the entries (see **Figure 12-13**).

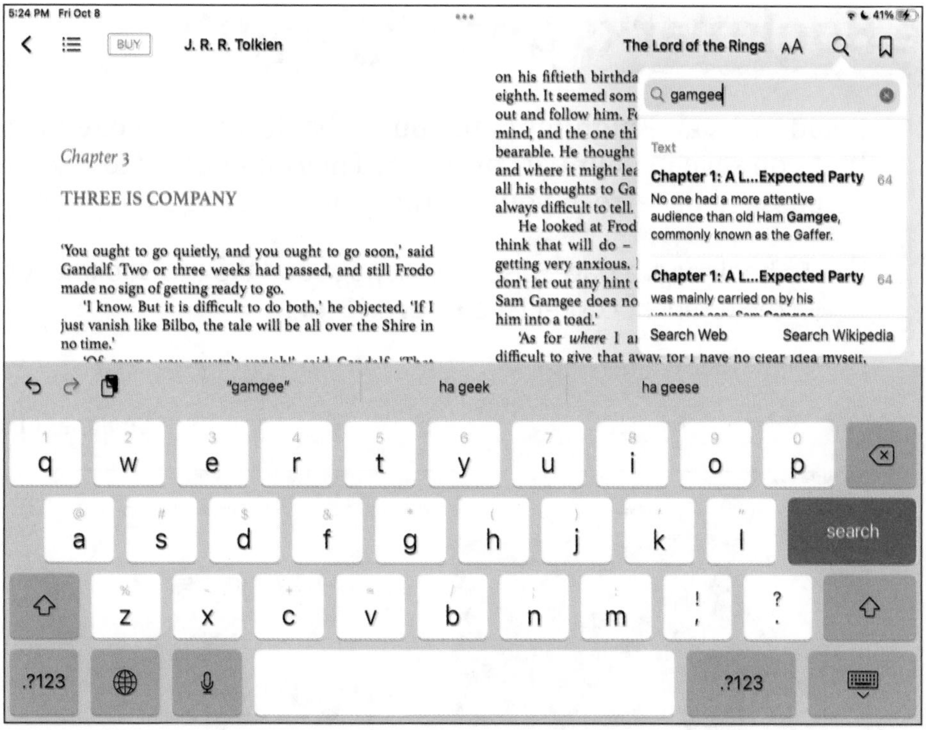

FIGURE 12-13

4. Flick your finger to scroll down the search results and then use either
the Search Web or Search Wikipedia button at the bottom of the
Search dialog if you want to search for information about the search
term online. Tap a result, and you're taken to the page containing that
result with a highlight applied to it.

> **TIP**
> You can also search for other instances of a particular word while
> in the book pages by pressing your finger on the word for just a
> moment and then releasing. A toolbar will appear. Tap Search to
> find your word.

Use Bookmarks and Highlights

Bookmarks and highlights in your e-books operate like favorite sites that you save in your web browser: They enable you to revisit a favorite passage or refresh your memory about a character or plot point.

1. To bookmark a page, display that page and tap the Bookmark button in the top-right corner (see **Figure 12-14**).

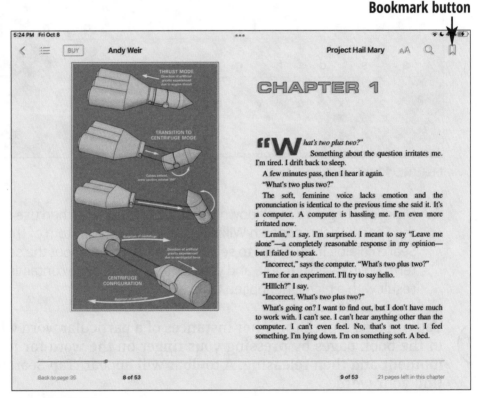

FIGURE 12-14

2. To highlight a word or phrase, press and release a word, and the toolbar shown in **Figure 12-15** appears.

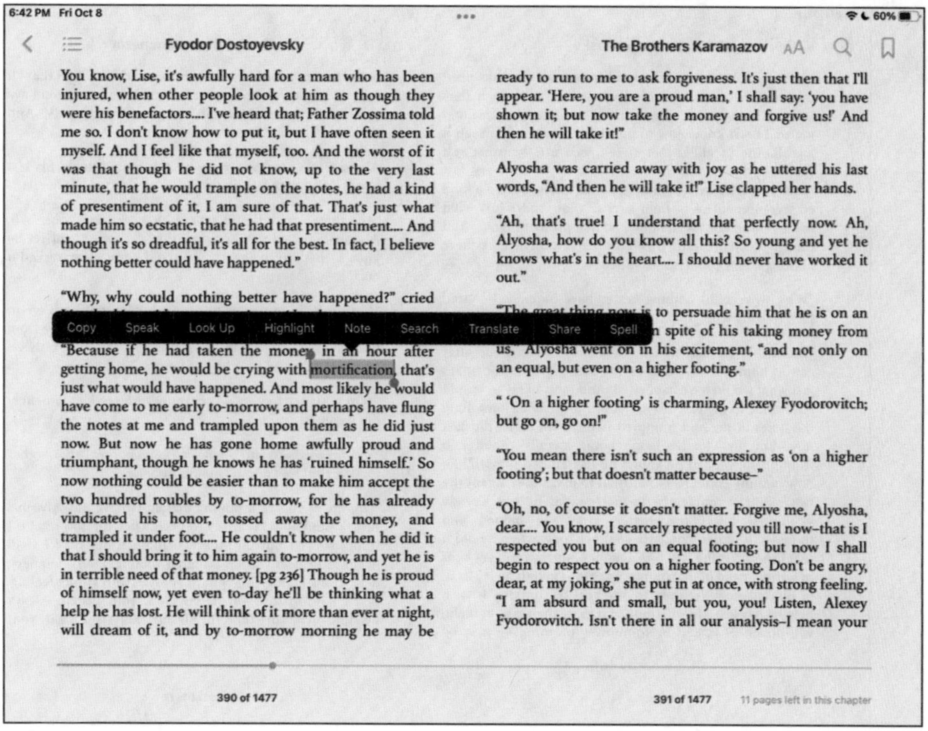

You know, Lise, it's awfully hard for a man who has been injured, when other people look at him as though they were his benefactors.... I've heard that; Father Zossima told me so. I don't know how to put it, but I have often seen it myself. And I feel like that myself, too. And the worst of it was that though he did not know, up to the very last minute, that he would trample on the notes, he had a kind of presentiment of it, I am sure of that. That's just what made him so ecstatic, that he had that presentiment.... And though it's so dreadful, it's all for the best. In fact, I believe nothing better could have happened."

"Why, why could nothing better have happened?" cried

Copy   Speak   Look Up   Highlight   Note   Search   Translate   Share   Spell

"Because if he had taken the money, in an hour after getting home, he would be crying with mortification, that's just what would have happened. And most likely he would have come to me early to-morrow, and perhaps have flung the notes at me and trampled upon them as he did just now. But now he has gone home awfully proud and triumphant, though he knows he has 'ruined himself.' So now nothing could be easier than to make him accept the two hundred roubles by to-morrow, for he has already vindicated his honor, tossed away the money, and trampled it under foot.... He couldn't know when he did it that I should bring it to him again to-morrow, and yet he is in terrible need of that money. [pg 236] Though he is proud of himself now, yet even to-day he'll be thinking what a help he has lost. He will think of it more than ever at night, will dream of it, and by to-morrow morning he may be

ready to run to me to ask forgiveness. It's just then that I'll appear. 'Here, you are a proud man,' I shall say: 'you have shown it; but now take the money and forgive us!' And then he will take it!"

Alyosha was carried away with joy as he uttered his last words, "And then he will take it!" Lise clapped her hands.

"Ah, that's true! I understand that perfectly now. Ah, Alyosha, how do you know all this? So young and yet he knows what's in the heart.... I should never have worked it out."

"The great thing now is to persuade him that he is on an equal footing with us in spite of his taking money from us," Alyosha went on in his excitement, "and not only on an equal, but even on a higher footing."

" 'On a higher footing' is charming, Alexey Fyodorovitch; but go on, go on!"

"You mean there isn't such an expression as 'on a higher footing'; but that doesn't matter because–"

"Oh, no, of course it doesn't matter. Forgive me, Alyosha, dear.... You know, I scarcely respected you till now–that is I respected you but on an equal footing; but now I shall begin to respect you on a higher footing. Don't be angry, dear, at my joking," she put in at once, with strong feeling. "I am absurd and small, but you, you! Listen, Alexey Fyodorovitch. Isn't there in all our analysis–I mean your

FIGURE 12-15

3. Tap the Highlight button. A colored highlight is placed on the word, and the toolbar shown in **Figure 12-16** appears.

4. Tap one of these buttons (from left to right):

- **Colors:** Displays a menu of colors that you can tap to change the highlight color as well as an underline option (the gray circle containing the underlined capital A).

- **Remove Highlight (looks like a trash can):** Removes the highlight.

- **Note (looks like a speech bubble):** Lets you add a note to the item.

- **Share:** Allows you to share the highlighted text with others via AirDrop, Messages, Mail, Notes, and possibly other third-party apps (such as Twitter, Facebook, and others) or to copy the text.

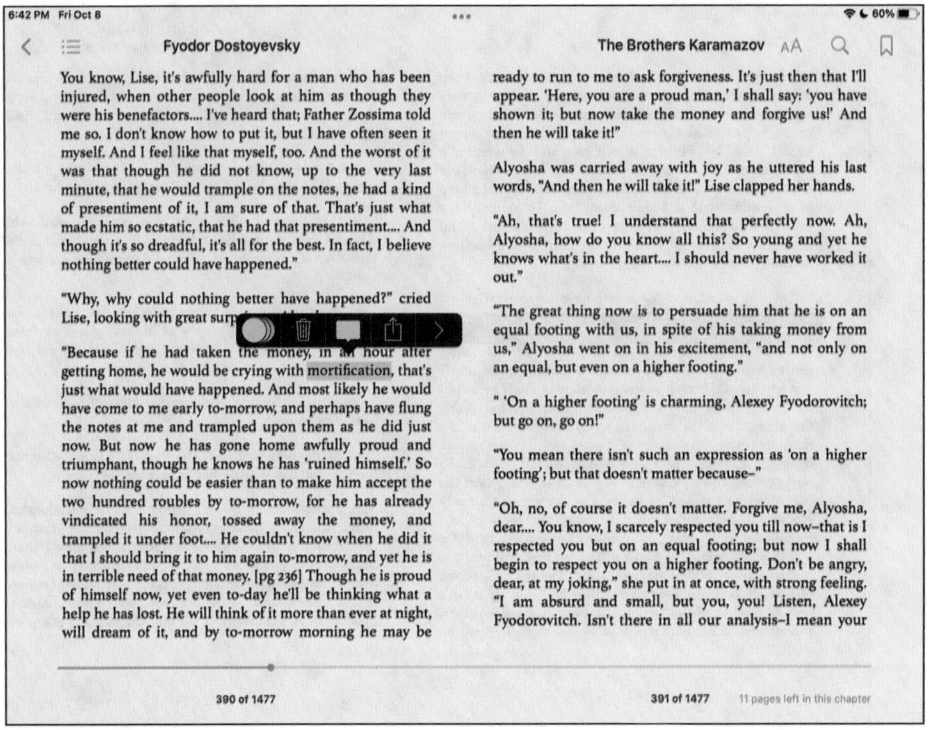

FIGURE 12-16

5. You can also tap the arrow button at the right side of the toolbar to access the Copy, Speak, Look Up, Highlight, Note, Search, Translate, Share, and Spell tools (some of which may not appear, depending on the book). Tap outside the highlighted text to close the toolbar.

6. To go to a list of bookmarks and notes (including highlighted text), tap the Table of Contents button in the upper left of the screen.

7. In the Table of Contents, tap the Bookmarks tab, shown in **Figure 12-17;** all bookmarks are displayed. If you want to see highlighted text and associated notes, you display the Notes tab.

8. Tap a bookmark in the bookmark list to go to that location in the book.

TIP

The Books app automatically bookmarks where you left off reading in a book so that you don't have to mark your place manually. If you use any other device registered to your Apple ID, you also pick up where you left off reading.

FIGURE 12-17

Set Reading Goals

iPadOS 15 includes a feature to help us stay on top of our daily reading: Reading Goals. This feature allows you to set a specific amount of time you'd like to spend reading each day, and it will keep track of the time for you. You can also set goals for the number of books you'd like to finish reading in a year.

1. Tap the Reading Now button in the lower left and then swipe down to the Reading Goals section.

2. Tap the Today's Reading area to adjust your goal or to share your progress with a significant other.

3. To adjust your reading goal time, tap the Adjust Goal button, scroll up or down to select a new time in the menu provided (see **Figure 12-18**), and tap the screen outside the menu to exit it.

4. Tap the small *x* in the upper-right to return to the Reading Goals section.

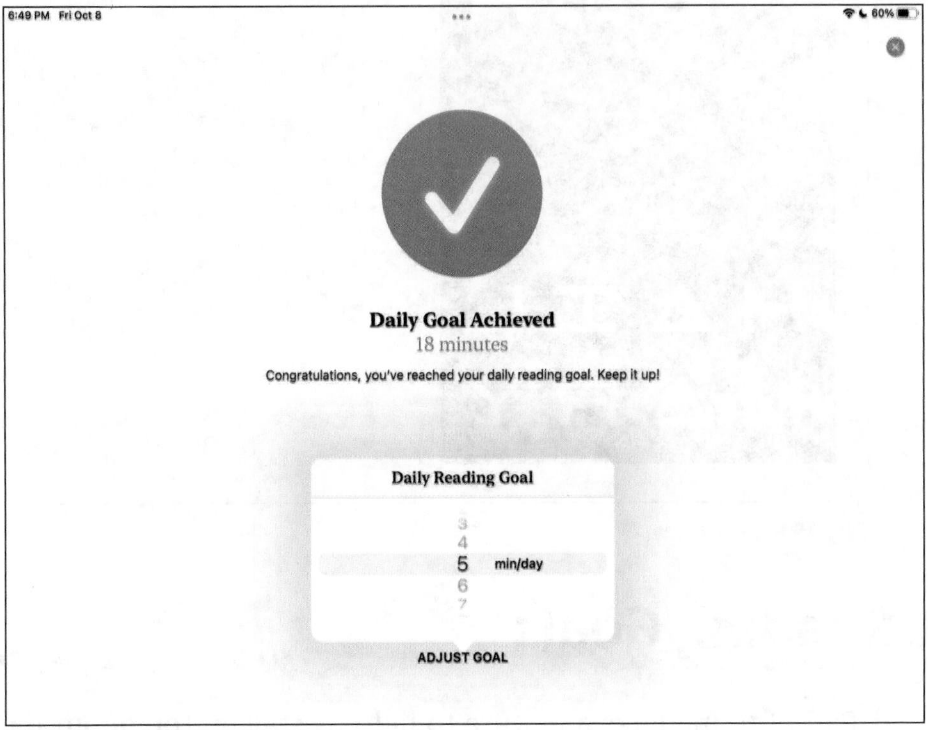

FIGURE 12-18

Chapter **13**

Enjoying Music and Podcasts

PadOS includes the Music app, which allows you to take advantage of your iPad's amazing little sound system to play your favorite music or other audio files.

In this chapter, you get acquainted with the Music app and its features that allow you to sort and find music and control playback. You also get an overview of AirPlay for accessing and playing your music over a home network or over any connected device (this also works with videos and photos). Finally, I introduce you to the Podcasts app for your listening pleasure.

View the Music Library

The Library in Music contains the music or other audio files that you've placed on your iPad, either by purchasing them through the iTunes Store or copying them from your computer. The following steps show you how to work with those files on your iPad:

TIP

The figures in this chapter show the Music app in landscape mode. If you prefer portrait mode, you can access the sidebar mentioned in the upcoming steps by tapping the arrow in the upper-right corner of the screen.

1. Tap the Music app, located in the Dock on the Home screen, and the Music window opens, as shown **Figure 13-1**.

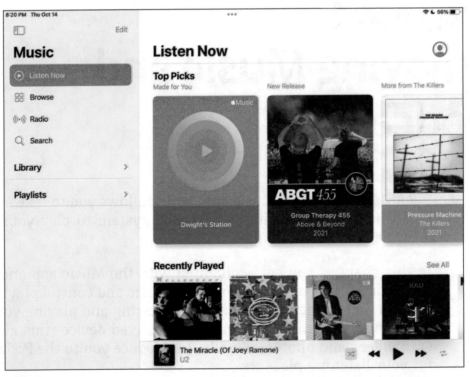

FIGURE 13-1

2. Tap the Library button in the sidebar on the left and tap a category (see **Figure 13-2**) to view music by Recently Added, Playlists, Artists, Albums, Songs, and other categories.

TIP

The iTunes Store has several free items that you can download and use to play around with the features in Music. You can also sync content (such as iTunes Smart Playlists stored on your computer or other Apple devices) to your iPad, and play it using the Music app. (See Chapter 3 for more about syncing, and see Chapter 11 for more about getting content from the iTunes Store.)

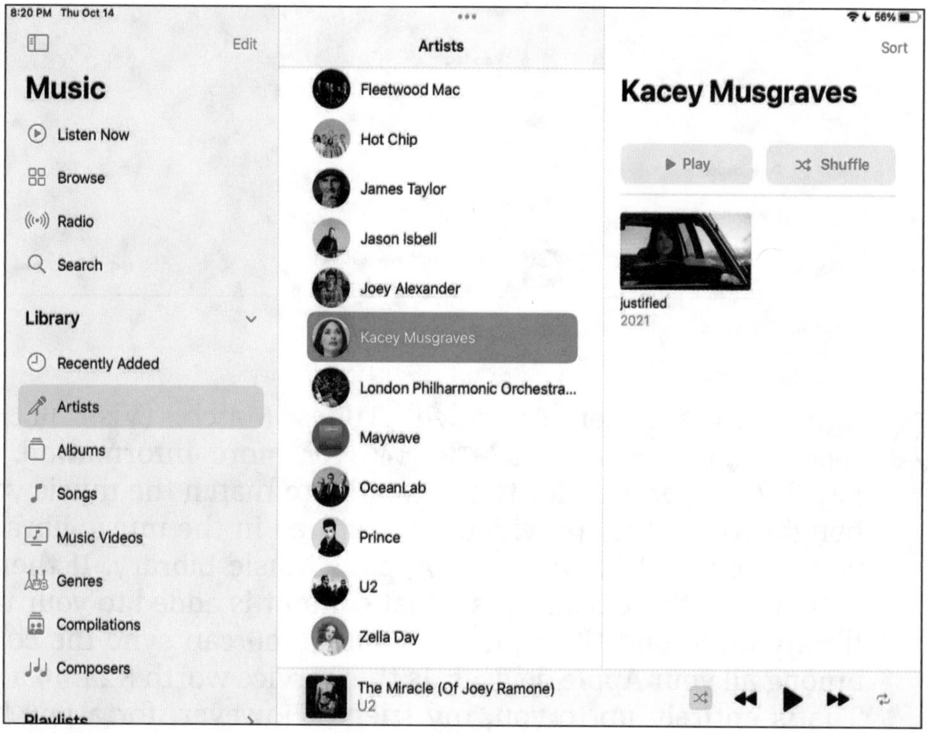

FIGURE 13-2

3. With the Library list expanded, tap Edit in the upper-right corner of the sidebar to edit the list of categories, as shown in **Figure 13-3**. Tap the check box to the left of categories that you'd like to sort your Music Library by; deselect those you don't want to use.

4. Tap Done in the upper-right corner of the sidebar when you're finished.

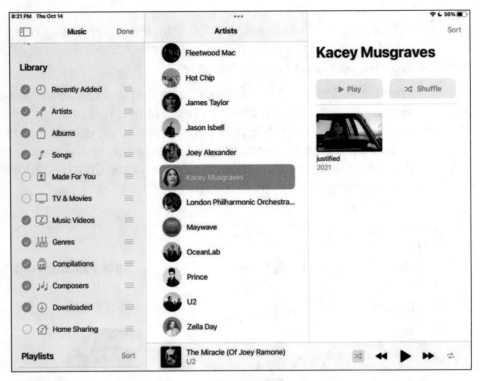

FIGURE 13-3

TIP

Apple offers a service called iTunes Match. (Visit `https://support.apple.com/en-us/HT204146` for more information.) You pay $24.99 per year for the capability to match the music you've bought from other providers (and stored in the music library on your computer) to what's in Apple's Music Library. If there's a match (and there usually is), that content is added to your music library on iCloud. Then, using iCloud, you can sync the content among all your Apple devices. Is this service worth $24.99 a year? That's entirely up to you, my friend. However, for a few bucks more, you can have the benefits of iTunes Match plus access to millions of songs across all your Apple devices by using another Apple service: Apple Music. There's more about Apple Music later in this chapter, but for more info about subscribing and what a full-blown Apple Music subscription offers, check out `www.apple.com/apple-music`.

Create Playlists

You can create your own playlists to put tracks from various sources into collections of your choosing:

1. Tap the Playlists button in the sidebar on the left of the screen.

2. Tap the New Playlist button. In the dialog that appears (see **Figure 13-4**), tap Playlist Name and enter a title for the playlist.

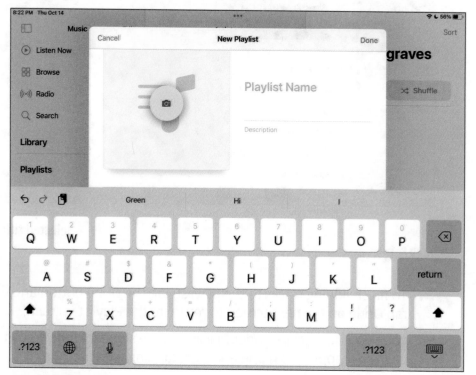

FIGURE 13-4

3. Tap Add Music; search for music by artist, title, or lyrics; or tap Library, Browse, or Listen Now to find what you're looking for.

4. In the list of selections that appears (see **Figure 13-5**), tap the plus sign to the right of each item you want to include (for individual songs or entire albums). Tap the arrow in the left corner of the window to go back and search for other items, if you like. Continue until you've selected all the songs you want to add to the playlist.

Tap here

Selected title

FIGURE 13-5

5. To finish adding tracks to the playlist, tap the Done button and then tap Done on the next screen to return to the Playlists screen.

6. Your playlist appears under Playlists in the sidebar, and you can now play it by tapping its name and then tapping a track to play it.

TIP

To search for and play a song in your music libraries from your Home screen (without even opening the Music app), use the Search feature. From your first Home screen, you can swipe down from the screen outside the Dock and enter the name of the song in the Search field. A list of search results appears. Just tap the Play button and rock on!

Search for Music

You can search for an item in your Music Library by using the Search feature:

1. With the Music app open, tap the Search button in the sidebar on the left. When the Search screen appears, tap the Search field at the top of the screen. Tap the Your Library tab to search for songs stored on your iPad, or tap Apple Music to search the Apple Music library. You may search for items in Apple Music, but you must be subscribed to Apple Music to play selections from it.

2. Enter a search term in the Search field. Results are displayed, narrowing as you type, as shown in **Figure 13-6.**

3. Tap an item to view or play it.

FIGURE 13-6

TIP In the Search field, you can enter an artist's name, a lyricist's or a composer's name, a word from the item's title, or even lyrics to find what you're looking for.

Play Music

After you know how to find your music, you can have some real fun by playing it!

TIP You can use Siri to play music hands free. Just press and hold the Home button (if your iPad has one) or the top button (if your iPad doesn't have a Home button), and when Siri appears, say something like "Play 'L.A. Woman'" or "Play 'Fields of Gold.'"

To play music on your iPad, follow these steps:

1. Locate the music that you want by using the methods described in previous tasks in this chapter.

2. Tap the item you want to play. If you're displaying the Songs category, you don't have to tap an album to open a song; you need only to tap a song to play it. If you're using any other categories, you have to tap items, such as albums (or multiple songs from one artist), to find the song you want to hear.

TIP Home Sharing is a feature of iTunes and the Music app that you can use to share music among up to five devices that have Home Sharing turned on. After Home Sharing is set up via iTunes or the Sharing pane in System Preferences (Mac users only), any of your devices can stream music and videos to other devices, and you can even click and drag content between devices using iTunes or the Music app. For more about Home Sharing, visit this site: https:// support.apple.com/en-us/HT202190.

3. Tap the item you want to play from the list that appears; it begins to play (see **Figure 13-7**). You can tell that the song is playing because the number to the left of its title turns into red audio equalizer bars and the name of the song appears at the bottom of the screen.

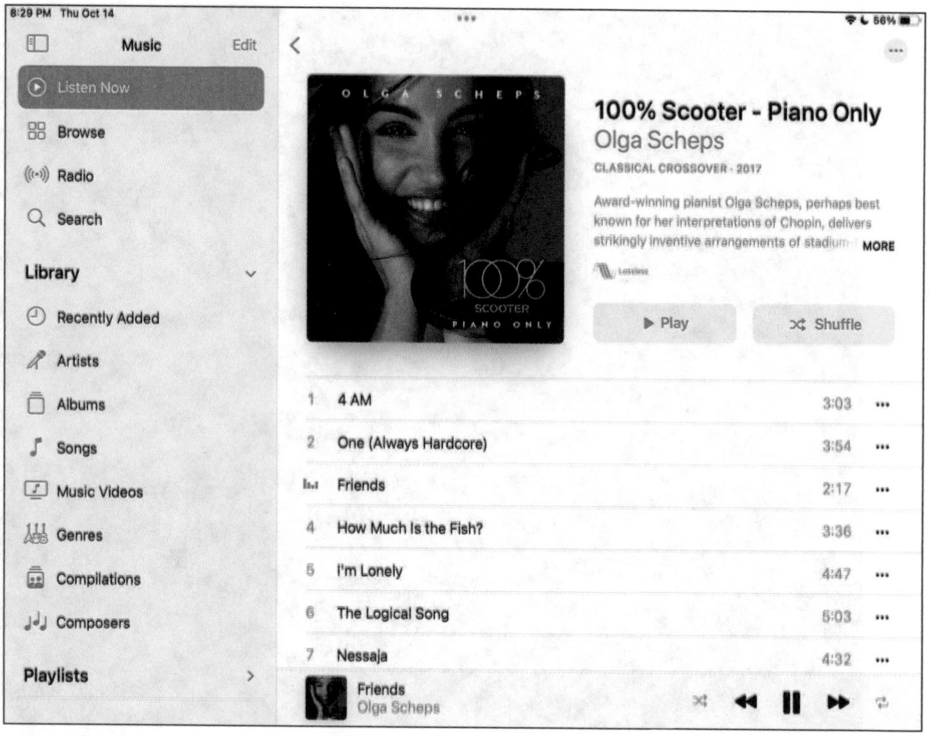

FIGURE 13-7

4. Tap the currently playing song title at the bottom of the screen to open it, displaying playback controls. Use the Previous and Next buttons near the bottom of the screen shown in **Figure 13-8** to navigate the audio file that's playing:

- The Previous button takes you back to the beginning of the item that's playing if you tap it, or rewinds the song if you press and hold it.

- The Next button takes you to the next item if you tap it, or fast-forwards the song if you press and hold it.

Use the Volume slider on the bottom of the screen (or the Volume buttons on the side of your iPad) to increase or decrease the volume.

5. Tap the Pause button to pause playback. Tap the button again to resume playing.

You can also use music controls for music that's playing from the lock screen.

FIGURE 13-8

6. Tap and drag the playhead line near the middle of the screen (underneath the song title) that indicates the current playback location. Drag the line to the left or right to "scrub" to another location in the song.

7. Do you like to sing along but sometimes flub the words? Tap the Lyrics button in the lower right (the button looks like a speech box with a quotation mark in it), and if the song is from the Apple Music library, the lyrics will scroll up the screen in sync with the song, as shown in **Figure 13-9.** You can swipe through the lyrics, or if you tap a lyric, Music will jump to that point in the song.

8. If you don't like what's playing, here's how to make another selection: Drag down from the top of the playback controls screen to view other selections in the album that's playing or to browse for other tunes.

Family Sharing allows up to six members of your family to share purchased content even if they don't share the same iTunes account. You can set up Family Sharing under iCloud in Settings. See Chapter 11 for more about Family Sharing.

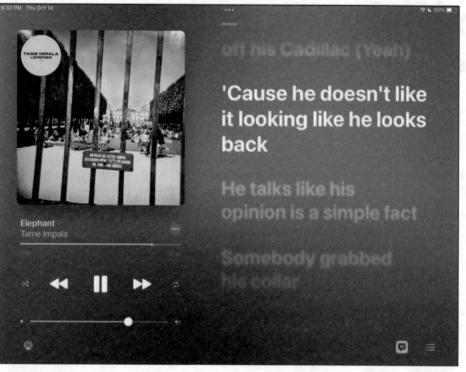

FIGURE 13-9

Shuffle Music

If you want to play a random selection of the music in an album on your iPad, you can use the Shuffle feature:

1. Tap the name of the currently playing song at the bottom of the screen.

2. Tap the Shuffle button, which looks like two lines crossing to form an *X* and is located to the left of the Previous button. Your content plays in random order.

3. To play the songs over again continuously, tap the Repeat button, which looks like two arrows circling one another and is located to the right of the Next button.

Listen with Your Earbuds

If you've set the volume slider as high as it goes but you're still having trouble hearing the music, consider using earbuds. They cut out extraneous noises and improve the sound quality of what you're listening to.

Some iPad models have 3.5mm headphone jacks; you can use 3.5mm stereo earbuds for them, inserting them into the headphone jack. If your iPad has a Lightning connector, you can use earbuds that have a Lightning connector, or you can use a Lightning-to-3.5mm adaptor with standard 3.5mm headphones. If your iPad has a USB-C connector, you can use a USB-C-to-3.5mm adaptor with standard 3.5mm headphones.

You might also look into purchasing Bluetooth earbuds, which allow you to listen wirelessly (this is your best bet, in my opinion). For a top-of-the-line wireless experience, try Apple's AirPods, AirPods Pro, or AirPods Max (go to www.apple.com/airpods for more info). They're a little pricey but are getting rave reviews, and for very good reason.

Listen with Spatial Audio

Spatial audio is a new technology (part of Dolby Atmos) that helps listeners feel as if they're sitting in the middle of the band, orchestra, or what-have-you. The difference between spatial audio and standard stereo can be eye-popping when you first hear it.

TIP

For more on Dolby Atmos, such as how to tell whether audio files are in the format or whether your device can play the format, visit https://support.apple.com/en-us/HT212182.

To enable Dolby Atmos for audio files that support the format:

1. Open the Settings app on your iPad.

2. Find and tap Music.

3. Tap Dolby Atmos, and then tap Automatic or Always On to have audio files that support Dolby Atmos play in that format.

To enable Spatial Audio while using AirPods Pro or AirPods Max:

1. Swipe from the top-right corner of your iPad's screen to open Control Center.

2. Press and hold down on the volume slider until the screen shown in **Figure 13-10** opens.

   If the audio file that's currently playing supports Dolby Atmos and spatial audio, the Spatial Audio button will appear in the lower right (see **Figure 13-10**).

3. To enable or disable spatial audio, tap the Spatial Audio button.

   If the button is blue, spatial audio is enabled; if it's gray, spatial audio is not enabled.

FIGURE 13-10

Use AirPlay

The AirPlay streaming technology is built into the iPad, iPod touch, Macs, PCs running iTunes, and iPhone. Streaming technology allows you to send media files from one device that supports AirPlay to be played on another.

1. Send a movie that you've purchased on your iPad or a slideshow of your photos to be played on your Apple TV, and then control the TV playback from your iPad.

2. Send music to be played over compatible speakers, such as Apple's HomePod (go to http://www.apple.com/homepod for more information). Check out the Apple TV Remote app in the App Store, which you can use to control your Apple TV from your iPad.

3. To stream music via AirPlay on your iPad with another AirPlay-enabled device on your network or in close proximity, tap the AirPlay button (looks like a pyramid with sound waves emanating from it) at the bottom of the playback control screen while listening to a song. Then select the AirPlay device to stream the content to, or choose your iPad to move the playback back to it.

 TIP If you get a bit antsy watching a long movie, one of the beauties of AirPlay is that you can still use your iPad to check email, browse photos or the Internet, or check your calendar while the media file is playing on the other device.

Find and Subscribe to Podcasts

First, what the heck is a podcast? A *podcast* is sort of like a radio show that you can listen to at any time. You'll find podcasts covering just about any subject imaginable, including news, sports, gardening, cooking, education, comedy, religion, and so much more. The Podcasts app is the vehicle by which you find and listen to podcasts on your iPad.

To search Apple's massive library of podcasts and subscribe to them (which is free, by the way):

1. Tap the Podcasts icon on the Home screen to open it.

2. There are three ways to discover podcasts:

- Tap Browse at the bottom of the screen. You find podcasts that are featured by the good folks at Apple, as shown in **Figure 13-11.**

- Tap Browse at the bottom of the screen and swipe down to Top Shows or Top Episodes. Tap See All and you'll be greeted with lists of the most popular podcasts. Tap the All Categories button in the upper-right corner to sift through the podcasts based on the category (such as Arts, Health & Fitness, or Music).

- Tap Search and then tap the Search field at the top of the screen. When the keyboard appears, type the name or subject of a podcast to see a list of results.

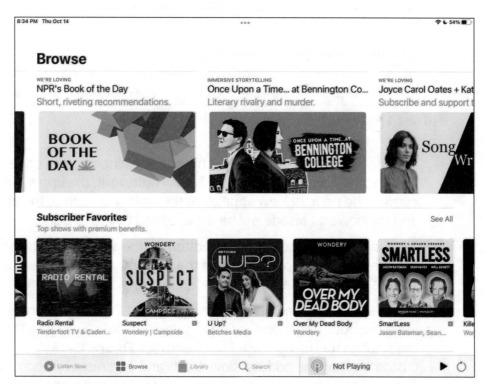

FIGURE 13-11

3. When you find a podcast that intrigues you, tap its name to see its information page, which will be similar to the one in **Figure 13-12.**

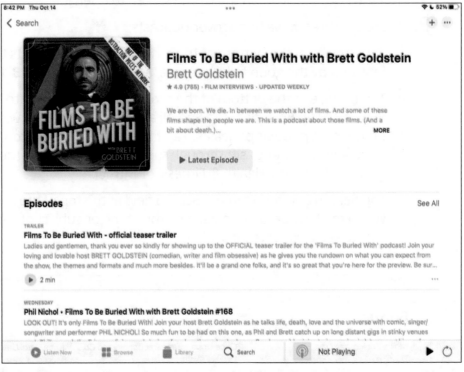

FIGURE 13-12

4. Tap the plus sign (+) button (which is the Subscribe button or, as Apple sometimes refers to it, the Follow button), in the upper-right corner. The podcast now appears in the Library section of the app, and the newest episode will be downloaded to your iPad.

5. Tap Library in the toolbar at the bottom of the screen, tap Shows on the left, and then tap the name of the podcast you subscribed to and view its information screen.

6. Tap the More button in the upper right (looks like a circle containing three dots) and then tap Settings (its icon looks like a gear) to see the settings for the podcast. From here (see **Figure 13-13**), you can customize how the podcast downloads and organizes episodes. Tap Done in the upper-right corner when you're finished with the Settings options.

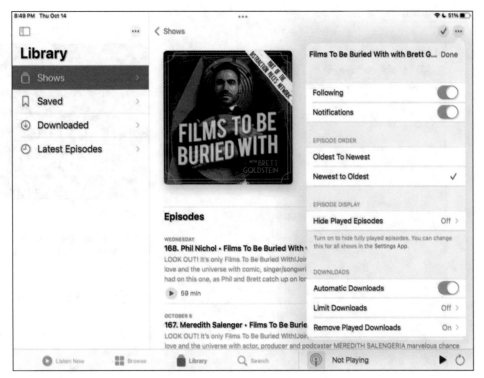

FIGURE 13-13

Play Podcasts

Playing podcasts is a breeze and works very much like playing audio files in the Music app.

1. Open the Podcasts app and tap Library at the bottom of the screen.

2. Tap the name of the podcast you'd like to listen to.

3. Tap the episode you want to play. The episode begins playing; you can see the currently playing episode in the bottom-right area of the screen.

4. Tap the currently playing episode in the lower right of the screen to open the playback controls, shown in **Figure 13-14.**

5. Drag the playhead line under the image to scrub to a different part of the episode, or tap the Rewind or Fast Forward buttons to the left and right of the Pause/Play button, respectively.

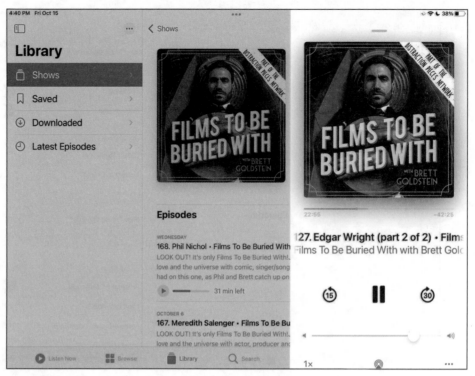

FIGURE 13-14

6. Adjust the playback speed by tapping the 1x icon in the lower left of the Play controls. Each tap increases or decreases playback speed.

7. Adjust the volume by dragging the Volume slider near the bottom of the screen or by using the Volume buttons on the side of your iPad.

Tap the Listen Now button in the toolbar at the bottom of the app's screen to see a list of the newest episodes that have been automatically downloaded to your iPad.

Chapter **14**

Taking and Sharing Photos

With its gorgeous screen, the iPad is a natural for taking and viewing photos. It supports JPEG and HEIF (High Efficiency Image Format) photos. You can shoot your photos by using the built-in cameras in the iPad with built-in square or panorama modes. With recent iPad models, you can edit your images using smart adjustment filters. You can also sync photos from your computer, save images that you find online to your iPad, or receive them by email, MMS, or iMessage.

The photo sharing feature lets you share groups of photos with people using iCloud on an iPadOS device, iOS device, or on a Mac or Windows computer with iCloud access. Your iCloud Photo Library makes all this storage and sharing easy.

When you have taken or downloaded photos to play with, the Photos app lets you organize and view them in albums, one by one, or in a slideshow. You can also view photos by the years in which they were taken, with images divided into collections by the location or time you took them. With iPadOS 15, videos and live photos will play as you browse through Photos, making it a more dynamic and interesting experience. You can also AirDrop, email, message, or tweet a photo to a friend, print it, share it via AirPlay, or post it to Facebook.

Finally, you can create time-lapse videos with the Camera app, allowing you to record a sequence in time, such as a flower opening as the sun warms it or your grandchild stirring from sleep. You can read about all these features in this chapter.

Take Pictures with the iPad Cameras

The cameras in the iPad are just begging to be used, no matter which model you have!

TIP

To go to the camera with the lock screen displayed, swipe down from the right corner of the screen and tap the Camera app icon in Control Center to go directly to the Camera app. You can also simply swipe from right to left on the lock screen to access Camera.

1. Tap the Camera app icon on the Home screen to open the app.

2. If the camera type on the lower-right side of the screen (see **Figure 14-1**) is set to Video or something other than Photo, swipe to choose Photo (the still camera).

TIP

The iPad's front- and rear-facing cameras allow you to capture photos and video (see Chapter 15 for more about the video features) and share them with family and friends. Newer models offer incredible cameras, even up to 12 megapixels, with such features as

» Autofocus

» Automatic image stabilization to avoid fuzzy moving targets

» True Tone Flash (with certain models), a sensor that tells the iPad when a flash is needed

Timer   Live photos

Switch camera   Shutter

FIGURE 14-1

The following are adjustments you can make after you've opened the Camera app:

» You can set the Pano (for panorama) and Square options using the camera type control below the Capture button (the large white or red circle). These controls let you create square images like those you see on Instagram. With Pano selected, tap to begin to take a picture and pan across a view, and then tap Done to capture a panoramic display.

» If your iPad supports it, tap the Flash button (looks like a lightning bolt) when using the rear camera and then select a flash option:

  • On, if your lighting is dim enough to require a flash

- Off, if you don't want your iPad to use a flash

- Auto, if you want to let your iPad decide for you

» To use the High Dynamic Range (HDR) feature (if your iPad supports it), tap the HDR setting and tap to turn it on. This feature uses several images, some underexposed and some overexposed, and combines the best ones into one image, sometimes providing a more finely detailed picture.

TIP

HDR pictures can be very large in file size, meaning that they'll take up more of your iPad's memory than standard pictures.

» If you want a time delay before the camera snaps the picture, tap the Time Delay button (looks like a timer), and then tap 3s or 10s for a 3- or 10-second delay, respectively.

» Tap the Live button (looks like concentric circles) to take Live Photos. As opposed to freezing a single moment in time, Live Photos lets you capture three-second moving images, which can create some truly beautiful photos. Be sure to hold your iPhone still for at least three seconds so that you don't move too soon and cause part of your Live Photo to show the movement of your iPhone as you get into position for the picture.

» Move the camera around until you find a pleasing image. You can do a couple of things at this point to help you take your photo:

- Tap the area of the grid where you want the camera to autofocus.

- Place two fingers apart from each other on the screen and then pinch them together (still touching the screen) to display a digital zoom control. Drag the circle in the zoom bar to the left to zoom in or out on the image.

» Tap the Shutter button. You've just taken a picture, and it's stored in the Photos app gallery automatically.

TIP

You can also use a Volume button (located on the right side of your iPad) to capture a picture or start or stop video camera recording.

» Tap the Switch Camera button above the Shutter button to switch between the front camera and rear camera. You can then take selfies (pictures of yourself), so go ahead and tap the Shutter button to take another picture.

» To view the last photo taken, tap the thumbnail of the latest image directly beneath the Shutter button; the Photos app opens and displays the photo.

» While viewing the image in Photos, tap the Share button (the box with an upward-pointing arrow, located near the upper-right corner of the screen) to display a menu that allows you to AirDrop (explained later in the chapter), email, or instant message the photo, assign it to a contact, use it as iPad wallpaper, tweet it, post it to Facebook, share via iCloud Photo Sharing or Flickr, or print it (see **Figure 14-2**).

FIGURE 14-2

>> You can tap images to select more than one.

>> To delete the image, have it displayed and tap the Trash button in the bottom-right corner of the screen. Tap Delete Photo in the confirming menu that appears.

TIP

You can use the iCloud Photo Sharing feature to automatically sync your photos across various devices. Turn on iCloud Photo Sharing by tapping Settings on the Home screen, tapping Photos, and then toggling the iCloud Photos switch to On (green).

View an Album

The Photos app organizes your pictures into albums, using such criteria as the folder or album on your computer from which you synced the photos, or photos captured using the iPad camera (saved in the Camera Roll album). You may also have albums for images that you synced from other devices through iTunes or shared via Photos.

To view your albums:

1. Tap the Photos app icon on the Home screen.

2. Tap My Albums in the sidebar on the left side of the screen to display your albums, as shown in **Figure 14-3.**

If you don't see the sidebar, tap the Sidebar button (if you're holding your iPad in landscape orientation) or the Photos button (if you're holding in portrait orientation) in the upper-left corner of the screen.

3. Tap an album. The photos in it are displayed.

TIP

You can associate photos with faces and events. When you do, additional tabs appear at the bottom of the screen when you display an album containing that type of photo.

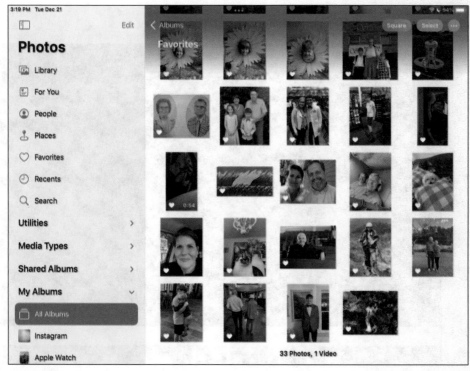

FIGURE 14-3

View Individual Photos

You can view photos individually by opening them from within an album.

To view individual photos:

1. Tap the Photos app icon on the Home screen.

2. Tap Albums or Library (refer to Figure **14-3**) in the sidebar.

3. Tap a photo to view it. The picture expands, as shown in **Figure 14-4.**

4. Flick your finger to the left or right to scroll through the album or library to look at the individual photos in it.

5. You can tap the Back button in the upper-left corner (looks like a left-pointing arrow) to return to the previous view.

FIGURE 14-4

TIP You can place a photo on a person's information record in Contacts. For more about how to do this, see Chapter 7.

Edit Photos

iPad Photos isn't Photoshop, but it does provide some tools for editing photos. To edit photos:

1. Tap the Photos app on the Home screen to open it.

2. Locate and display a photo you want to edit.

3. Tap the Edit button in the upper right of the screen; the Edit Photo screen shown in **Figure 14-5** appears.

4. At this point, you can take several possible actions with these tools:

Filters

Adjustments

Auto-enhance

Crop

FIGURE 14-5

- **Crop:** To crop the photo to a portion of its original area, tap the Crop button. You can then tap any corner of the image and drag inward or outward to remove areas of the photo. Tap Crop and then Save to apply your changes.

- **Filters:** Apply any of nine filters (such as Vivid, Mono, or Noir) to change the look and feel of your image. These effects adjust the brightness of your image or apply a black-and-white tone to your color photos. Tap the Filters button in the middle of the tools on the left side of the screen and scroll to view available filters. Tap one and then tap Apply to apply the effect to your image.

- **Adjustments:** Swipe the options to the right of the screen to see adjustment options such as Light, Color, or B&W. There is a slew of tools that you can use to tweak contrast, color intensity, shadows, and more.

- **Depth:** With this slider, you can control the depth of field of any photo shot in portrait mode (if your iPad model supports it). A lower value, such as ƒ1.8, gives you more background blur. A higher number, such as ƒ16, reveals a more detailed background.

- **Auto-enhance:** The icon for this feature looks like a magic wand, and it pretty much works like one. Tapping the wand allows your iPhone to apply automatic adjustments to your photo's exposure, saturation, contrast, and so on.

5. If you're pleased with your edits, tap the Done button. A copy of the edited photo is saved.

TIP

Each of the editing features has a Cancel button. If you don't like the changes you made, tap this button to stop making changes before you save the image.

Organize Photos

You'll probably want to organize your photos to make it simpler to find what you're looking for:

1. If you want to create your own album, open the Recents album.

2. Tap the Select button in the top-right corner and then tap individual photos to select them. Small check marks appear on the selected photos (see **Figure 14-6**).

3. Tap the Share button (the box containing an upward-pointing arrow) in the bottom of the screen, tap Add to Album, and then tap the New Album button.

Check marks indicate selected items

FIGURE 14-6

TIP

If you've already created albums, you can choose to add the photo to an existing album at this point.

4. Enter a name for a new album and then tap Save. If you create a new album, it appears in the Photos main screen with the other albums that are displayed.

TIP

You can also choose several other Share options or Delete when you've selected photos in Step 2 of this task. This allows you to share or delete multiple photos at a time.

Share Photos with Mail, Social Media, or Other Apps

You can easily share photos stored on your iPad by sending them as email attachments or in a text message; you can post them on Facebook, share them via iCloud Photo Sharing or Flickr, tweet them on Twitter, and so on.

To share photos in this manner:

1. Tap the Photos app icon on the Home screen.

2. Locate the photo you want to share.

3. Tap the photo to select it and then tap the Share button. (It looks like a box with an upward-pointing arrow.) The menu shown in **Figure 14-7** appears. Tap to select additional photos, if you want them.

FIGURE 14-7

4. Tap the Mail, Message, Twitter, iCloud Photo Sharing, Facebook, Flickr, or any other option you'd like to use. Obviously, some items appear here only if you have their app installed.

5. In the message form that appears, make any modifications that apply in the To, Cc/Bcc, or Subject fields and then type a message for email or enter your social media posting.

6. Tap the Send or Post button, and the message and photo are sent or posted.

TIP

You can also copy and paste a photo into documents, such as those created in the Pages word-processor app. To do this, tap a photo in Photos and tap Share. Tap the Copy command. In the destination app, press and hold the screen and tap Paste when it appears.

Share a Photo Using AirDrop

AirDrop provides a way to share content, such as photos, with others who are nearby and who have an AirDrop-enabled device (iPhones, iPads, and more recent Macs that can run macOS 10.10 or later).

Follow the steps in the previous task to locate a photo you want to share.

1. Tap the Share button.

2. If an AirDrop-enabled device is in your immediate vicinity (within 30 feet or so), you see the device listed underneath the selected image (see **Figure 14-8**). Tap the device name and your photo is sent to the other device.

AirDrop-enabled devices nearby

FIGURE 14-8

TIP

Other iOS or iPadOS devices must have AirDrop enabled to use this feature. To enable AirDrop, open Control Center (swipe up from the bottom of any screen) and tap AirDrop, as shown in **Figure 14-9.** Choose Contacts Only or Everyone to specify the people you can use AirDrop with.

Tap to enable/disable AirDrop

FIGURE 14-9

Share Photos Using iCloud Photo Sharing

iCloud Photo Sharing allows you to automatically share photos using your iCloud account:

1. Open the Photos app.

2. Select a photo or photos you would like to share, and tap the Share button.

3. In the Share screen that opens, tap Add to Shared Album.

4. Enter a comment if you like (see **Figure 14-10**) and then tap Post. The photos are posted to your iCloud Photo Library.

FIGURE 14-10

Print Photos

If you have a printer that's compatible with Apple's AirPrint technology, you can print photos from your iPad.

1. With Photos open, locate the photo you want to print and tap it to maximize it.

2. Tap the Share button. On the menu that appears, scroll to near the bottom of the list of options and then tap Print.

3. In the Print Options dialog that appears (see **Figure 14-11**), tap an available printer in the list or tap the Printer button. The iPad presents you with a list of any compatible wireless printers on your local network.

4. Tap the plus or minus symbols in the Copy field to set the number of copies to print.

5. Select a paper size to print on from the Paper Size menu.

6. Tap the Print button, and your photo is sent to the printer.

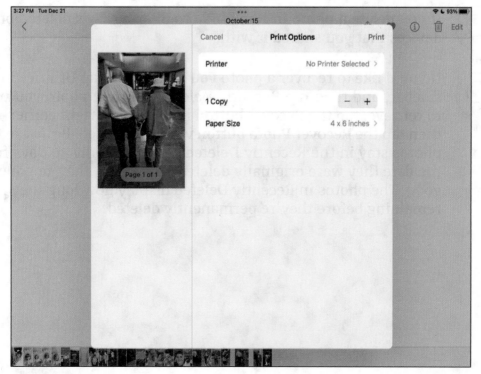

FIGURE 14-11

Delete Photos

You may find that it's time to get rid of some of those old photos of the family reunion or the latest community center project. If the photos weren't transferred from your computer but instead were taken, downloaded, or captured as screenshots on the iPad, you can delete them.

1. Tap the Photos app icon on the Home screen.

2. Tap Library or open an album.

3. Locate and tap a photo that you want to delete, and then tap the Trash icon. In the confirming dialog that appears, tap the Delete Photo button to finish the deletion.

If you delete a photo in iCloud Photo Sharing, it is deleted on all devices that you shared it with.

If you'd like to recover a photo you've deleted, tap Utilities in the sidebar, and then tap Recently Deleted. Tap the photo you want to retrieve, tap the Recover button in the lower-right corner, and then tap the Recover Photo button when prompted. Be aware that photos stay in the Recently Deleted album for only 30 days from the date they were originally deleted. After that, they're gone for good. The photos in Recently Deleted display how long they have remaining before they're permanently deleted.

Chapter **15**

Creating and Watching Videos

U sing the TV app (formerly known as Videos), you can watch movies or TV shows, as well as media that you've synced from iCloud on your Mac or PC, and even media that's provided from other content providers, such as cable and streaming video services. The TV app aims to be your one-stop shop for your viewing pleasure.

In addition, iPads sport both a front and rear video camera that you can use to capture your own videos, which iPadOS now allows you to edit in the same way you can edit photos: You can apply adjustments, filters, and crop your videos. Speaking of editing, you can also download the iMovie app for iPad (a more limited version of the longtime mainstay on Mac computers) that allows you to do an editing deep dive with the capability to add titles, music, transitions, and much more. Some iPad models sport cameras that support up to 4K video, which produces rich detail with 8 million pixels per frame. The latest iPad and iPad mini models all support HD video up to 1080p.

A few other features of video in newer iPad models include image stabilization to avoid the shakes when recording, more frames shot per second for smoother video, and continuous autofocus video, which means that your iPad continually autofocuses as you're recording.

In this chapter, you find out about shooting and watching video content from a variety of sources. For practice, you may want to refer to Chapter 11 first to find out how to purchase or download one of many available TV shows or movies from the iTunes Store.

Capture Your Own Videos with the Built-In Cameras

The camera lenses on newer iPads have perks for photographers, including large apertures and highly accurate sensors, which make for better images all around. In addition, auto image stabilization makes up for any shakiness in the hands holding the iPad, and auto-focus has sped up thanks to the super-fast processors being used. Videographers will appreciate the fast frames-per-second capability as well as the slow-motion feature.

1. To capture a video, tap the Camera app on the Home screen. With an iPad, two video cameras are available for capturing video, one from the front and one from the back of the device. (See more about this topic in the next task.)

2. The Camera app opens (see **Figure 15-1**). Tap and slide the camera-type options on the lower right of the screen until Video is selected and you see the red Record button. This button is how you switch from the still camera to the video camera.

3. If you want to switch between the front and back cameras, tap the Switch Camera button above the Record button (see **Figure 15-1**).

4. Tap the red Record button to begin recording the video. (The red dot in the middle of this button turns into a red square when the camera is recording.) The duration of your recording is displayed at the top of the screen. Use the Zoom slider to zoom in and out if you need to get closer to or farther away from your subject. When you're finished, tap the Record button again. Your new video is now listed under the

Record button. Tap the video to play it, share it, or delete it. In the future, you can find and play the video in your Library or in the Videos album under Media Types when you open the Photos app.

Record button

Switch Camera button

Camera-type options

FIGURE 15-1

Before you start recording, remember where the camera lens is — while holding the iPad and panning, you can easily put your fingers directly over the lens! Also, you can't pause your recording; when you stop, your video is saved, and when you start recording, you're creating a new video file.

Edit Videos

The iPadOS Photos app isn't as full featured as Apple's Final Cut or Adobe's Premier, but it does provide some tools for editing videos.

1. Tap the Photos app (where your videos are stored) on the Home screen, locate your video, and tap to open it.

2. Tap the Edit button in the upper-right corner of the screen; the Edit screen appears. The one shown in **Figure 15-2** is for a video shot in Landscape mode.

FIGURE 15-2

3. At this point, you can take several possible actions with the tools provided:

- **Crop/rotate:** To rotate or flip the image, tap the rotate or flip icon in the upper-left corner (next to Cancel when viewing in Portrait mode). To crop the video to a portion of its original area, tap the Crop button. You can then tap any corner of the image and drag inward or outward to remove areas of the video. Tap Crop and then Save to apply your changes.

- **Filters:** Apply any of nine filters (such as Vivid, Mono, or Noir) to change the look of your video images. These effects adjust the brightness of your video or apply a black-and-white tone to your color videos. Tap the Filters button on the left side of the screen and then scroll through the list on the right side to view available filters. Tap one to apply the effect to your video.

- **Adjustments:** Tap Light, Color, or B&W to access a slew of tools that you can use to tweak contrast, color intensity, shadows, and more.

- **Auto-enhance:** The icon for this feature looks like a magic wand, and it pretty much works like one. Tapping the wand allows your iPad to apply automatic adjustments to your video's exposure, saturation, contrast, and so on.

- **Trim:** Use the trim tool to remove parts of your video you no longer want to view.

4. If you're pleased with your edits, tap the Done button. A copy of the edited video is saved.

TIP

Each of the editing features has a Cancel button. If you don't like the changes you made, tap this button (in the upper-left corner) to stop making changes before you save the image. How about if you make changes you later regret? Just open the video, tap Edit, and then tap the red Revert button in the upper right to discard changes to the original.

Play Movies or TV Shows with the TV App

Open the TV app for the first time, and you'll be greeted with a Welcome screen. Tap Get Started, and you'll be asked to sign in to your television provider, if you haven't done so already.

Signing in will allow you to use the TV app to access content in other apps (like ESPN or Disney), if such services are supported by your TV provider. This way, you need to use only the TV app to access content and sign in, as opposed to having multiple apps to juggle and sign in to.

TIP

Should you decide to skip signing in to your TV provider and worry about it later (or if you've already opened the TV app and cruised right past this part), you can access the same options by going to Settings ⇨ TV Provider, tapping the name of your provider, and then entering your account information. If you're not sure of your account information, you'll need to contact your provider for assistance.

The TV app offers a couple of ways to view movies and TV shows: via third-party providers (many require a subscription, such as HBO Max, Disney+, and Netflix) or items you've purchased or rented from the iTunes Store.

Content from third-party providers

To access content from third-party providers like Apple TV+, NBC, ABC, PBS, and more, tap the Watch Now button in the bottom left of your screen (see **Figure 15-3**). Swipe to see hit shows and browse by genres like Comedy, Action, and others.

FIGURE 15-3

Tap a show that interests you and then tap an episode to see a description, as I've done in **Figure 15-4.** Tap an episode to begin playing it, and if you have the app that supports the video, it will open automatically. You may be prompted to connect apps from providers like PBS and ABC to the TV app so that you can watch their videos in TV. If you want to do so, tap Connect, but if not, just tap Not Now. If you don't have the app installed that you need to watch the video, you'll be asked if you'd like to download and install it, as shown in **Figure 15-5.**

FIGURE 15-4

TIP

If your iPad is on the same Wi-Fi network as your computer and both are running iTunes, with the iPad and iTunes set to use the same Home Sharing account, you see the Shared List. With this setup, you can stream videos from iTunes on your computer to your iPad.

Content from the iTunes Store

To access video you've purchased or rented from the iTunes Store, follow these steps:

1. Tap the TV app icon on the Home screen to open the application, and then tap Library at the bottom of the screen.

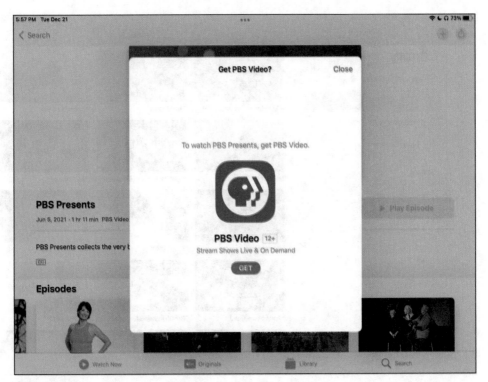

FIGURE 15-5

2. On a screen like the one in **Figure 15-6,** tap a selection from within the categories listed and then tap the video you want to watch. You can also tap the Library button in the upper left to view items in select categories, such as Rentals, TV Shows, or Movies, depending on the content you've downloaded.

Information about the movie or TV show episodes appears, as shown in **Figure 15-7.**

3. For TV Shows, tap the episode that you'd like to play; for Movies, the Play button appears right on the description screen. Tap the Play button, and the movie or TV show begins playing (see **Figure 15-8**). (If you see a small, cloud-shaped icon instead of a Play button, tap it, and the content is downloaded from iCloud.)

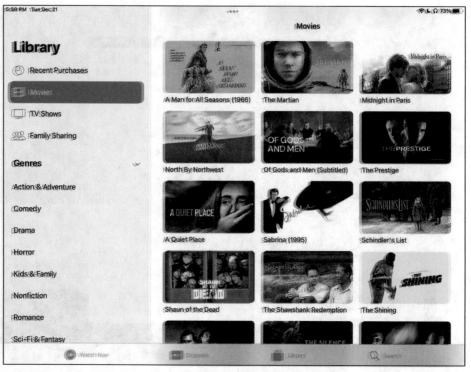

FIGURE 15-6

TIP

The progress of the playback is displayed on the Progress bar, showing how many minutes you've viewed and how many remain. If you don't see the bar, tap the screen once to display it briefly, along with a set of playback tools at the bottom of the screen.

4. With the playback tools displayed, take any of these actions:

- To pause playback, tap the Pause button (which looks like two white, vertical bars next to one another).

- To move to a different location in the video playback, drag the video slider or tap one of the buttons labeled 15 to go backward or forward 15 seconds.

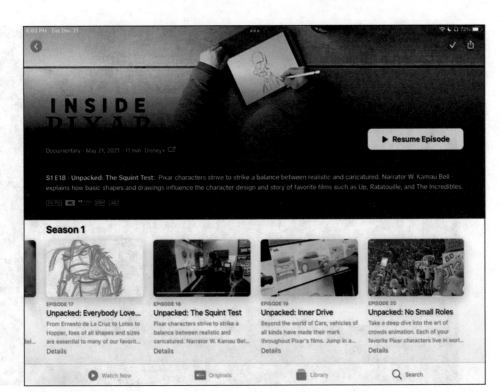

FIGURE 15-7

TIP

If a video has chapter support, another button called Scenes appears here for displaying all chapters so that you can move more easily from one to another.

- Tap the circular button on the Volume slider and drag the button left or right to decrease or increase the volume, respectively.

TIP

If your controls disappear during playback, just tap the screen, and they'll reappear.

5. To stop the video and return to the information screen, tap the Done button to the left of the Progress bar.

TIP

If you've watched a video and stopped it before the end, it opens by default to the last location where you were viewing. To start a video from the beginning, tap and drag the circular button (the *playhead*) on the Progress bar all the way to the left.

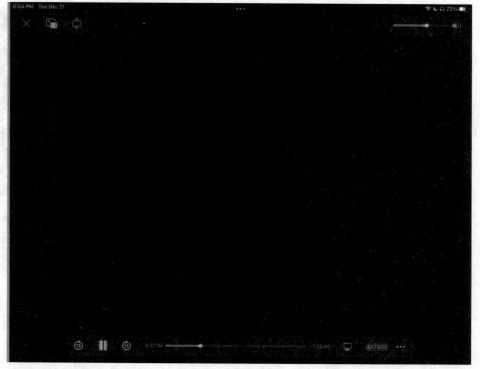

FIGURE 15-8

Turn On Closed-Captioning

iTunes and the iPad offer support for closed-captioning and subtitles. Look for the CC logo on media that you download to use this feature.

TIP

Video you record on your iPad doesn't have closed-captioning capability.

If a movie has either closed-captioning or subtitles, you can turn on the feature in your iPad.

1. Begin by tapping the Settings icon on the Home screen.

2. Tap Accessibility, scroll down, and tap Subtitles & Captioning.

3. On the menu that displays, tap the Closed Captions + SDH switch to turn on the feature (the switch toggles to green). Now when you play a movie with closed-captioning, you can tap the Audio and Subtitles button to the left of the playback controls to manage these features. Tap the Style option to see and control how your subtitles will appear onscreen.

Delete a Video from the iPad

You can buy videos directly from your iPad, or you can sync via iCloud, Finder (a Mac running macOS Catalina or newer), or iTunes (a PC or a Mac running macOS Mojave or earlier) to place content you've bought or created on another device on your iPad.

When you want to get rid of video content on your iPad because it's hogging all your storage space, you can delete it:

1. Open the TV app and go to the TV show or movie you want to delete.

2. Tap the Downloaded button (looks like an arrow and a blue circle containing a check mark), shown in **Figure 15-9.**

3. Tap Remove Download in the options that appear, and the downloaded video will be deleted from your iPad.

If you buy a video using iTunes, sync to download it to your iPad, and then delete it from your iPad, it's still saved in your iTunes Library. You can sync your computer and iPad again to download the video again. Remember, however, that rented movies, when deleted, are gone with the wind. Also, video doesn't sync to iCloud as photos and music do.

TIP

The iPad has a much smaller storage capacity than your typical computer, so downloading lots of TV shows or movies can fill its storage area quickly. If you don't want to view an item again, delete it to free up space.

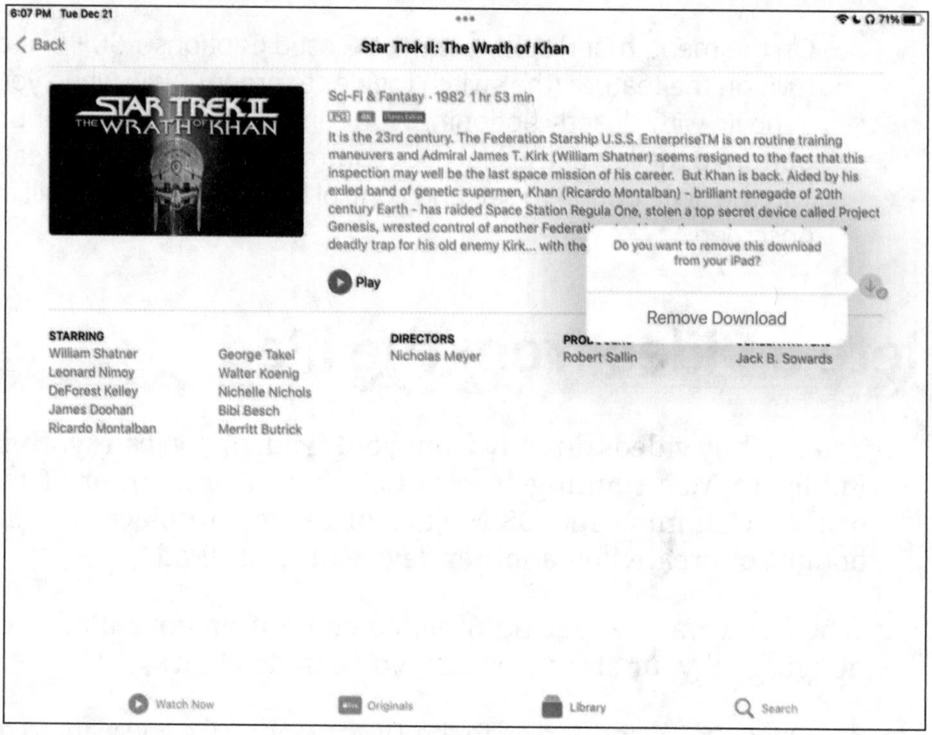

< Back   **Star Trek II: The Wrath of Khan**

**STAR TREK II
THE WRATH OF KHAN**

Sci-Fi & Fantasy · 1982 1 hr 53 min

[PG] [4K] [Tunnel Extra]

It is the 23rd century. The Federation Starship U.S.S. EnterpriseTM is on routine training maneuvers and Admiral James T. Kirk (William Shatner) seems resigned to the fact that this inspection may well be the last space mission of his career. But Khan is back. Aided by his exiled band of genetic supermen, Khan (Ricardo Montalban) - brilliant renegade of 20th century Earth - has raided Space Station Regula One, stolen a top secret device called Project Genesis, wrested control of another Federati...
deadly trap for his old enemy Kirk... with the

> Do you want to remove this download
> from your iPad?
>
> **Remove Download**

▶ Play

STARRING		DIRECTORS	PRODUCERS	
William Shatner	George Takei	Nicholas Meyer	Robert Sallin	Jack B. Sowards
Leonard Nimoy	Walter Koenig			
DeForest Kelley	Nichelle Nichols			
James Doohan	Bibi Besch			
Ricardo Montalban	Merritt Butrick			

▶ Watch Now   Originals   Library   Q Search

FIGURE 15-9

4

Living with Your iPad

Chapter **16**

Keeping on Schedule with Calendar and Clock

Whether you're retired or still working, you have a busy life full of activities (perhaps even busier if you're retired, for some unfathomable reason). You need a way to keep on top of all those activities and appointments. The Calendar app on your iPad is a simple, elegant, electronic daybook that helps you do just that.

In addition to being able to enter events and view them in a list or by the day, week, or month, you can set up Calendar to send alerts to remind you of your obligations and search for events by keywords. You can even set up repeating events, such as birthdays, monthly get-togethers with friends, or weekly babysitting appointments with the kids in your life. To help you coordinate calendars on multiple devices, you can also sync events with other calendar accounts. And by taking advantage of the Family Sharing feature, you can create a Family calendar that everybody in your family can view and add events to.

Another preinstalled app that can help you stay on schedule is Clock. Though simple to use, Clock helps you view the time in multiple locations, set alarms, check yourself with a stopwatch feature, and use a timer.

In this chapter, you master the simple procedures for getting around your calendar, creating a Family calendar, entering and editing events, setting up alerts, syncing, and searching. You also discover the simple ins and outs of using Clock.

View Your Calendar

Calendar offers several ways to view your schedule:

1. Start by tapping the Calendar app icon on the Home screen to open it. Depending on what you last had open and the orientation in which you're holding your iPad, you may see today's calendar, List view, the year, the month, the week, an open event, or the Search screen with search results displayed.

2. Tap the Today button on the upper right of the screen to display Today's view (if it isn't already displayed) and then tap the List view button in the upper left to see all scheduled events for that day. The Today view with List view open, shown in **Figure 16-1,** displays your daily appointments for every day in a list, with times listed on the left. Tap an event in the list to get more event details, or tap the List view button (upper left) to exit List view.

TIP

If you'd like to display events only from a particular calendar, such as the Birthday or US Holidays calendars, tap the Calendars button in the upper left of the screen (see **Figure 16-1**) and select a calendar to view by tapping the circle(s) to the left of the listed calendar(s).

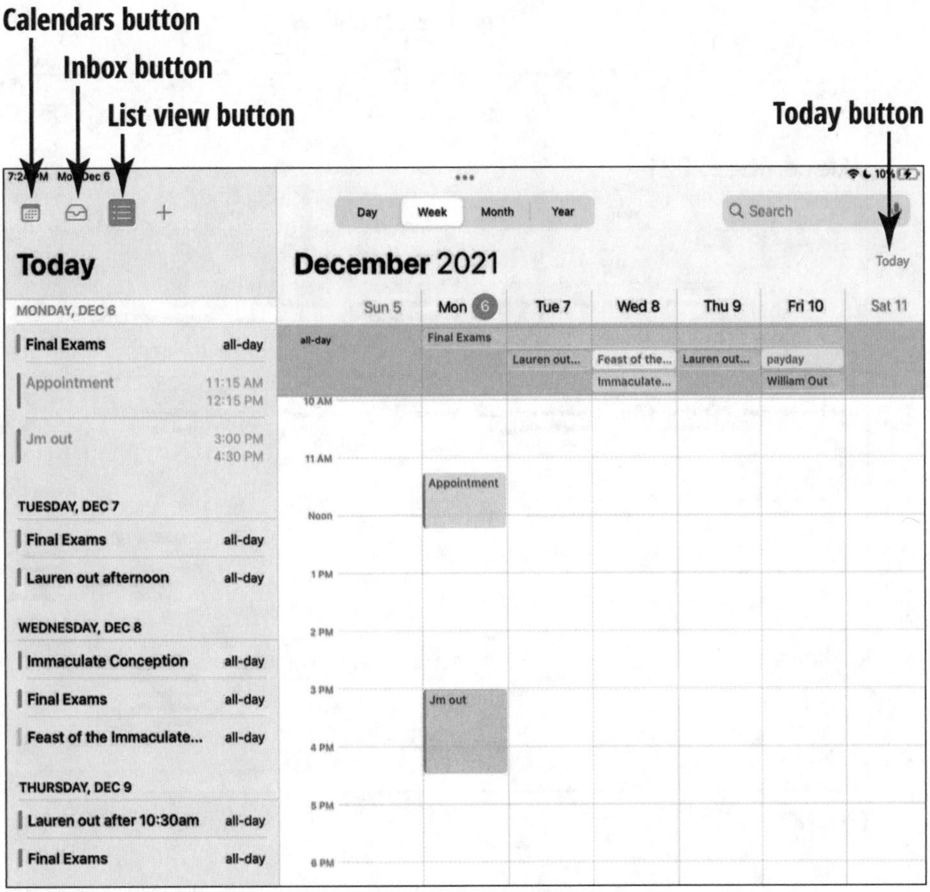

FIGURE 16-1

3. Tap the Week button to view all events for the current week. In this view, appointments appear against the times listed along the left side of the screen.

4. Tap the Month button to get an overview of your busy month (see **Figure 16-2**). In this view, you see the name and timing of each event.

5. Tap the Year button to see all months in the year so that you can quickly move to one, as shown in **Figure 16-3.**

6. To move from one month or year to the next (depending on which view you're in), you can also scroll up or down the screen with your finger.

7. To jump back to today, tap the Today button in the upper-right corner of the screen. The month containing the current day is displayed.

Tap to select a view

	Sun	Mon	Tue	Wed	Thu	Fri	Sat

December 2021   Today

Sun	Mon	Tue	Wed	Thu	Fri	Sat
5	6	7	8	9	10	11
	Final Exams					
	*Appointment 11:00AM	Lauren out afternoon	Feast of the Immaculat...	Lauren out after 10:30a...	payday	
	*Jim out 3 PM		Immaculate Conception		William Out	
12	13	14	15	16	17	18
Feast of Our Lady of Gu...	William Out	Dwight Spivey's birthday	* Timecard! 10:00AM	* Timecard!	William Out	
	*Check Ryan's invoi... 10:00AM	Happy birthday!			* Timecard! 10:00AM	
		Dwight Bday				
		**Faculty & Staff & Lun... 10:00AM				
19	20	21	22	23	24	25
					Christmas Holiday	Christmas Day
					payday	Christmas Day
					Christmas Eve	Christmas
					Day off for Christmas O...	Christmas Day
					Christmas Eve	
					2 more...	
26	27	28	29	30	31	
Christmas Holiday					Day off for New Year's...	
Kwanzaa		Childermas	* Timecard! 10:00AM	* Timecard! 10:00AM	New Year's Eve	
					New Year's Eve	
					* Timecard! 10:00AM	
					Jan 1	
					Victoria	

FIGURE 16-2

Calendar looks slightly different when you hold your iPad in portrait and landscape orientations. Turn your iPad in both directions to see which orientation you prefer to work in, and make sure to try this with each view option.

TIP

To view any invitation that you accepted, which placed an event on your calendar, tap the Inbox button in the upper-left corner (refer to **Figure 16-1**) and a list of invitations is displayed on the left of the screen in the Inbox sidebar. You can use text within emails (such as a date, flight number, or phone number) to add an event to Calendar. Tap the Inbox button again to close the Inbox sidebar.

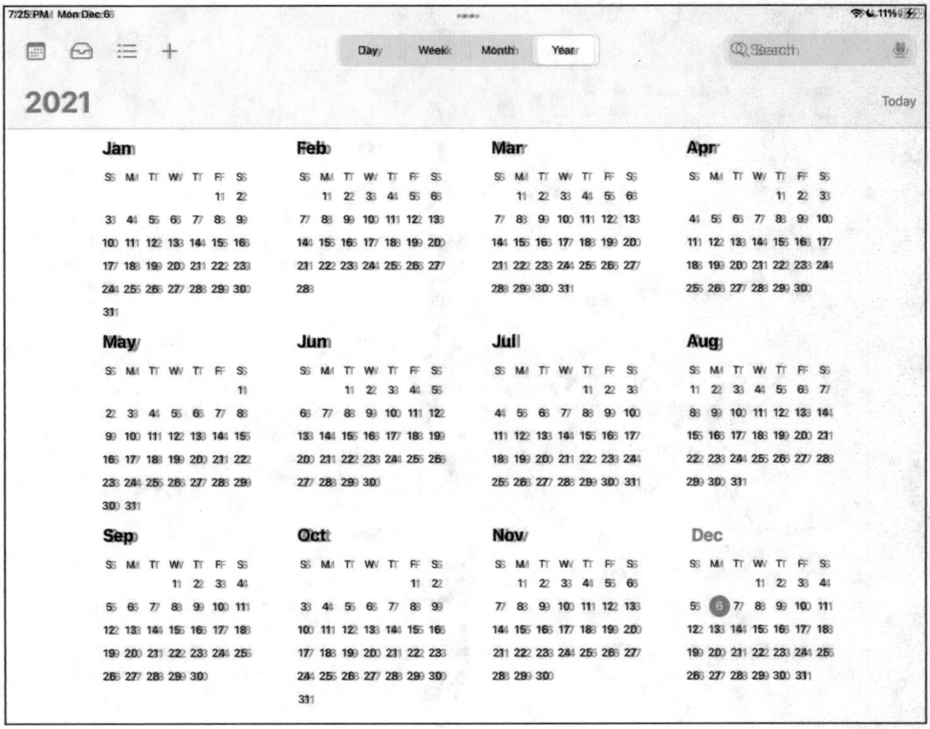

FIGURE 16-3

Add Calendar Events

Calendars are fun, but adding events to them makes them fun–ctional (see what I did there?). To add events to your calendar:

1. With any view displayed, tap the Add button (which looks like a plus symbol) in the upper-left corner of the screen to add an event. The New Event dialog appears.

2. Enter a title for the event and, if you want, a location.

3. Tap the All-day switch to turn it on for an all-day event, or tap the Starts and Ends fields to set start and end times for the event. As shown in **Figure 16-4,** the scrolling setting for day, hour, and minute appears.

4. Place your finger on the date, hour, minute, or AM/PM column and move your finger to scroll up or down.

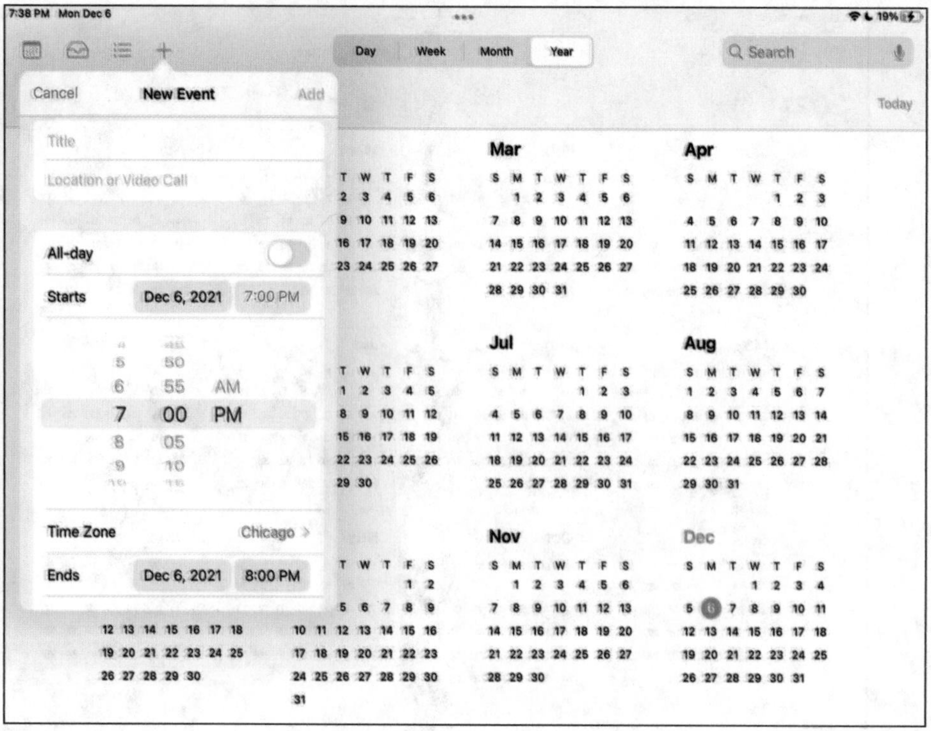

FIGURE 16-4

5. To select which calendar to use for the event, add a note, or change other settings, scroll down in the New Event dialog and do the following:

- To select a different calendar, tap the Calendar button, tap the calendar you'd like to use for this event, and then tap New Event in the upper left.

- To add a note, tap in the Notes field, type your note, and then tap the Add button to save the event.

- To change another setting, tap its button, tap any options you'd like to adjust, and then tap New Event in the upper-left corner.

6. When you're ready, tap the Add button to save the event.

TIP

You can edit any event at any time by simply tapping it in any view of your calendar. When the details are displayed, tap Edit in the upper-right corner. The Edit Event dialog appears, offering the same settings as the New Event dialog. Tap the Done button to save your changes, or tap Cancel to return to your calendar without saving any changes.

Add Events with Siri

Play around with this feature and Calendar; it's a lot of fun!

1. Press and hold the Home button (top button for iPad models without a Home button) or say "Hey Siri."

2. Speak a command, such as "Hey Siri. Create a meeting on October 3 at 2:30 p.m."

3. The event is automatically added to Calendar. You can edit or delete it just as you can other events that you've manually added.

TIP

You can schedule an event with Siri in several ways:

» Say "Create event." Siri asks you first for a date and then for a time.

» Say "I have a meeting with John on April 1." Siri may respond by saying "I don't find a meeting with John on April 1; shall I create it?" You can say "Yes" to have Siri create it.

Create Repeating Events

If you want an event to repeat, such as a weekly or monthly appointment, you can set a repeating event.

1. With any view displayed, tap the Add button (+) to add an event. The New Event dialog (refer to **Figure 16-4**) appears.

2. Enter a title and location for the event and set the start and end dates and times, as shown in the earlier section, "Add Calendar Events."

3. Scroll down the page, if necessary, and then tap the Repeat field; the Repeat dialog, shown in **Figure 16-5,** is displayed.

4. Tap a preset time interval — Every Day, Every Week, Every 2 Weeks, Every Month, or Every Year — and you return to the New Event dialog. Tap Custom and make the appropriate settings if you want to set any other interval, such as every two months on the 6th of the month.

5. Should you like to set an expiration date for the repeated event, tap End Repeat (this option appears only if you had set the event to repeat) and make the necessary settings.

6. Tap Done and you'll return to the Calendar.

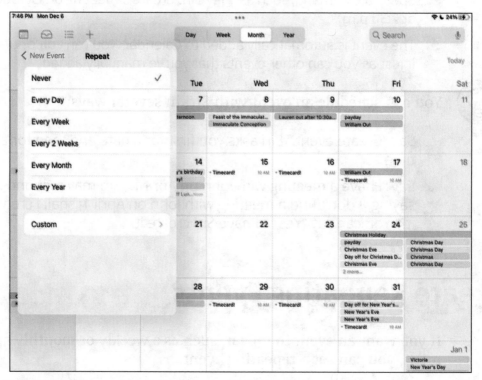

FIGURE 16-5

View an Event

Tap an event anywhere — on a Day view, Week view, Month view, or List view — to see its details. To make changes to the event you're viewing, tap the Edit button in the upper-right corner.

Add an Alert to an Event

If you want your iPad to alert you when an event is coming up, you can use the Alert feature.

1. Tap the Settings icon on the Home screen and choose Sounds.

2. Scroll down to Calendar Alerts and tap it; then tap any Alert Tone, which causes your iPad to play the tone for you. After you've chosen the alert tone you want, tap Sounds to return to Sounds settings. Press the Home button (or swipe up from the bottom of the screen for iPad models without a Home button) and then tap Calendar, and create an event in your calendar or open an existing one for editing, as covered in earlier tasks in this chapter.

3. In the New Event (refer to **Figure 16-4**) or Edit Event dialog, tap the Alert field. The Alert dialog appears, as shown in **Figure 16-6.**

4. Tap any preset interval and you'll return to the New Event or Edit Event dialog.

The Alert setting appears in the dialog, and a Second Alert option appears if you'd like to set one.

5. Tap Done in the Edit Event dialog or Add in the New Event dialog to save all settings.

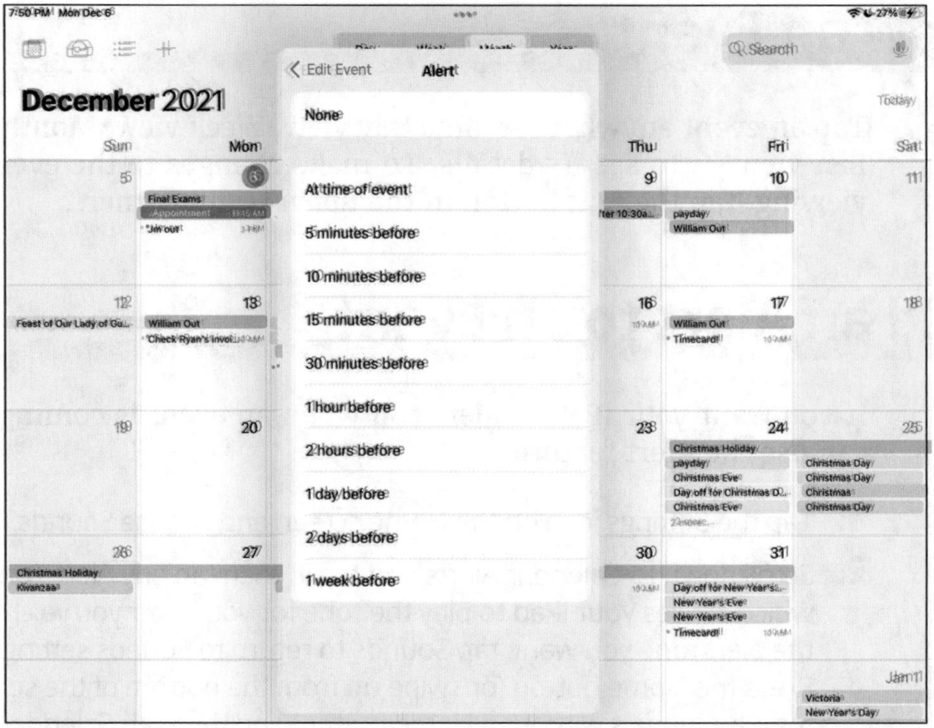

FIGURE 16-6

TIP

If you work for an organization that uses a Microsoft Exchange account, you can set up your iPad to receive and respond to invitations from colleagues. When somebody sends an invitation that you accept, it appears on your calendar. Check with your organization's network administrator (who will jump at the chance to get their hands on your iPad) or the iPad User Guide to set up this feature if it sounds useful to you.

TIP

iCloud offers individuals functionality similar to that of Microsoft Exchange.

Search for an Event

Having trouble remembering what day next week you scheduled that lunch date? You can do a search of your calendars:

1. With Calendar open in any view, tap the Search field in the top-right corner to display the onscreen keyboard.

2. Type a word or words to search by and then tap the blue Search key. While you type, the Results dialog appears under the Search field, as shown in **Figure 16-7**.

Results that display with a crosshatch pattern are events in the past.

3. Tap any result to display the event details.

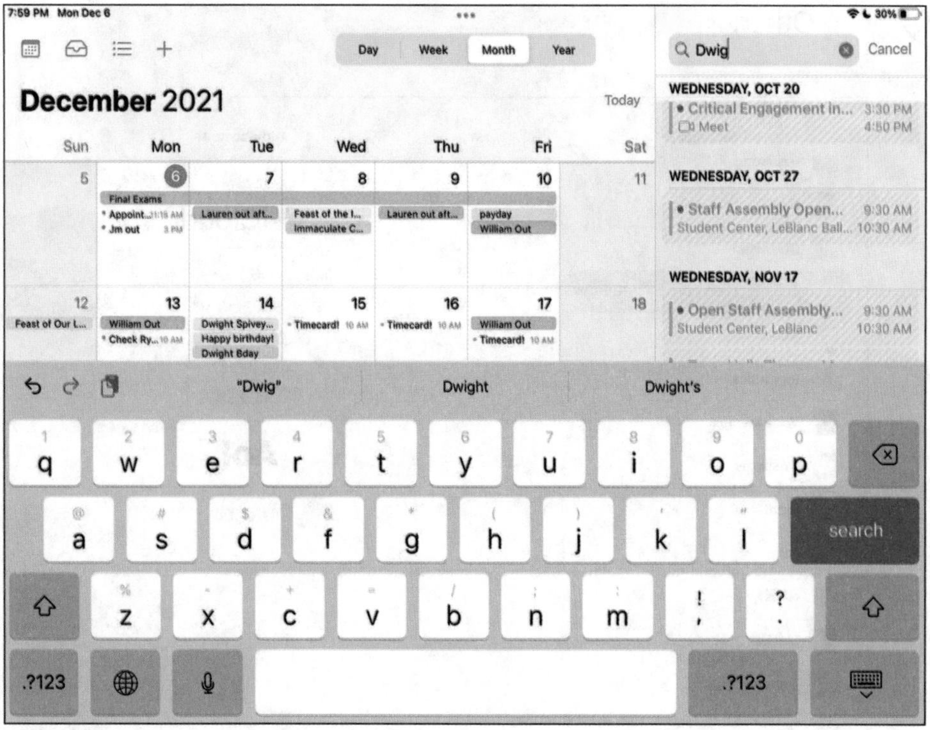

FIGURE 16-7

Create a Calendar Account

If you use a calendar available from an online service, such as Yahoo! or Google, you can subscribe to that calendar to read events saved there on your iPad.

1. Tap the Settings icon on the Home screen to get started.

2. Tap Calendar on the left, and then tap the Accounts option.

3. Tap Add Account and the Add Account options, shown in **Figure 16-8**, appear.

4. Tap a selection, such as Outlook.com, Google, or Yahoo!, depending on the calendar service you'd like to use.

Turn on Calendars for other accounts that aren't listed by tapping Other.

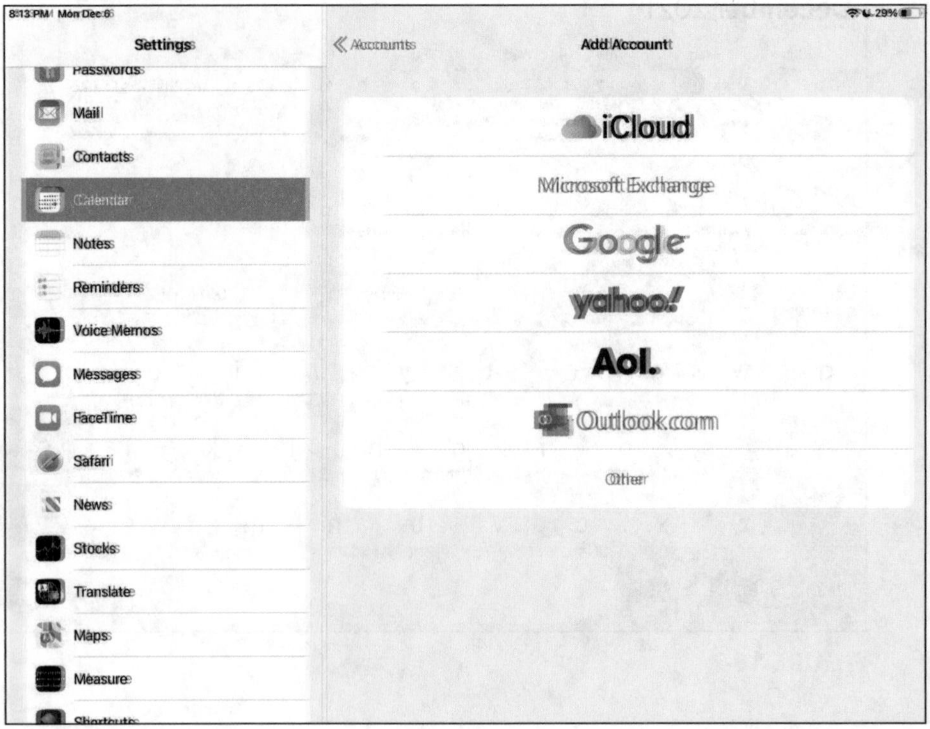

TIP

FIGURE 16-8

5. In the next screen that appears (see **Figure 16-9**), enter your account information for the service (the screen you see will vary, depending on the service you selected in Step 4). If you don't yet have an account for the service, there will be a way on the screen for you to create a new account.

6. Tap Next. The iPad verifies your account information.

7. On the following screen (see **Figure 16-10**), toggle the On/Off switch for the Calendars field to On (green); your iPad retrieves data from your calendar at the interval you have set to fetch data. Tap Save to save your account settings.

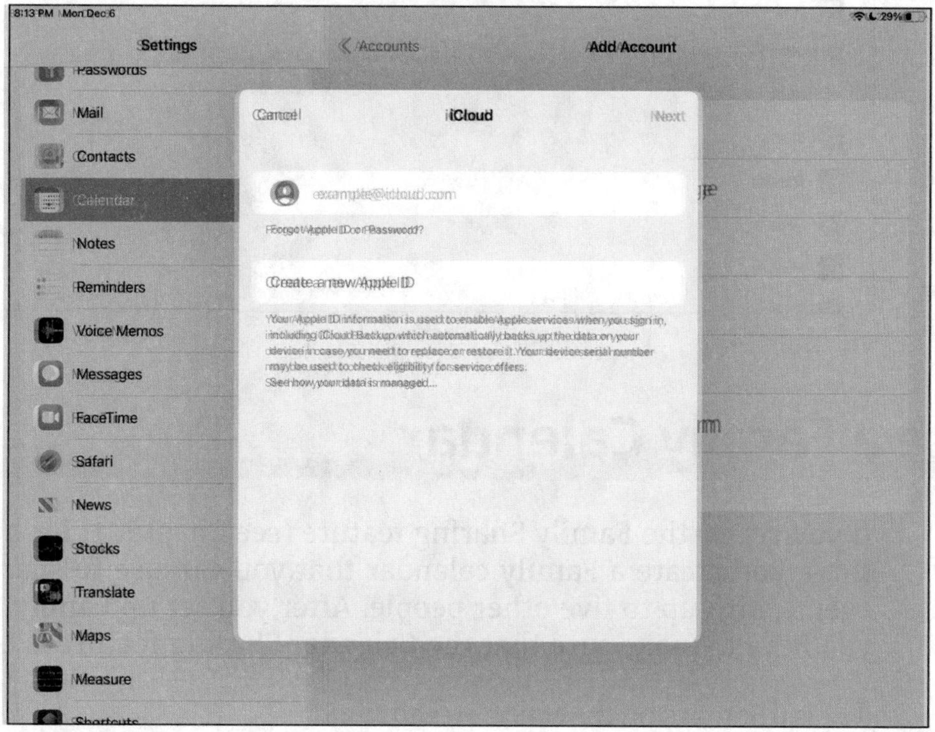

FIGURE 16-9

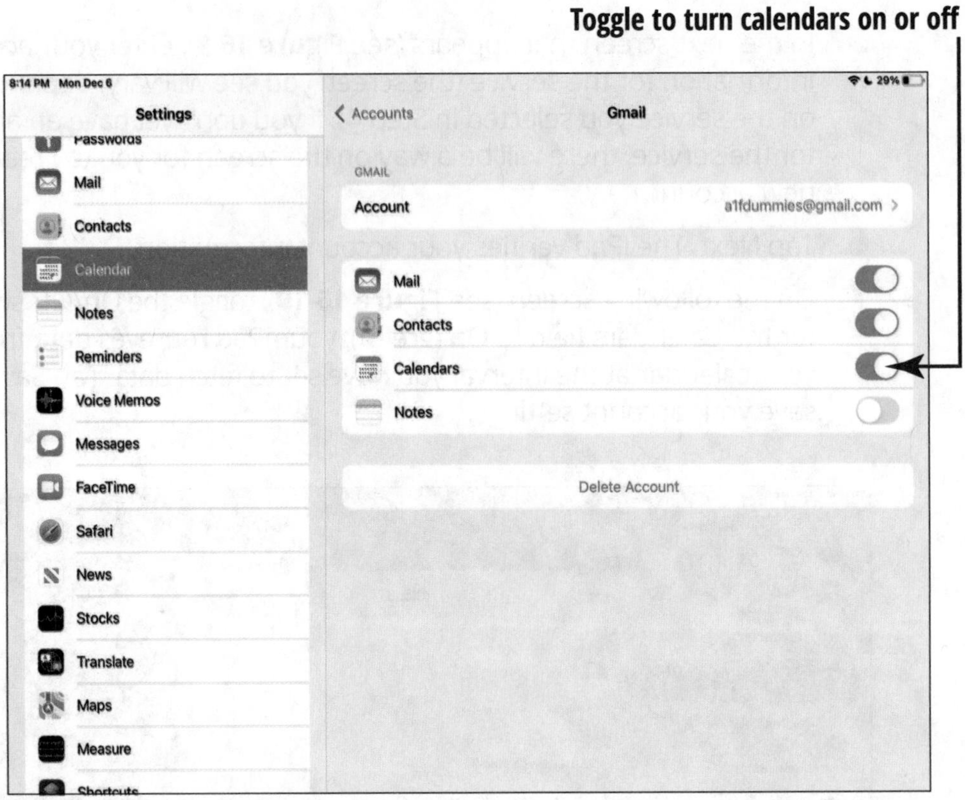

Toggle to turn calendars on or off

FIGURE 16-10

Use a Family Calendar

If you set up the Family Sharing feature (see Chapter 11 for how to do this), you create a Family calendar that you can use to share family events with up to five other people. After you set up Family Sharing, you have to make sure that the Calendar Sharing feature is on.

1. Tap Settings on the Home screen.

2. Tap the Apple ID (you may need to swipe up to see it on the left) and check that Family Sharing is set up (see **Figure 16-11**). You'll see Family Sharing rather than Set Up Family Sharing if it has been set up. If you see Set Up Family Sharing, go to Chapter 11 for instructions on setting up Family Sharing.

3. Tap iCloud. In the iCloud settings, tap the switch for Calendars to turn it on if it isn't already on.

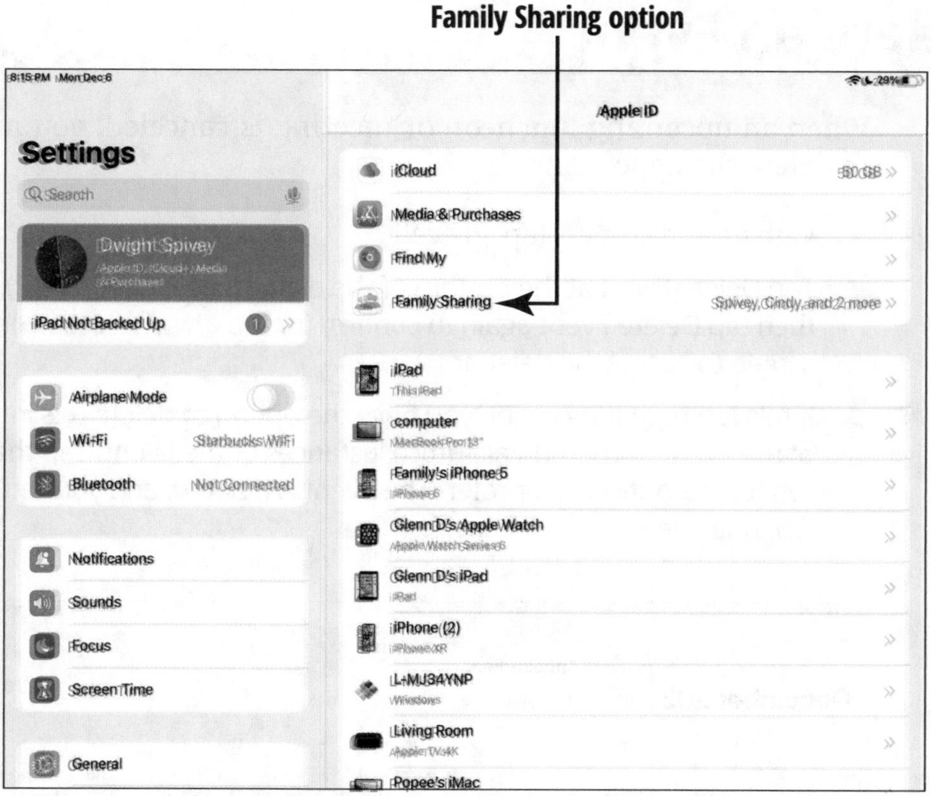

Family Sharing option

FIGURE 16-11

4. Tap the Home button or swipe up from the bottom of the screen (for iPad models without a Home button) and then tap Calendar to open the app. Tap the Calendars button in the upper left of the screen. Scroll down and make sure that Family is selected. Tap the Calendars button again to close the sidebar when finished.

5. Now when you create a new event in the New Event dialog, tap Calendar and choose Family or Show All Calendars. The details of events contain a notation that an event is from the Family calendar.

TIP If you store birthdays for people in the Contacts app, by default the Calendar app then displays these when the day comes around so that you won't forget to pass on your congratulations! You can turn off this feature by tapping Calendars in the Calendar app and deselecting Birthday Calendar.

Delete an Event

When an upcoming luncheon or meeting is canceled, you may want to delete the appointment.

1. With Calendar open, tap an event.

2. Tap Delete Event at the bottom of the dialog (see **Figure 16-12**), and then tap Delete Event again to confirm (or tap anywhere else on the screen to cancel the deletion).

3. If this is a repeating event, you have the option to delete this instance of the event or this and all future instances of the event. Tap the button for the option you prefer. The event is deleted, and you return to Calendar view.

Tap Delete Event

FIGURE 16-12

TIP

If an event is moved but not canceled, you don't have to delete the old one and create a new one. Simply edit the existing event to change the day and time in the Edit Event dialog (tap the event and then tap Edit).

Display the Clock App

Clock is a preinstalled app that resides on the Home screen along with other preinstalled apps, such as Apple Books and Camera.

1. Tap the Clock app to open it. If this is the first time you've opened Clock, you see the World Clock tab (see **Figure 16-13**).

2. You can add a clock for many (but not all) locations around the world. With Clock displayed, tap the Add button (looks like a plus symbol) in the upper-right corner.

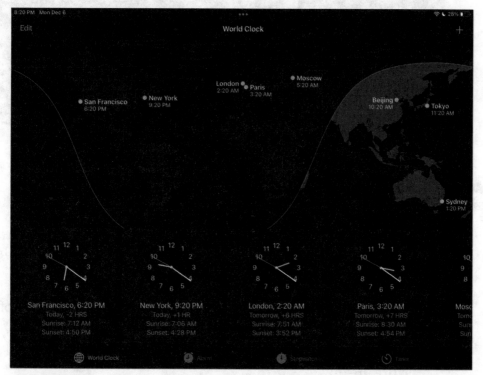

FIGURE 16-13

3. Tap a city on the list, or tap a letter on the right side to display locations that begin with that letter (see **Figure 16-14**) and then tap a city. You can also tap in the Search field and begin to type a city name to find and tap a city. The clock appears in the last slot at the bottom.

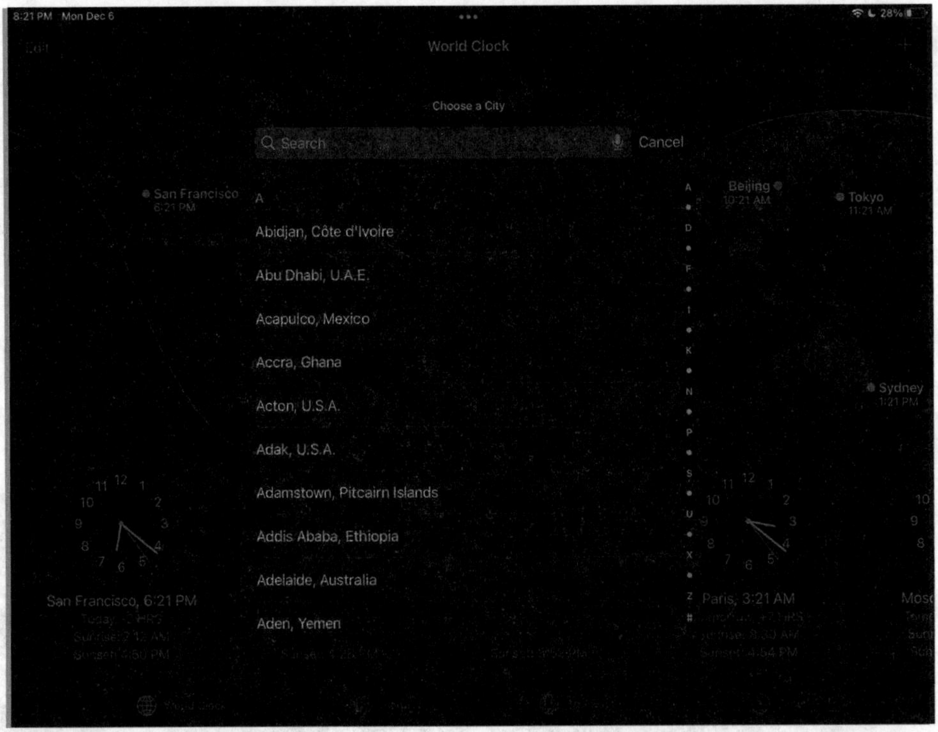

FIGURE 16-14

Delete a Clock

Maybe you no longer need to know what time it is in San Francisco, which is one of the default clocks on your iPad. You can delete that clock if you want:

1. To remove a location, tap the Edit button in the top-left corner of the World Clock screen.

2. Tap the minus symbol next to a location to delete it (see **Figure 16-15**).

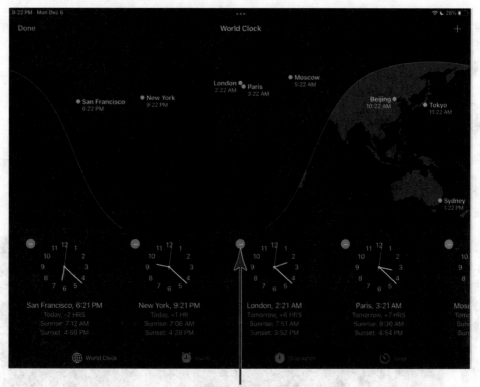

Delete button

FIGURE 16-15

Set an Alarm

It seems like nobody has a bedside alarm clock anymore; everyone uses their smart device instead. Here's how you set an alarm:

1. With the Clock app displayed, tap the Alarm tab at the bottom of the screen.

2. Tap the Add button (the + in the upper-right corner). In the Add Alarm dialog shown in **Figure 16-16,** take any of the following actions, tapping Back after you make each setting to return to the Add Alarm dialog:

   • Tap Repeat if you want the alarm to repeat at a regular interval, such as every Monday or every Sunday.

- Tap Label if you want to name the alarm, such as "Take Pill" or "Call Glenn."

- Tap Sound to choose the tune the alarm will play.

- Tap the On/Off switch for Snooze if you want to use the Snooze feature.

3. Place your finger on any of the three columns of sliding numbers at the top of the dialog and scroll to set the time you want the alarm to occur (don't forget to verify AM or PM!); then tap Save. The alarm appears in the Alarm tab.

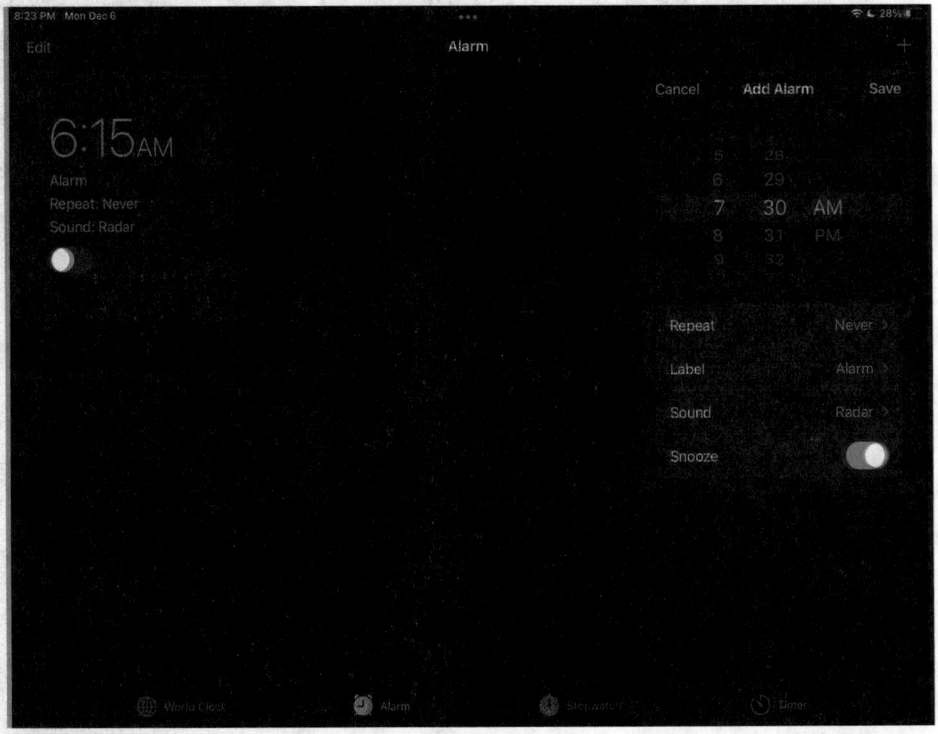

FIGURE 16-16

To delete an alarm, tap the Alarm tab and tap Edit. All alarms appear. Tap the red circle with a minus in it, and the alarm is deleted. Be careful: When you tap the Delete button, the alarm is unretrievable and will need to be re-created from scratch if you mistakenly removed it.

Use Stopwatch and Timer

Sometimes life seems like a countdown, or a ticking clock counting the minutes you've spent on a certain activity. You can use the Timer and Stopwatch tabs of the Clock app to do a countdown to a specific time, such as the moment when your chocolate chip cookies are done baking, or to time an activity, such as reading.

These two work very similarly: Tap the Stopwatch or Timer tab from the Clock's screen and then tap the Start button (see **Figure 16-17**). When you set the Timer, the iPad uses a sound to notify you when time's up. When you start the Stopwatch, you have to tap the Stop button when the activity is done.

Start button

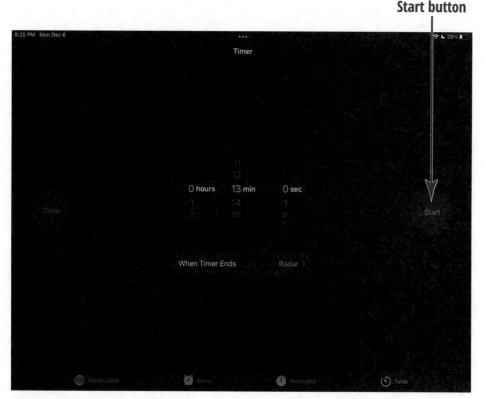

FIGURE 16-17

TIP

Stopwatch allows you to log intermediate timings, such as a lap in the pool or the periods of a timed game. With Stopwatch running, just tap the Lap button, and the first interval of time is recorded. Tap Lap again to record a second interval, and so on.

Chapter **17**

Working with Reminders and Notifications

The Reminders app and the Notification Center warm the hearts of those who need help remembering all the details of their lives.

Reminders is a kind of to-do list that lets you create tasks and set reminders so that you don't forget important commitments.

You can even be reminded to do things when you arrive at or leave a location, or receive a message from someone. For example, you can set a reminder so that when your iPad detects that you've left the location of your golf game, an alert reminds you to pick up your grandchildren, or when you arrive at your cabin, the iPad reminds you to turn on the water . . . you get the idea. iPadOS 15 introduces tags for reminders. Tags, such as #groceries or #kids, help you organize and find reminders quickly.

Notification Center allows you to review all the things you should be aware of in one place, such as mail messages, text messages, calendar appointments, and alerts.

If you occasionally need to escape all your obligations, or focus on only certain tasks, try the new Focus and Notification Summary features. Turn on these features, and you won't be bothered with alerts and notifications until you're ready to be.

In this chapter, you discover how to set up and view tasks in Reminders, as well as how Notification Center can centralize all your alerts in one easy-to-find place.

Create a Reminder

Creating an event in Reminders is pretty darn simple:

1. Tap Reminders on the Home screen.

2. Tap the New Reminder button with a plus sign to the left of it at the bottom of the screen to add a reminder (see **Figure 17-1**). A new reminder appears in the Reminders list, together with the onscreen keyboard.

3. Enter a task name or description using the onscreen keyboard, and then tap Done in the upper-right corner.

Tap here to add tasks and reminders

FIGURE 17-1

Edit Reminder Details

The following task shows you how to add specifics about an event for which you've created a reminder.

1. Tap a reminder and then tap the Details button (an *i* in a circle) that appears to the right of the reminder to open the Details dialog shown in **Figure 17-2.**

I deal with reminder settings in the following task.

2. Tap Notes and enter any notes about the event using the onscreen keyboard.

3. Toggle the Flag switch to enable or disable a flag for the reminder. Swipe up or down within the Details dialog if you don't see the Flag switch (or any other options discussed in this section) upon first glance.

Flags help denote the most important events.

4. Tap Priority and then tap None, Low (!), Medium (!!), or High (!!!) from the choices that appear. Tap Details in the upper left of the Priority dialog to return to the Details screen.

TIP

Priority settings display the associated number of exclamation points associated with an event in a list to remind you of its importance.

5. Tap List and then tap which list you want the reminder saved to, such as your calendar, iCloud, Exchange, or a category of reminders that you've created (see **Figure 17-3**). Tap Details in the upper left of the List dialog to return to the Details screen.

6. Tap Done in the upper right of the Details dialog to save the changes you made to the event.

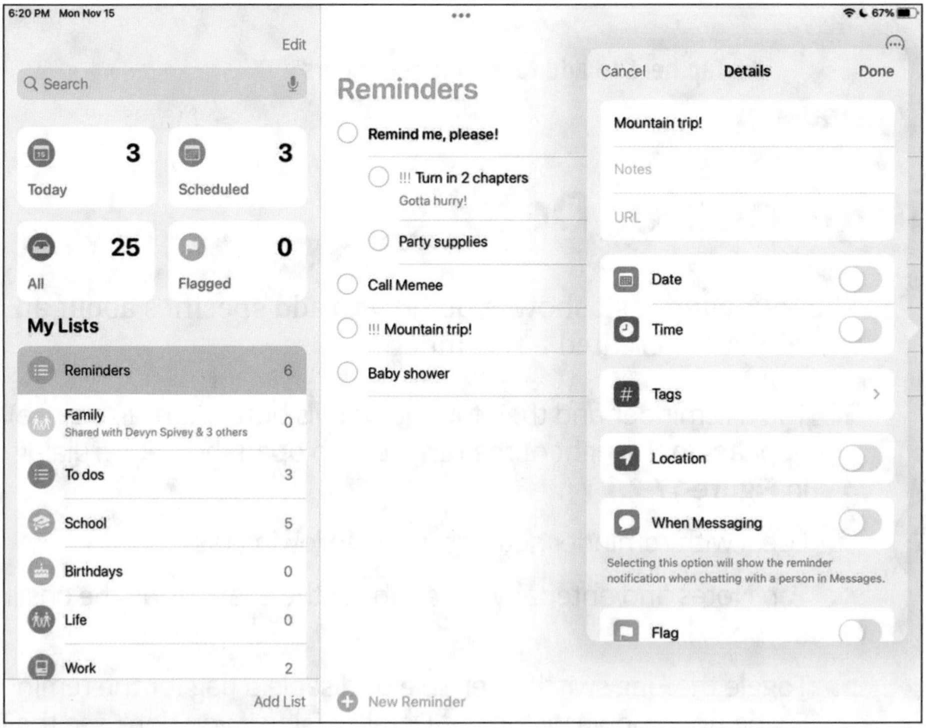

FIGURE 17-2

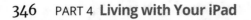

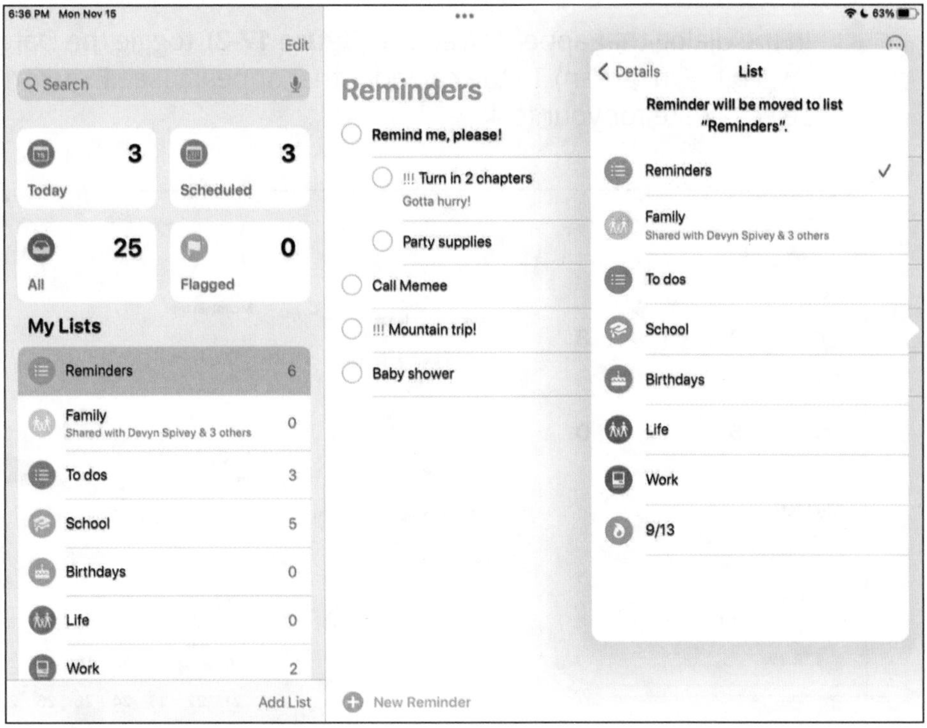

FIGURE 17-3

TIP

The Reminders app in iPadOS 15 includes a quick toolbar that appears just above the keyboard, which allows you to quickly add a time, location, tags, a flag, or images to the reminder you've tapped in a list. Just tap the icon for whichever item you want to activate, and make the appropriate settings as prompted.

Schedule a Reminder by Time, Location, or When Messaging

One of the major purposes of Reminders is to remind you of upcoming tasks. To set options for a reminder, follow these steps:

1. Tap a task and then tap the Details button (looks like a small *i* in a circle) that appears to the right of the task.

2. In the dialog that appears (refer to **Figure 17-2**), toggle the Date switch to On (green). In the calendar that appears (see **Figure 17-4**), select a date for your task.

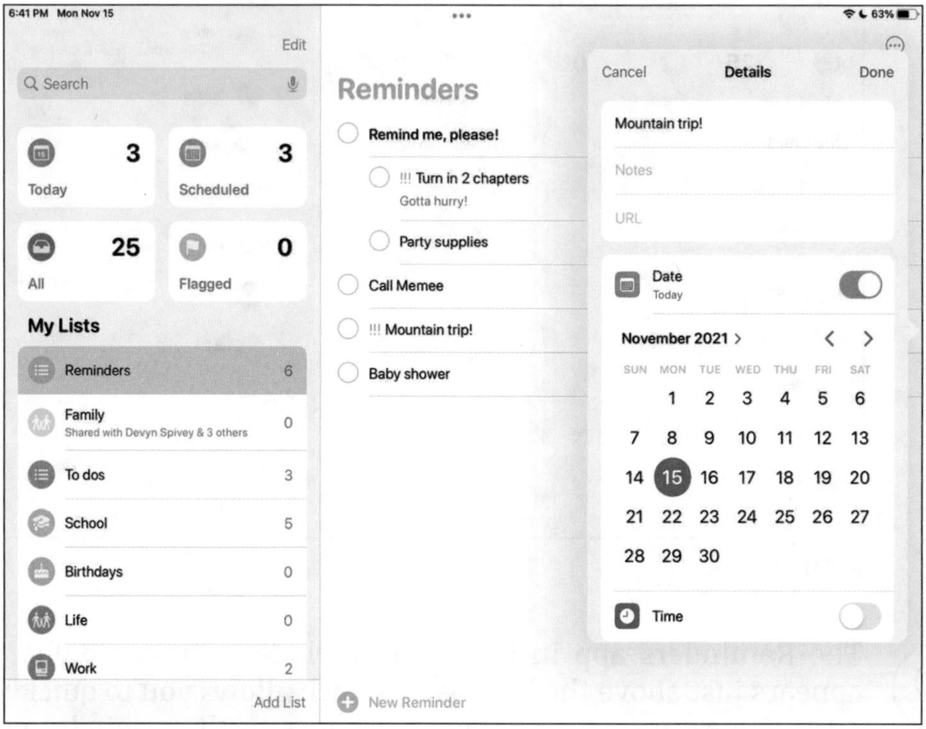

FIGURE 17-4

3. Toggle the Time switch to On (green) to display the hour and minute dials (see **Figure 17-5**). Use the dials to select a time for the reminder. Select AM or PM as appropriate.

4. If this is something you frequently need to be reminded of, tap Repeat and select an appropriate option. Tap Details in the upper left of the Repeat window to return to the previous screen.

5. Tap the Tags button and add as many tags as you like to your reminder. To add a tag, just type the word using the onscreen keyboard and tap Return. Tap Done in the upper right when finished.

There's no need to add a hashtag (#) in front of the word for your tag; Reminders automatically adds it.

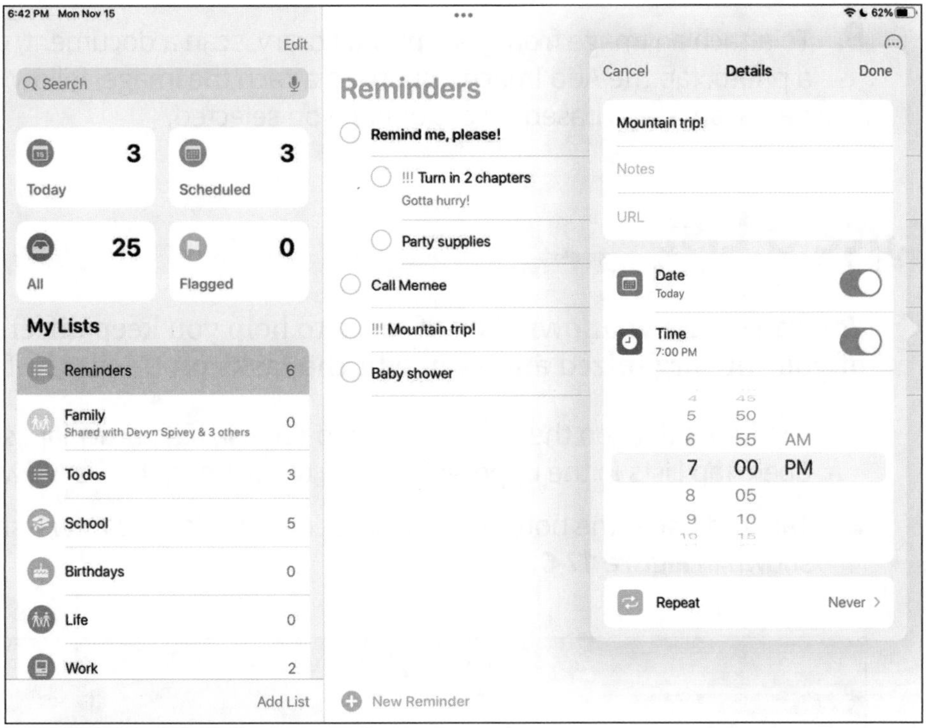

FIGURE 17-5

6. Toggle the Location switch to On and then tap one of the buttons to set a location for your task. Or use the Custom field to enter a location manually, and then tap Details in the upper left to return to the Details screen.

TIP You have to be in range of a GPS signal for the location reminder to work properly.

7. Scroll down if necessary and then toggle the When Messaging switch to On; then tap Choose Person. Select a person or group from your Contacts.

This option will remind you of the item when you're engaged in messaging with the person or group selected. This is a super helpful tool if you, like I, have trouble remembering to share information with people.

8. Add subtasks to this task by tapping the Subtasks option near the bottom of the screen.

9. To attach an image from your photo library, scan a document, or take a photo, tap the Add Image option. To attach the image, follow the necessary steps based on the option you selected.

Create a List

You can create your own lists of tasks to help you keep different parts of your life organized and even edit the tasks on the list in List view.

1. Tap Reminders on the Home screen to open it. If a particular list is open, tap Lists in the upper-left corner to return to the List view.

2. Tap Add List at the bottom of the screen to display the New List form shown in **Figure 17-6.**

FIGURE 17-6

3. Tap the List Name text field and then enter a name for the list.

4. Tap a color; the list name will appear in that color in List view.

5. Tap an icon to customize the icon for the list.

This feature helps you to better organize your lists by using icons for birthdays, medications, groceries, and a host of other occasions and subjects (see **Figure 17-7**).

6. Tap Done in the upper-right corner to save the list. Tap the New Reminder button to enter a task.

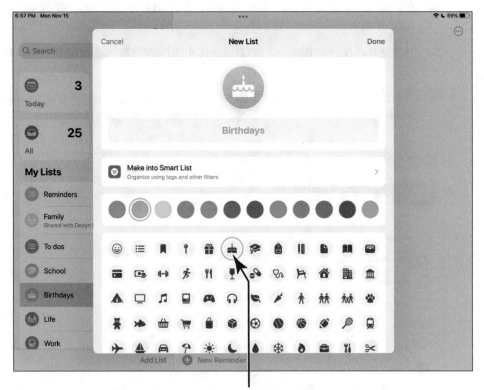

Tap to customize list icons

FIGURE 17-7

Sync with Other Devices and Calendars

To make all these settings work, you need to set up your default calendar and enable reminders in your iCloud account.

TIP

Your default Calendar account is also your default Reminders account.

1. To determine which tasks are brought over from other calendars (such as Outlook), tap Settings on the Home screen.

2. Tap your Apple ID and then tap iCloud. In the dialog that appears, be sure that Reminders is set to On (green).

3. In the main Settings list on the left, find and tap Calendar; then tap Accounts.

4. Tap the account you want to sync Reminders with and then toggle the Reminders switch to On, if available (as shown in **Figure 17-8**).

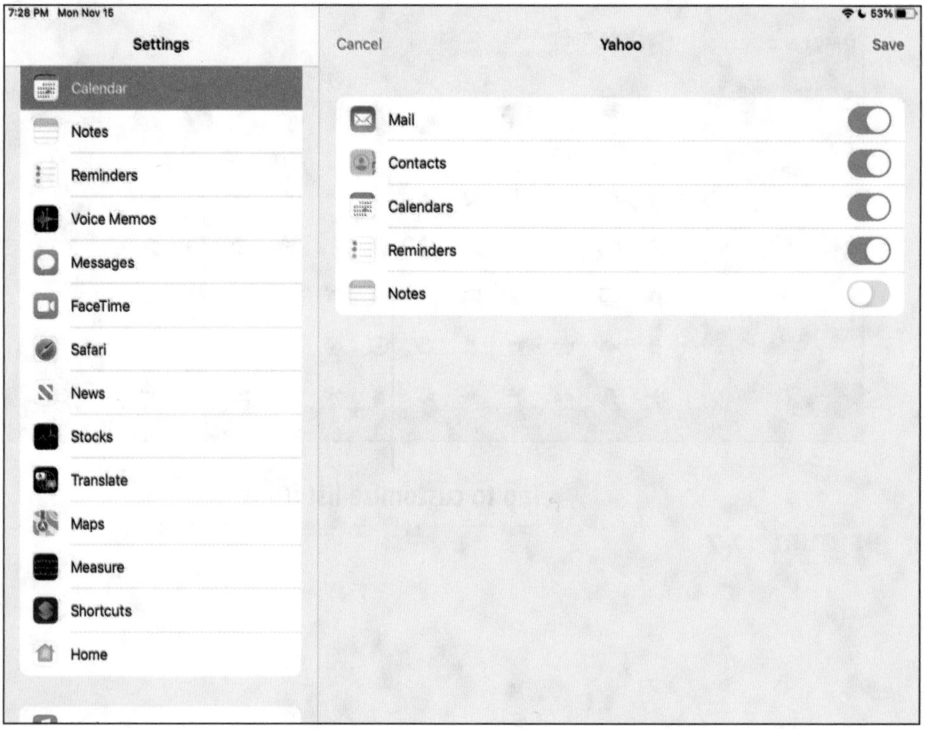

FIGURE 17-8

Mark as Complete or Delete a Reminder

You may want to mark a task as completed or just delete it entirely.

1. With Reminders open and a list of tasks displayed, tap the circle to the left of a task to mark it as complete.

The completed task disappears from the list in a second or two.

2. To view completed tasks, tap the More button in the upper right (looks like a blue circle containing three tiny dots) and tap Show Completed in the options (shown in **Figure 17-9**). To hide completed tasks, just tap the More button and then tap Hide Completed.

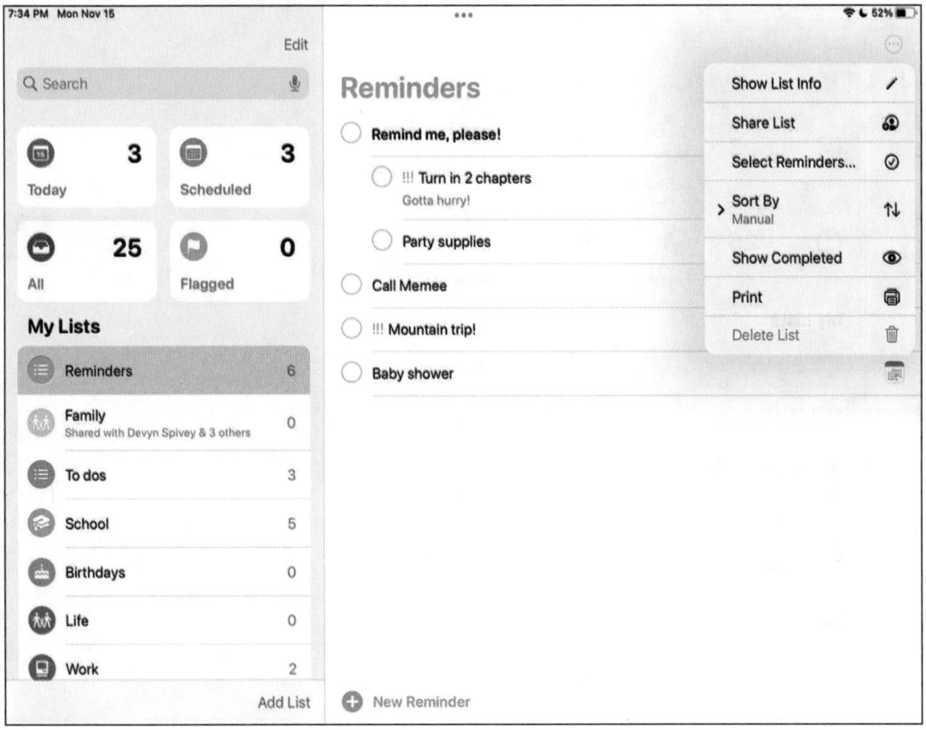

FIGURE 17-9

3. To delete a single task, with the list of tasks displayed, swipe the task you want to delete to the left. Tap the red Delete button to the right of the task (see **Figure 17-10**) and it will disappear from your list.

TIP

Be aware that if you delete a task, it's gone for good. There is no area in Reminders to retrieve deleted tasks. If you simply want to remove the item from the list without deleting it entirely, be sure to mark it as completed, as instructed in Step 1.

4. To delete more than one task, with the list of tasks displayed, tap the More button and tap Select Reminders in the options. In the screen shown in **Figure 17-11,** tap the circle to the left of the tasks you want to select, and then tap the Delete button in the lower-right corner.

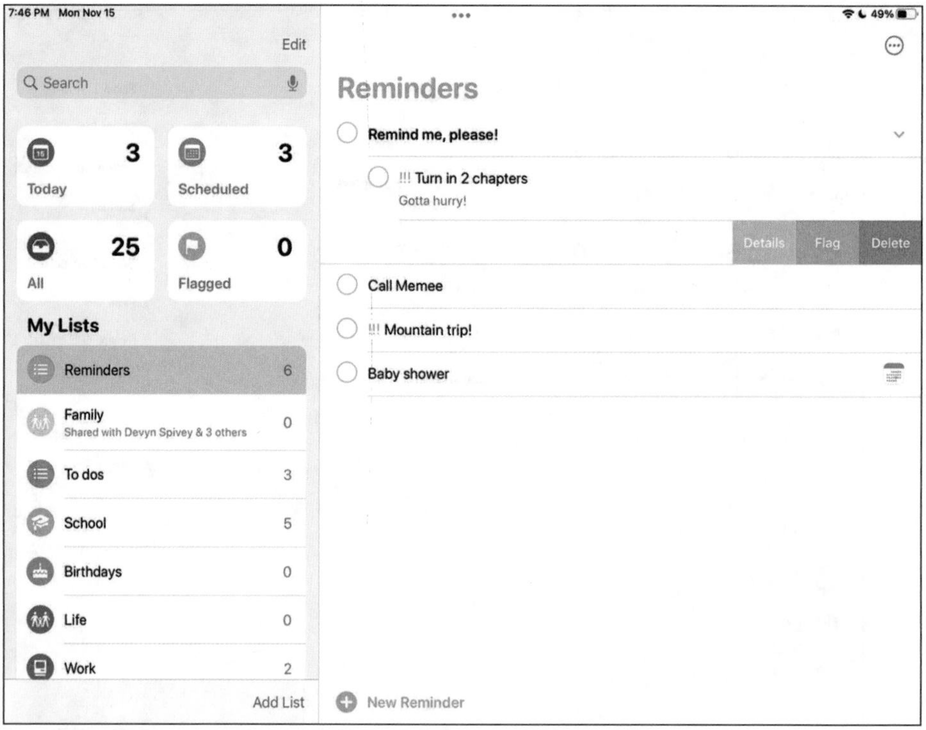

FIGURE 17-10

Tap to select   Tap to delete

FIGURE 17-11

Get Notified!

Notification Center is a list of various alerts and scheduled events; it even provides information (such as stock quotes) that you can display by swiping down from the top of your iPad screen. Notification Center is on by default, but you don't have to include every type of notification there if you don't want to. For example, you may never want to be notified of incoming messages but always want to have reminders listed here — it's up to you.

Notifications are enabled for every app when they're installed, so after you start using your iPad, you could spend half your day reading or dismissing notifications that you could have waited to see later.

To your rescue comes the much-anticipated Notification Summary feature, new in iPadOS 15, which allows you to set up notifications so that you receive them for only some apps as a summary at scheduled times during your day.

Jump right in to see how notifications work.

Notification summaries

Because notification summaries are the latest cool thing, this section takes a look at enabling them and determining which apps are included in the summary.

To enable the Notification Summary feature (if it's not enabled already):

1. Open Settings, tap Notifications, and then tap Scheduled Summary.

2. Toggle the Scheduled Summary switch to On (green), as shown in **Figure 17-12.**

3. Adjust your schedules, if you like.

   By default, you get two summaries a day: one at 8 AM and another at 6 PM. From the Schedule section of the Scheduled Summary window, you can

   - Tap the plus sign (+) in a green circle (Add Summary) to add another schedule.

   - Tap the minus sign (–) in a red circle (delete), and then tap the red Delete button to delete a schedule.

   - Tap a time to the right of a schedule to adjust when the schedule occurs.

4. To add apps to Notification Summary:

   a. Scroll down to the Apps in Summary section of the Scheduled Summary screen.

   b. Tap the Daily Notifications Avg. tab (see **Figure 17-12**) or the A to Z tab to see a list of apps by an average of how many notifications you receive from them or by alphabetical order, respectively.

c. Toggle the switch to On (green) for each app that you want to appear in the Notification Summary.

Note the line with the red dot below each app in the Daily Notifications Avg. tab. You can't do anything with that line or dot; it's only an indicator of the daily average of notifications that the app generates.

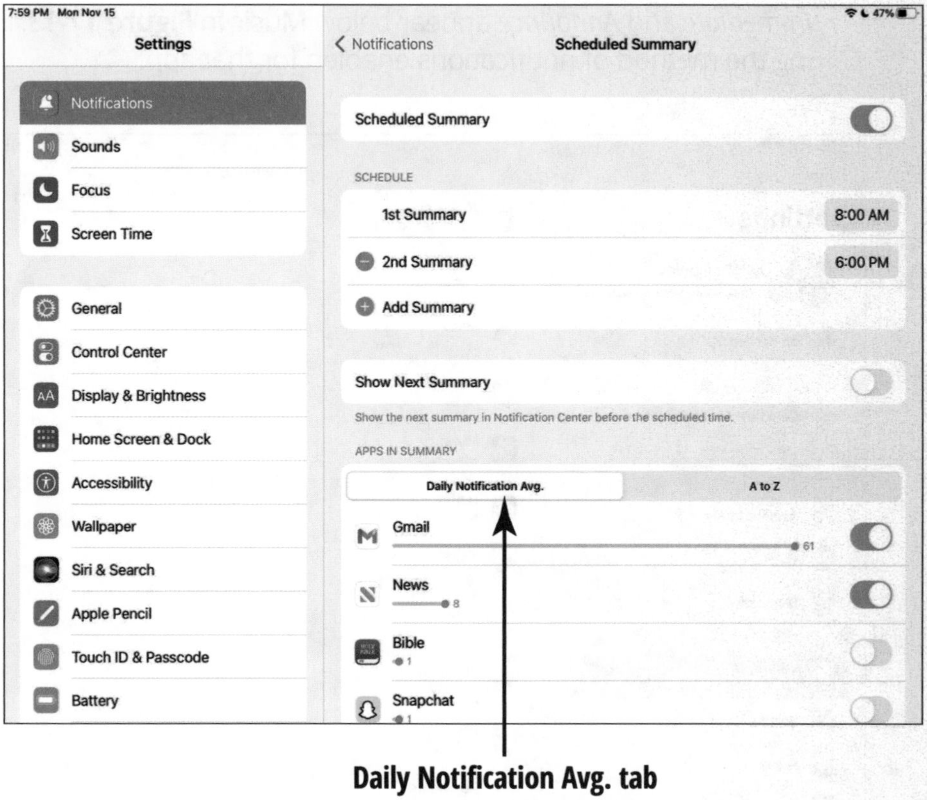

7:59 PM Mon Nov 15	🥐 📶 47% ◼

Settings   ❮ Notifications   **Scheduled Summary**

🔔 Notifications

🔊 Sounds

🌙 Focus

⏳ Screen Time

⚙️ General

🎛 Control Center

AA Display & Brightness

▦ Home Screen & Dock

♿ Accessibility

🖼 Wallpaper

🔍 Siri & Search

✏️ Apple Pencil

⬜ Touch ID & Passcode

🔋 Battery

Scheduled Summary ⬤

SCHEDULE

  1st Summary   8:00 AM

⊖ 2nd Summary   6:00 PM

⊕ Add Summary

Show Next Summary ◯

Show the next summary in Notification Center before the scheduled time.

APPS IN SUMMARY

Daily Notification Avg.	A to Z

M **Gmail** ————————●61 ⬤

N **News** ——●8 ⬤

📖 **Bible** ●1 ◯

👻 **Snapchat** ●1 ◯

Daily Notification Avg. tab

FIGURE 17-12

You can feel comfortable adding all your apps to Notifications Summary, if you like. Time-sensitive messages, such as phone calls and texts, will break through anyway.

TIP

Set notification types

Some Notification Center settings let you control what types of notifications are included:

1. Tap Settings and then tap Notifications.

The Notification Style section lists the apps included in Notification Center. The app's state is listed directly under its name. For example, *Immediate* and *Announce* appear below Music in **Figure 17-13**, indicating the method of notifications enabled for that app.

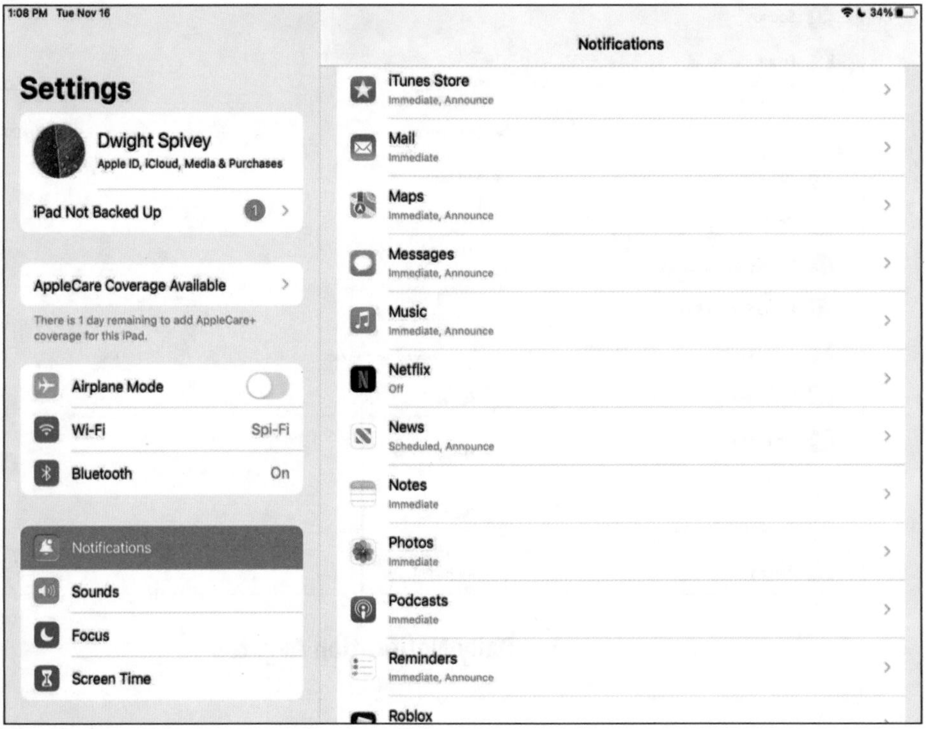

FIGURE 17-13

2. Tap any app to open its settings.

3. Set an app's Allow Notifications switch (see **Figure 17-14**) to On (green) or Off to include or exclude it, respectively, from Notification Center.

Settings	‹ Notifications Music

🔔 Notifications

🔊 Sounds

🌙 Focus

⏳ Screen Time

⚙️ General

🔲 Control Center

🅰️ Display & Brightness

🔳 Home Screen & Dock

♿ Accessibility

✳️ Wallpaper

🔵 Siri & Search

✏️ Apple Pencil

📱 Touch ID & Passcode

🔋 Battery

Allow Notifications ⬤

NOTIFICATION DELIVERY

🔔 **Immediate Delivery** ✓
Deliver right away

📋 **Scheduled Summary**
Deliver at 8 AM and 6 PM

Notifications are delivered immediately.

ALWAYS DELIVER IMMEDIATELY

💧 **Time Sensitive Notifications** ⬤

Time Sensitive notifications are always delivered immediately and remain on the Lock Screen for an hour.

ALERTS

Lock Screen	Notification Center	Banners
✓	✓	✓

Banner Style   Temporary ›

Sounds   ⬤

FIGURE 17-14

4. In the Notification Delivery section, tap Immediate Delivery (to receive notifications for this app immediately) or Scheduled Summary (to add the app to the Notification Summary; see the preceding task in this chapter for more info).

5. In the Alerts section, you can choose to display alerts on the Lock Screen, Notification Center, as Banners, or a combination of two or more.

If you don't want any alerts, simply don't make a selection.

TIP

If you enable Banners, choose a style by tapping the Banner Style option. Banners will appear and then disappear automatically if you tap the Temporary style. If you choose Persistent, you have to take an action to dismiss the alert when it appears (such as swiping it up to dismiss it or tapping to view it). Tap the Back button in the upper left to return to the previous screen.

6. Toggle the Sounds and Badges switches to On or Off to suit your taste.

7. Tap Show Previews to determine when or if previews of notifications should be shown on your iPad's screen.

Options are Always (which is default), When Unlocked (previews appear only when your iPad is unlocked), or Never. Tap the name of the app at the top of the screen to go to the previous screen.

8. Select a Notification Grouping option. This feature allows you to group notifications if you like, which can keep things much cleaner, as opposed to seeing every single notification listed. Options are

- **Automatic**: Notifications are grouped according to their originating app, but they may also be sorted based on various criteria. For example, you may see more than one group for Mail if you receive multiple emails from an individual; those email notifications may merit their own grouping.

- **By App**: Notifications are grouped according to their originating app — period. You'll see only one grouping for the app, not multiple groups based on the varying criteria, as described for the Automatic setting.

- **Off**: All notifications for this app are listed individually.

Tap the name of the app at the top of the screen to return to the previous screen.

9. Tap Notifications at the top of the screen to return to the main Notifications settings screen. When you've finished making settings, press the Home button or swipe up from the bottom of the screen (for iPads without a Home button).

View Notification Center

After you've made settings for what should appear in Notification Center, you'll want to take a look at those alerts and reminders regularly.

1. From any screen, press and hold your finger at the top of the screen and drag down to display Notification Center (see **Figure 17-15**).

Swipe from left-to-right on the date at the top of the Notification Center to view other notifications such as weather, reminders, Siri app suggestions, and more.

TIP

2. To close Notification Center, swipe upward from the bottom of the screen.

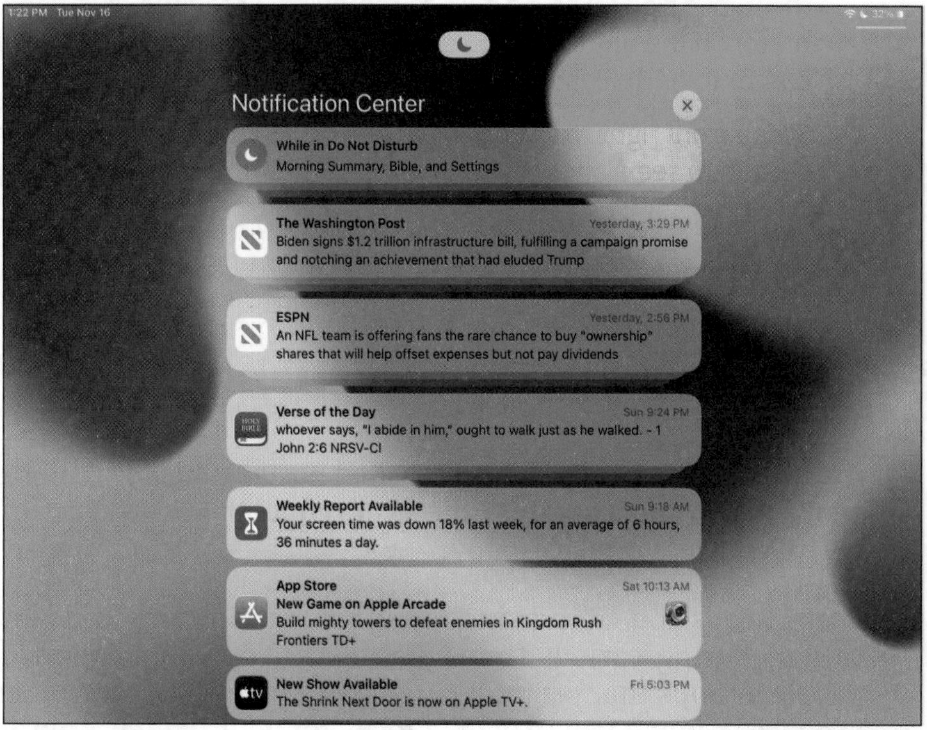

FIGURE 17-15

To determine what is displayed in Notification Center, see the previous task.

There are two sections in Notification Center for you to play with: Notification Center and Today.

1. Swipe down from the top of the screen to open Notification Center.

Notifications are displayed by default.

2. Swipe from left to right on the date/time at the top of Notification Center to access the Today tab to view information in widgets that pertain to today, such as Reminders, weather, stock prices, Calendar items, and other items you've selected to display in Notification Center (see the preceding task).

TIP

You select which widgets appear on the Today screen. From the first Home screen, swipe from left to right to access the Today screen, tap the Edit button, and then select the items you want to see. Tap the minus sign (–) on an item to remove it, or tap the plus sign (+) button in the upper left to add widgets. Tap Done in the upper-right corner to finish customizing your Today screen.

3. Swipe from right to left on the screen to go back to the Notifications section to see all notifications that you set up in the Settings app.

   You'll see only notifications that you haven't responded to, deleted in the Notifications section, or viewed in their originating app.

Stay Focused and Undisturbed

iPadOS 15 brings a new feature, called Focus, which is really an extension of (and incorporates) the ever-popular Do Not Disturb feature that iPad users already enjoy.

Focus keeps you from being disturbed by incoming calls and notifications during various times and tasks. You can customize a list of people or apps that can still contact or notify you, even when a focus is enabled. When you turn on a focus for your iPad, it's automatically turned on for every other Apple device that you're signed into using the same Apple ID.

Do Not Disturb is a simple but useful setting that you can use to stop alerts, phone calls, text messages, and FaceTime calls from appearing or making a sound. You can make settings to allow calls from certain people or several repeat calls from the same person in a short time to come through. (The assumption here is that such repeat calls may signal an emergency or an urgent need to get through to you.)

Set up a focus

To set up a focus:

1. Go to Settings and tap Focus.

2. Tap either Do Not Disturb or the particular focus you'd like to edit.

3. In the Allowed Notifications section (see **Figure 17-16**), tap People or Apps to customize who or what app can contact or notify you, even when Do Not Disturb or the particular focus is on.

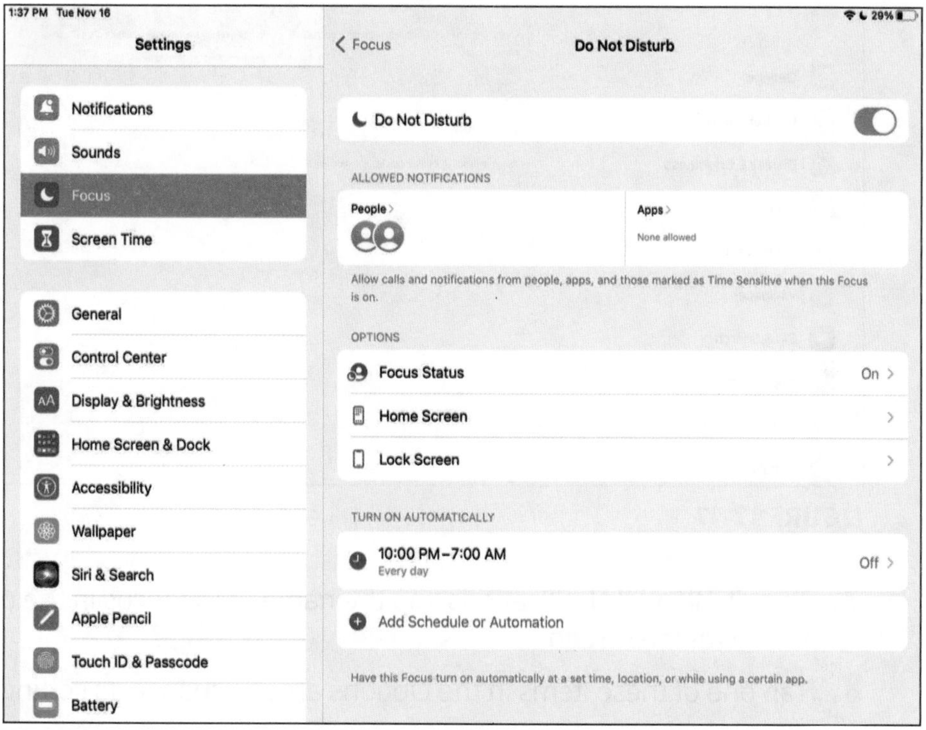

FIGURE 17-16

4. On the next screen, tap the Add Person or Add App button.

5. Tap the names of people or apps for which you want to allow exceptions, and then tap Done in the upper-right corner.

   The Allowed People or Allowed Apps area displays the people or apps for which you've allowed exceptions, as shown in **Figure 17-17**.

6. Tap the minus sign (–) in the upper-left corner of an icon to remove an individual person or app from the list, or tap Remove All to wipe the slate clean.

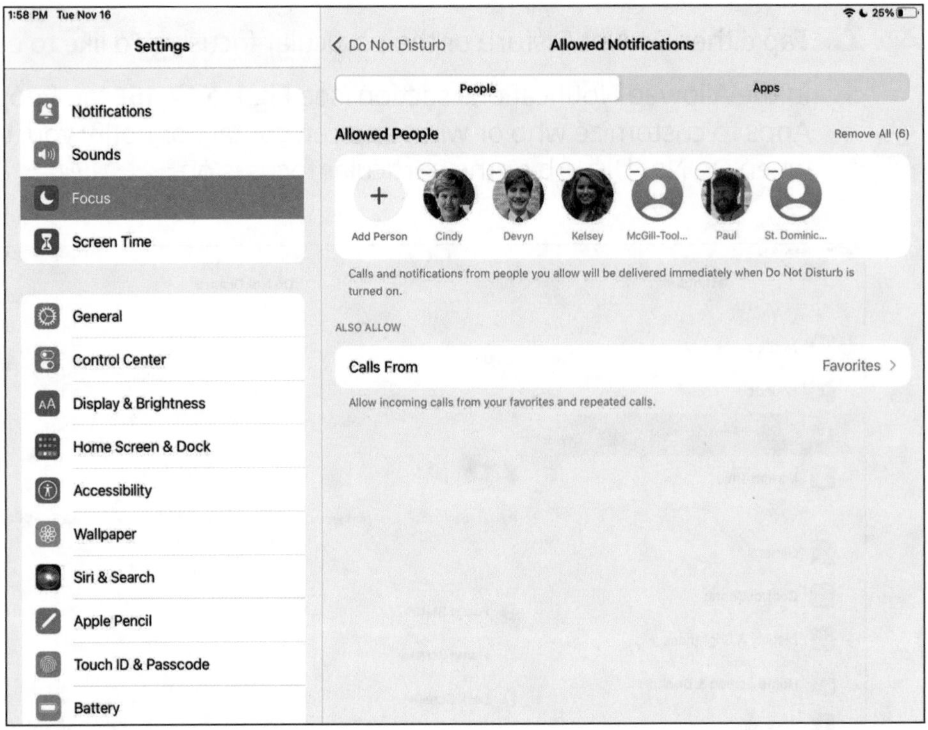

FIGURE 17-17

7. To exit Allowed Notifications, tap the name of the focus in the upper middle of the screen.

8. Tap one of these items in the Options area to change its settings:

- **Focus Status:** Decide whether to allow others to see the status of your devices. For example, if you've enabled a focus that silences notifications, the other people will see this on their Apple devices.

- **Home Screen:** Hide notification badges on Home screens, or allow only certain Home screens to be visible when this focus is on.

- **Lock Screen:** Dim the lock screen or allow notifications to be viewed on it.

9. If you prefer to turn on the focus at a specific time, use the options in the Turn On Automatically section to set a schedule.

Turn on a focus

To turn on a focus:

1. Open Control Center by swiping down from the upper-right corner of your screen.

2. Tap Focus.

3. Tap a focus in the list to turn it on.

   When a focus is on, its button is white, as shown in **Figure 17-18.**

4. Tap the more icon (three dots) to the right of a focus name to access more options, as shown in **Figure 17-19.**

   These options may vary, depending on the focus.

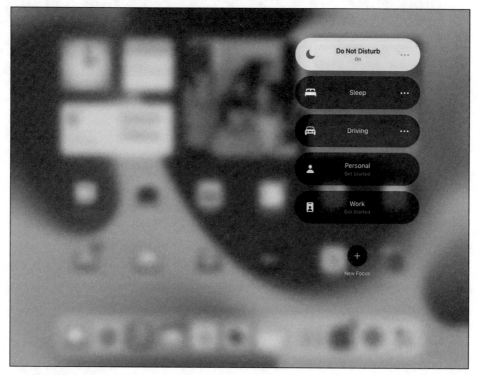

FIGURE 17-18

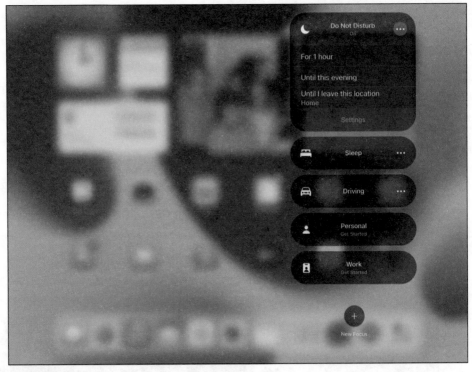

FIGURE 17-19

Chapter **18**
Making Notes

N otes is the app that you can use to do everything from jotting down notes at meetings to keeping to-do lists. It isn't (yet) a robust word processor (such as Apple Pages or Microsoft Word), but for taking notes on the fly, jotting down shopping lists, or writing a few pages of your novel-in-progress while you sip a cup of coffee on your deck, it's becoming an increasingly useful tool with each new iteration.

In this chapter, you see how to enter and edit text in Notes and how to manage those notes by navigating among them, searching for content, or sharing or deleting them. I also help you explore the shortcut menu that allows you to create bulleted checklists, add pictures and drawings to notes, and apply styles to text in a note.

iPadOS 15 also introduces Quick Notes, which is a feature that allows you to — you guessed it!— quickly create notes. The unique part is that you can do so from anywhere and any app on your iPad; you don't have to be in the Notes app to make a Quick Note.

Time to get started!

Open a Blank Note

To open a blank note:

1. To get started with Notes, tap the Notes app icon on the Home screen. If you've never used Notes, it opens with a blank Notes list displayed. (If you have used Notes, it opens to the last note you were working on. If that's the case, you may want to jump to the next task to display a new, blank note.) You see the view shown in **Figure 18-1.**

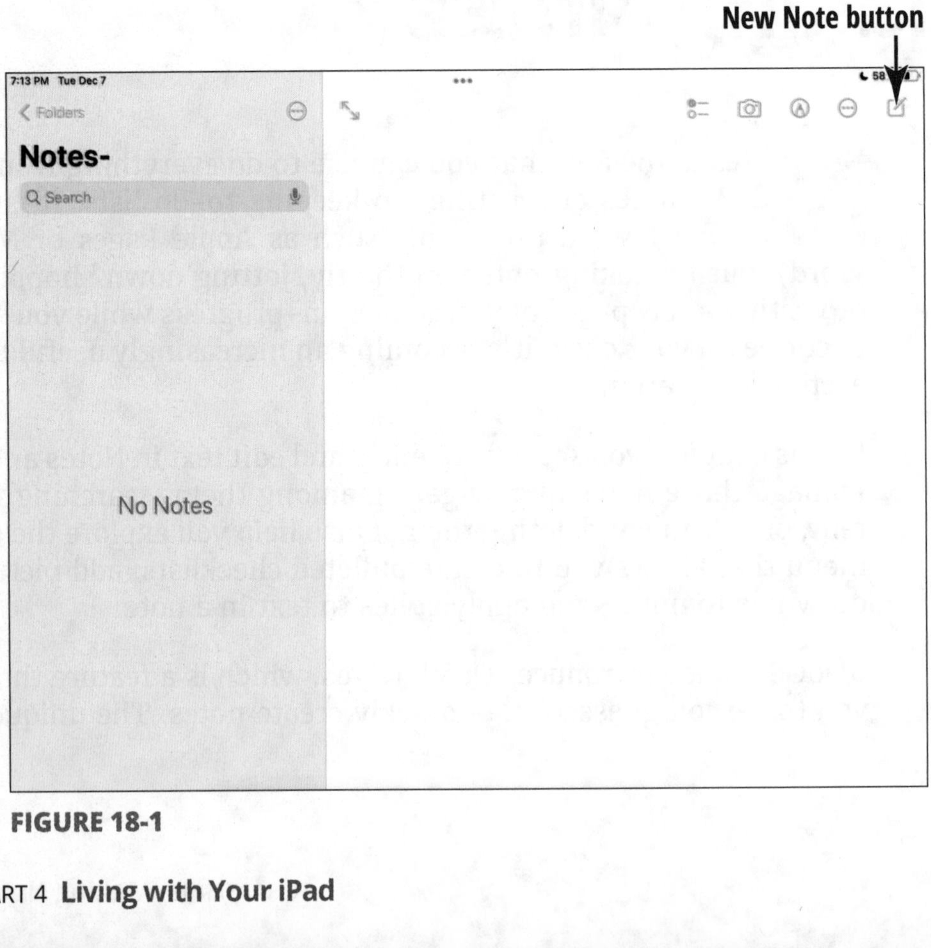

New Note button

FIGURE 18-1

2. Tap the New Note button in the upper-right corner of the open note (looks like a piece of paper with a pencil writing on it; refer to **Figure 18-1**). A blank note opens and displays the onscreen keyboard, shown in **Figure 18-2.**

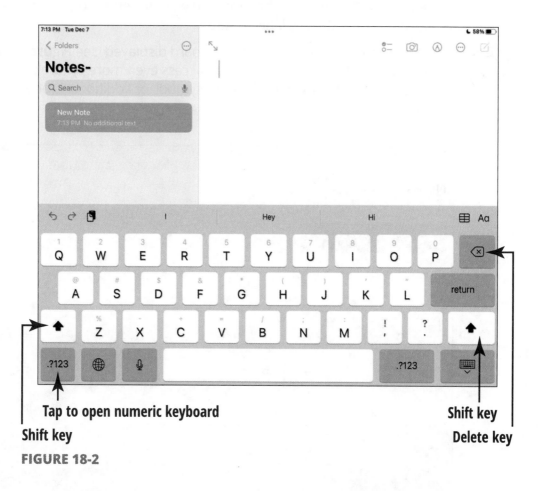

Tap to open numeric keyboard

Shift key

Shift key

Delete key

FIGURE 18-2

TIP

Notes can be shared among Apple devices via iCloud. In Settings, both devices must have Notes turned on under iCloud. New notes are shared instantaneously if both devices are connected to the Internet; this makes it easy to begin a note on one device and move to another device, picking up right where you left off.

3. Tap keys on the keyboard to enter text or, with Siri enabled, tap the Dictation key (the one with the microphone on it) to speak your text. If you want to enter numbers or symbols, tap the key labeled .?123 on the keyboard (refer to **Figure 18-2**). The numeric keyboard, shown in **Figure 18-3,** appears. Whenever you want to return to the alphabetic keyboard, tap the key labeled ABC.

TIP

When you have the numerical keyboard displayed (see **Figure 18-3**), you can tap the key labeled #+= to access even more symbols, such as the percentage sign or the euro symbol, or additional bracket styles.

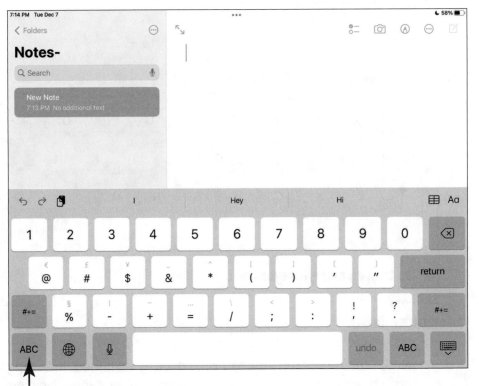

Tap for alphabetic keyboard

FIGURE 18-3

TIP

Allow me to introduce you to a cool keyboard trick: the ability to access alternate characters on a key with a simple pull-down. For example, if you need to type the number 4, simply touch the R key, quickly pull down on it, and then release, as opposed to engaging the numerical keyboard.

4. To capitalize a letter, tap the Shift key, which looks like a bold, upward-facing arrow (refer to **Figure 18-2**), and then tap the letter. Tap the Shift key once again to turn the feature off.

TIP

You can activate the Enable Caps Lock feature in Settings ⇨ General ⇨ Keyboard so that you can then turn on Caps Lock by double-tapping the Shift key. (This upward-pointing arrow is available only in the alphabetic keyboard.)

5. When you want to start a new paragraph or a new item in a list, tap the Return key (refer to **Figure 18-2**).

6. To edit text, tap to the right of the text you want to edit and either use the Delete key (refer to **Figure 18-2**) to delete text to the left of the cursor or enter new text. No need to save a note — it's kept automatically until you delete it.

TIP

You can press a spot on your note and, from the menu that appears, choose Select or Select All. Then you can tap the button labeled BIU to apply bold, italic, or underline formatting.

Use Copy and Paste

The Notes app includes two essential editing tools that you're probably familiar with from using other smart devices and computers: Copy and Paste.

1. With a note displayed, press and hold your finger on a word.

TIP

To extend a selection to adjacent words, press one of the little handles that extend from an edge of the selection and drag to the left, right, up, or down.

2. Tap Select or Select All in the options that appear.

3. On the next toolbar that appears (see **Figure 18-4**), tap the Copy button.

Tap here to copy

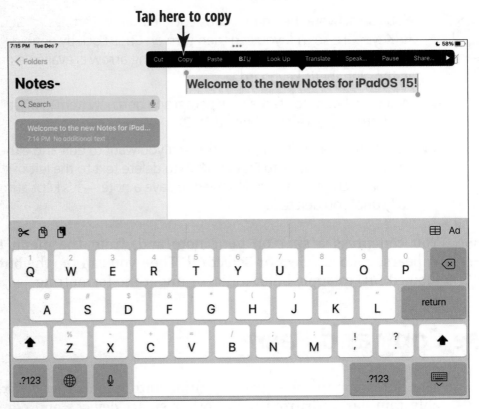

FIGURE 18-4

4. Tap in the document where you want the copied text to go and then press and hold your finger on the screen.

5. On the toolbar that appears (see **Figure 18-5**), tap the Paste button. The copied text appears (see **Figure 18-6**).

Tap here to paste

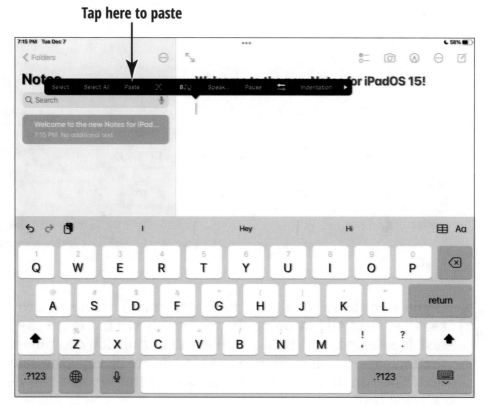

FIGURE 18-5

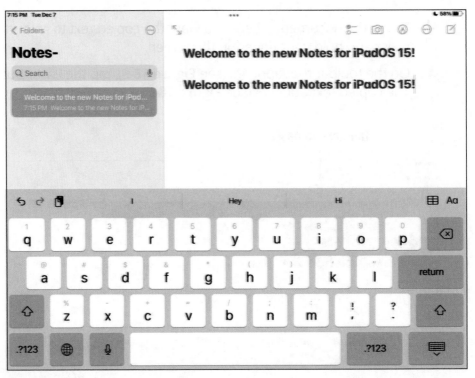

FIGURE 18-6

TIP

If you want to select all text in a note to either delete or copy it, tap the Select All button on the toolbar shown in **Figure 18-5.** All text is selected, and then you use the Cut or Copy command on the toolbar, shown in **Figure 18-4,** to delete or copy the selected text. You can also tap the Delete key on the keyboard to delete selected text.

Insert a Picture

To insert a photo into a note:

1. Tap the Camera button in the top right of the note. In the menu that appears, tap Choose Photo or Video (see **Figure 18-7**).

2. Tap to choose the photos you want to insert, as shown in **Figure 18-8.**

3. Tap Done, and the photos are inserted into your note.

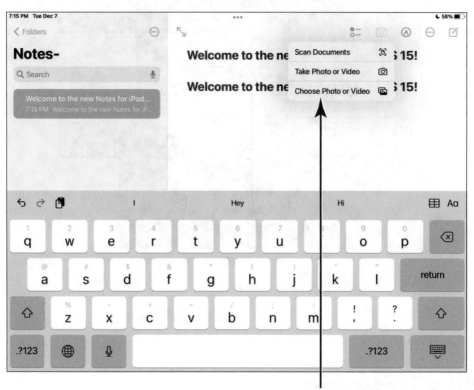

Tap Choose Photo or Video

FIGURE 18-7

If you want to take a photo or video, tap Take Photo or Video in Step 2 and take a new photo or video. Tap Use Photo (lower-right corner) to insert it into your note, or tap Retake (lower-left corner) to start over.

Selected photo

FIGURE 18-8

Add a Drawing

Notes has advanced to the point where you can now create a drawing to add to your note.

1. With a note open, tap the Markup button (looks like the tip of a marker or pen) on the top right of the keyboard to display the short-cut toolbar, and the drawing tools appear.

2. Tap a drawing tool (Pen, Marker, or Pencil). The selected tool will be the tallest among the group.

3. Tap a Color button in the color palette.

4. Tap a color and then draw on the screen using your finger (or with a stylus, such as an Apple Pencil), as shown in **Figure 18-9.**

5. When you've finished drawing, tap Done in the upper-left corner.

6. You can delete a drawing from a note by pressing the drawing until the toolbar appears. Tap the Delete button, shown in **Figure 18-10,** to remove the drawing.

FIGURE 18-9

Tap to delete

FIGURE 18-10

> **TIP** Tapping the Ruler tool places a ruler-shaped item onscreen that you can use to help you draw straight lines. Use two fingers on the screen to rotate the ruler. Tap the Ruler tool again to dismiss it when you're finished using it.

Apply a Text Style

Text styles, including Title, Heading, Subheading, Body, Monospaced, Bulleted List, Dashed List, and Numbered List, are available on the shortcut toolbar (which is just sitting on the top right of the onscreen keyboard). With a note open and the shortcut toolbar displayed, press on the text and choose Select or Select All.

Tap the Text Style button on the shortcut bar (labeled with Aa) and then tap to choose a style from the options, shown in **Figure 18-11**.

Notes is a very nice application and is getting better with every iOS iteration, but it's limited when compared to full-blown word processing apps. So if you've made some notes and want to graduate to building a more robust document in a word processor, you have a couple of options. One way is to download the Pages word-processor app for iPad (it's free) from the App Store (if it's not already installed) and copy your note into it (using the copy-and-paste feature discussed earlier in this chapter). Alternatively,

TIP

you can send the note to yourself in an email message, sync it to your computer, or use the Share button to send it your computer via AirDrop. Open the note and copy and paste its text into a full-fledged word processor, and you're good to go.

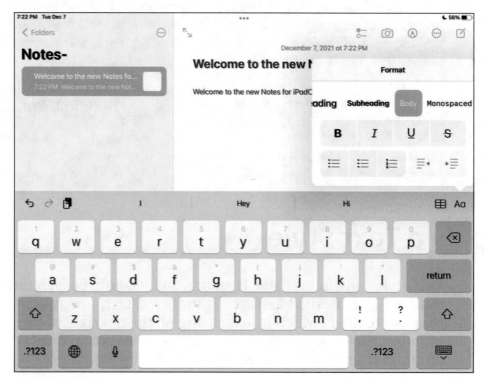

FIGURE 18-11

Create a Checklist

The Checklist formatting feature in Notes allows you to add circular buttons in front of text and then tap those buttons to check off completed items on a checklist.

1. With a note open, tap the Checklist button (the two circles with dashes next to them; one circle contains a check mark) in the shortcut toolbar at the top of the note.

2. Enter text and press Return on the keyboard. A second checklist bullet appears.

3. When you're done entering Checklist items, tap the Checklist button again to turn the feature off.

TIP

You can apply the Checklist formatting to existing text if you press on the text, tap Select or Select All, and then tap the Checklist button.

Now that your checklist is completed, simply tap the circle next to completed items in the checklist to place a check in them, marking them complete, as shown in **Figure 18-12.**

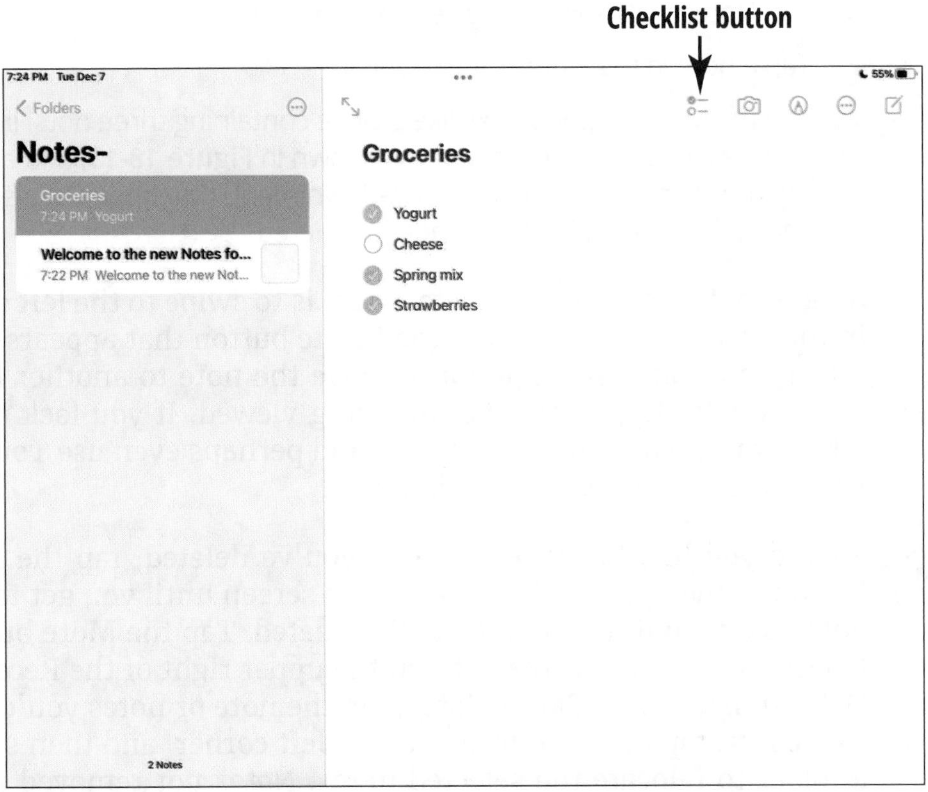

Checklist button

FIGURE 18-12

You can allow Notes to automatically sort checked items in your list by moving them to the bottom of the list. Doing so keeps the remaining items from getting lost in the shuffle. To enable this feature, go to Settings ⇨ Notes ⇨ Sort Checked Items and tap Automatically. Tap Manually to disable the feature.

Delete a Note

There's no sense in letting your Notes list get cluttered, making it harder to find the ones you need. When you're done with a note, it's time to delete it.

1. Tap Notes on the Home screen to open Notes.

2. Tap a note in the Notes list to open it.

3. Tap the More button (looks like a circle containing three dots) in the upper-right corner of the note, as shown in **Figure 18-13,** and then tap the Delete button in the drop-down menu that appears (also shown in **Figure 18-13**). The note is deleted.

An alternative method to delete a note is to swipe to the left on a note in the Notes list and then tap the Delete button that appears (it looks like a trash can). You could also move the note to another folder or lock the note to prevent it from being viewed. If you lock the note, you'll want to provide a password, and perhaps even use Touch ID or Face ID, to secure it from prying eyes.

Should you like to retrieve a note you've deleted, tap the Back button in the upper-left corner of the screen until you get to the Folders list, and then tap Recently Deleted. Tap the More button (a circle containing three dots) in the upper right of the Recently Deleted list, choose Select Notes, tap the note or notes you'd like to recover, tap Move To in the lower-left corner, and then select a folder to relocate the selected items. Notes not removed from Recently Deleted will be permanently deleted in 30 days.

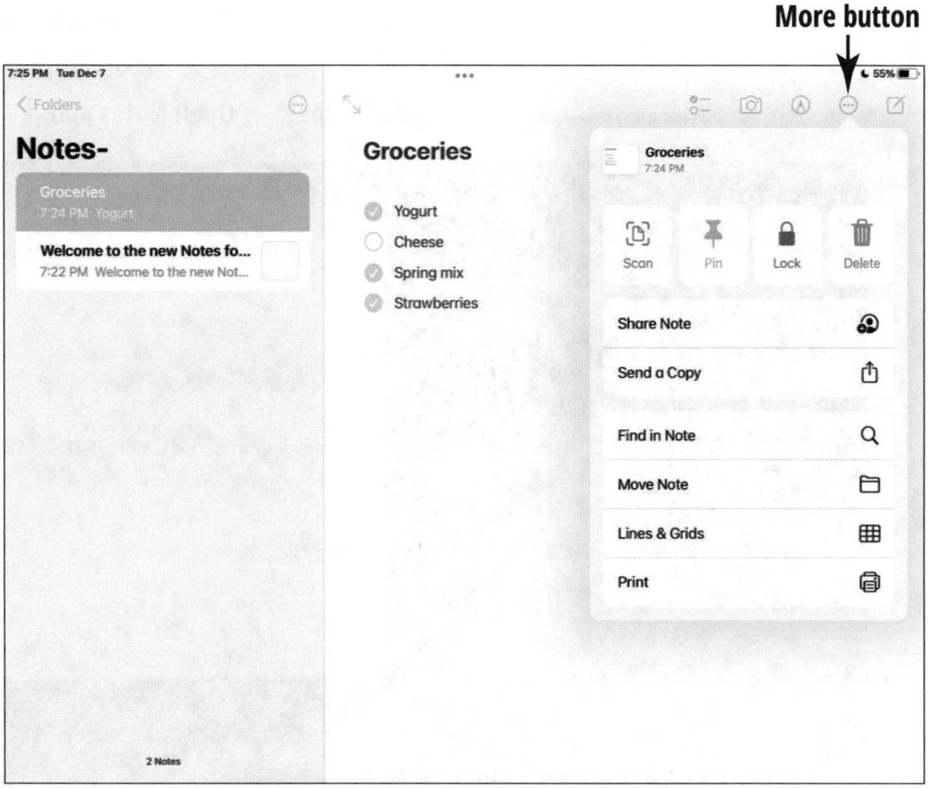

FIGURE 18-13

Speeding Along with Quick Notes

Sometimes a thought strikes and you just have to immediately jot it down before you forget it (which is happening to me more frequently with each passing day). I'm guessing that those kinds of fleeting thoughts were behind Apple's motivation for iPadOS 15's new feature, Quick Notes.

From the Home screen or within most apps, a simple swipe up from the right corner and to the center of the screen opens a Quick Note like the one shown in **Figure 18-14,** where you can type, scribble, or draw until you get that idea down.

Tap to close

Open Notes app

New Quick Note

More button

Swipe this way to open Quick Notes

Drawing tool

FIGURE 18-14

While working within a Quick Note, you can

» Tap the drawing tool icon in the lower right of the window (refer to **Figure 18-14**) to open the drawing tools to change writing instruments and colors, as well as to access other tools.

» Tap the More button (which looks like a circle containing three dots; refer to **Figure 18-14**) in the upper-right corner to share or delete your note.

- » Tap the New Note button (refer to **Figure 18-14**) to open a new note.

- » Swipe right or left in the Quick Notes window to move from note to note.

- » Drag the Quick Notes window to anywhere on the screen where you want to position it.

- » Tap the Notes button, which looks like a two-by-two stack of boxes (refer to **Figure 18-14**), to open the Quick Notes folder in the Notes app.

- » Tap Done in the upper-left corner of the window to close Quick Notes.

Your Quick Notes are stored in the Quick Notes folder within the Notes app. You can find and organize them all there, and you can also move them to other folders within Notes. However, doing so will change the Quick Note to a regular note.

TIP

You can't lock Quick Notes, so if you want to lock a note you created in that app, just move it to a different folder within the Notes app.

Chapter **19**

Using Utilities

U tilities are simple apps that can be very useful indeed to help with common tasks, such as recording ideas for your first novel or measuring the height of your dining room chairs.

In this chapter, you find out how to make recordings using the Voice Memos app, and how to take measurements with the Measure app in iPadOS. Also, in case you lose your iPad, I tell you about a feature that helps you find it, mark it as lost, or even disable it if it has fallen into the wrong hands. I offer a quick introduction to the Home app, which enables you to set up and control all your smart devices. Finally, this chapter takes a look at using the Translate app to assist with conversing in languages you don't natively speak or are still learning.

Record Voice Memos

The Voice Memos app allows you to record memos, edit memos by trimming them down, share them through email or instant message with Messages, synchronize recordings and edits across Apple devices (iPad, iPhone, and Mac), and label recordings so that you find them easily. iPadOS 15 also enables you to organize recordings by creating folders in the app, and to speed playback if you want to listen to your recordings quickly.

TIP

If you use iCloud with Voice Memos, memos you record on your iPhone, iPad, or Mac will sync with all your Apple devices (if they're signed into iCloud with your Apple ID).

To record voice memos, follow these steps:

1. Tap the Voice Memos icon (on the second Home screen, by default) to open the app.

2. In the Voice Memos app (see **Figure 19-1**), tap the red Record button at the bottom left of the screen to record a memo.

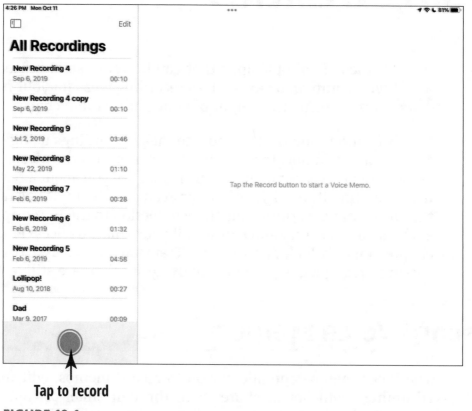

Tap to record

FIGURE 19-1

This button changes to a red Pause button when you're recording, and the screen changes to show you the recording in progress. A red waveform moving from right to left indicates that you're in recording mode (see **Figure 19-2**).

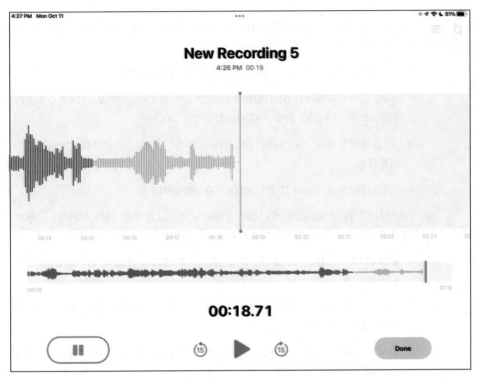

New Recording 5
4:26 PM 00:19

00:18.71

FIGURE 19-2

3. While recording, you can

- Tap the name of the recording (called New Recording by default) to give it a new more descriptive name.

- Tap the red Pause button to pause the recording; then tap Resume to continue recording. While paused, you can also tap the Play button to play what you've recorded so far, and then tap Resume to continue recording.

- While paused, drag the waveform to a place in the recording you'd like to record over and then tap the Replace button to begin recording from there.

- Tap Done to stop recording, and the new recording appears in the Voice Memos list.

4. Tap a recording (called a memo) in the All Recordings list to open its controls. From here you can

- Tap the play icon to play back the recording.

- Tap the forward or reverse icons to move forward or backward, respectively, 15 seconds in the recording.

- Tap the trash can icon (at the top of the screen) to delete the memo.

- Tap the name of the memo to rename it.

5. Tap the Options icon in the upper-right corner (shown in **Figure 19-3**) in the memo playback controls. Options are

- **Playback Speed:** Drag the slider to slow down or speed up playback.

- **Skip Silence:** Toggle this switch to On (green) to have gaps in the audio removed.

- **Enhance Recording:** Toggle this switch to On to remove background noise from the recording.

Tap the blue word *Reset* (see **Figure 19-3**) in the upper-left corner to return to the default settings, if you like.

TIP

Deleted voice memos are kept for 30 days in the Recently Deleted folder in the Voice Memos list. You can retrieve a deleted memo by tapping the Recently Deleted button, tapping the name of the memo you want to retrieve, and then tapping Recover.

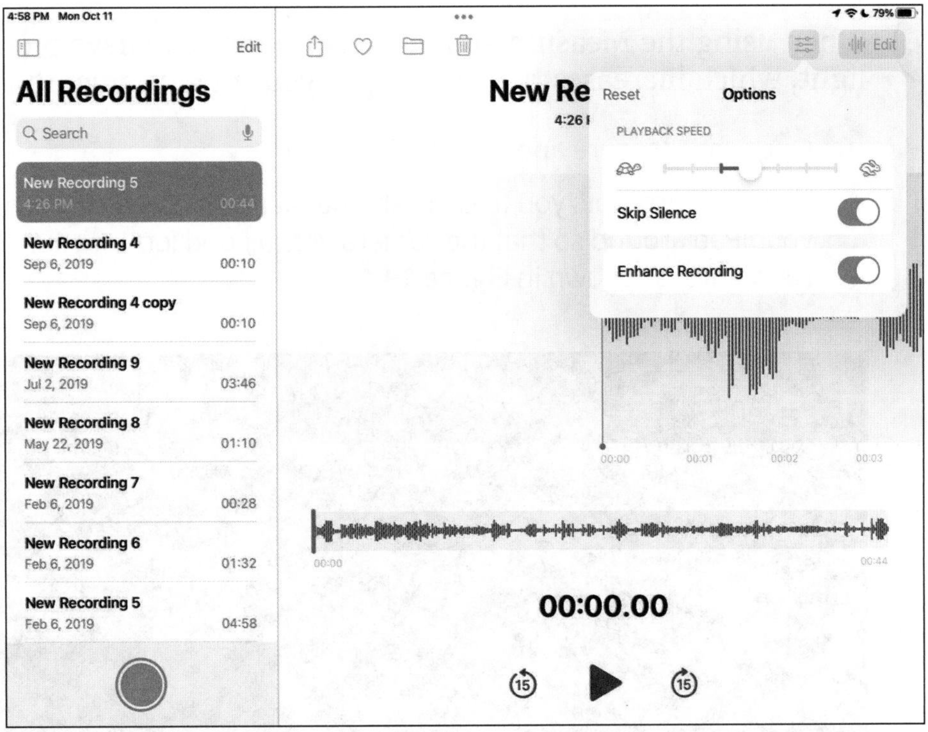

FIGURE 19-3

Measure Distances

iPadOS uses the latest advancements in augmented reality (AR) and your iPad's camera to offer you a cool new way to ditch your measuring tape: the Measure app! This app allows you to use your iPad to measure distances and objects simply by pointing your iPad at them. This app is fun to play with and surprisingly accurate to boot (although you still may want to hang onto your trusty measuring tape).

TIP

As of this writing, the Measure app can measure only in straight lines, but Apple is working to allow more flexibility in upcoming iPadOS updates.

TIP

When using the Measure app, make sure that you have plenty of light, which increases the accuracy of your measurements.

1. Open the Measure app by tapping its icon.

2. Your iPad prompts you to calibrate the Measure app by panning your iPad around so that the camera gets a good look at your surroundings, as shown in **Figure 19-4**.

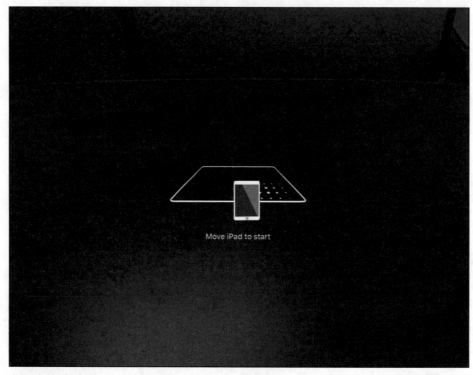

Move iPad to start

FIGURE 19-4

3. After the app is calibrated, you need to add the first reference point for your measurement. Do so by aiming the white targeting dot in the center of the screen to the location of your first reference point, as shown in **Figure 19-5.** Tap the Add a Point button (white button containing the +) to mark the point.

4. Next, mark the second reference point by placing the targeting dot on the location and tapping the Add a Point button again.

TIP

Should you make a mistake or simply want to start afresh, tap the Clear button in the upper-right corner to clear your reference points and begin again.

FIGURE 19-5

5. The length of your measurement is displayed as a white line, and the distance is shown in the middle of it (see **Figure 19-6**).

6. You can continue to make measurements by aiming the targeting dot at a previous reference point, tapping the Add a Point button, and moving your iPad to the next reference point, where you again tap the Add a Point button to make a new measurement (as shown in **Figure 19-7**).

7. When you've finished measuring, tap the white Capture button (just above the Add a Point button) to save an image of your measurements to the Camera Roll in the Photos app.

Measure is a very handy app and is only going to get more useful as Apple updates it.

FIGURE 19-6

FIGURE 19-7

Find a Missing Apple Device

The Find My app can pinpoint the location of your Apple devices and your Apple-using friends. This app is extremely handy if you forget where you left your iPad or someone absconds with it. Find My not only lets you track down the critter but also lets you wipe out the data contained in it if you have no way to get the iPad (or other Apple device) back.

TIP

You must have an iCloud account to use Find My. If you don't have an iCloud account, see Chapter 3 to find out how to set one up.

TIP

If you're using Family Sharing, someone in your family can find your device and play a sound. This works even if the volume on the device is turned down. See Chapter 11 for more about Family Sharing. Also, see Apple's support article called "Share your location with your family" at https://support.apple.com/en-us/HT201087 (as of this writing) for help with this service.

Follow these steps to set up the Find My feature for your iPad:

1. Tap Settings on the Home screen.

2. In Settings, tap your Apple ID at the top of the screen and then tap Find My.

3. In the Find My settings, tap Find My iPad and then tap the On/Off switch for Find My iPad to turn the feature on (see **Figure 19-8**).

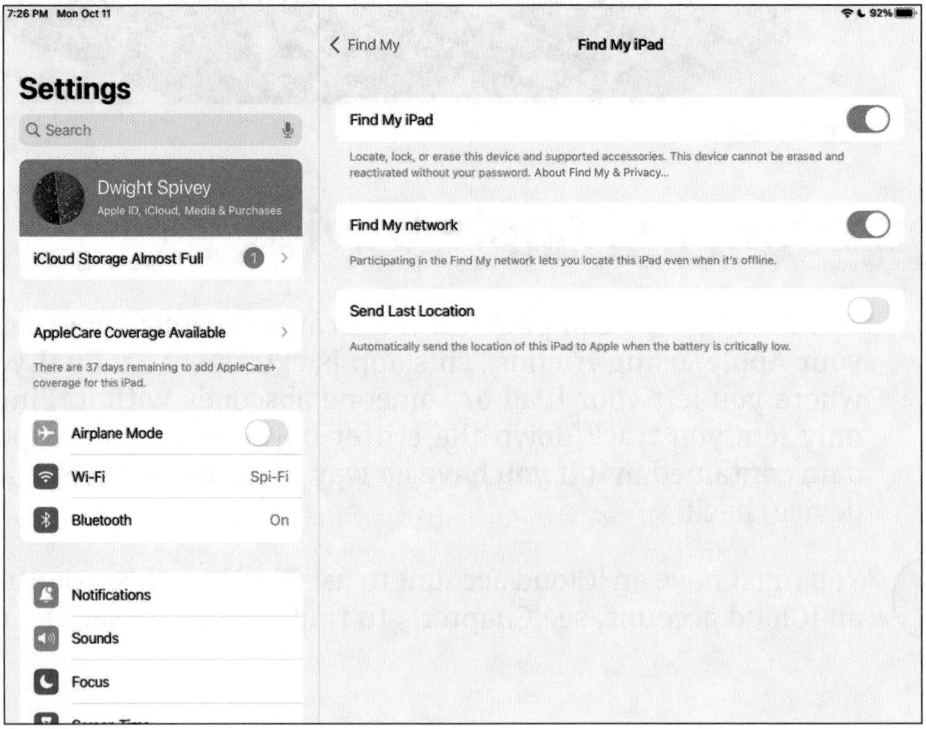

![Screenshot of the iPad Settings showing the Find My iPad options]

7:26 PM Mon Oct 11	🔋 92%

Settings

🔍 Search 🎤

Dwight Spivey
Apple ID, iCloud, Media & Purchases

iCloud Storage Almost Full ① >

AppleCare Coverage Available >
There are 37 days remaining to add AppleCare+ coverage for this iPad.

✈️ Airplane Mode ⚪

📶 Wi-Fi   Spi-Fi

🔵 Bluetooth   On

🔔 Notifications

🔊 Sounds

🌙 Focus

‹ Find My   **Find My iPad**

Find My iPad ⚫

Locate, lock, or erase this device and supported accessories. This device cannot be erased and reactivated without your password. About Find My & Privacy...

Find My network ⚫

Participating in the Find My network lets you locate this iPad even when it's offline.

Send Last Location ⚪

Automatically send the location of this iPad to Apple when the battery is critically low.

FIGURE 19-8

TIP

You may also want to turn on the Find My Network option. This feature allows Apple devices to be found using their built-in Bluetooth technology, even when not connected to Wi-Fi or a cellular network. When you mark your device as missing on www.icloud.com and another Apple user is close by the device, the two devices connect anonymously via Bluetooth and you're notified of its location. It's pretty cool stuff and completely private for all involved parties.

TIP

You may also want to enable the Send Last Location switch, which lets your iPad send its location to Apple just as its battery is running low.

4. From now on, if your iPad is lost or stolen, you can go to www.icloud.com from your computer, iPhone, or another iPad and enter your Apple ID and password. You can also use the Find My app on an iPad, iPhone, or Mac.

5. In your computer's browser, the iCloud Launchpad screen appears. Click the Find iPhone button (yes, iPhone) to display a map of your device's location and some helpful tools (see **Figure 19-9**). I have no idea why Apple hasn't updated this button name to simply Find My, but rest assured that it works for all your Apple devices if they're signed in to the same Apple ID.

6. Click the All Devices option at the top of the window and click your iPad in the list. In the window that appears, choose one of three options:

- To wipe information from the iPad, click the Erase iPad button.

- To lock the iPad from access by others, click the Lost Mode button.

- Click Play Sound to have your iPad play a "ping" sound that might help you locate it if you're in its vicinity. If you choose to play a sound, it plays for two minutes, helping you track down your iPad in case it fell behind the couch or somebody holding your iPad is within earshot. You can also tap OK on your iPad (after you find it) to stop the sound before the two minutes is up.

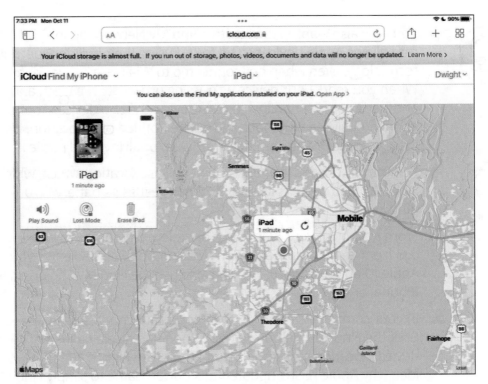

FIGURE 19-9

TIP

The Erase iPad option deletes all data from your iPad, including contact information and content (such as music and photos). However, even after you've erased your iPad, it can display your phone number on the Lock screen along with a message so that any Good Samaritan who finds it can contact you (you'll be prompted to add your phone number, message, or both after you initiate the erasure). If you've created an iTunes or iCloud backup, you can restore your iPad's contents from those sources.

TIP

The Lost Mode feature allows you to send whomever has your iPad a note saying how to return it to you. You'll be prompted to add your contact information and message after you mark the iPad as lost.

An Overview of the Home App

Since the smart home movement began a few years ago, controlling your home remotely meant juggling several apps: one for your lights, one for your garage doors, one for your thermostat, one for your oven, and on and on. Although some developers have tried to create apps that worked with multiple smart home platforms by multiple manufacturers, none had the clout or the engineering manpower to pull things together — until Apple jumped in.

The Home app on your iPad is designed to work with multiple smart home platforms and devices, and you can control all the smart devices in your home from one easy-to-use app.

Here's a list of the types of devices you can control with your iPad: lighting, locks, windows and window shades, heating and cooling systems, speakers, humidifiers and air purifiers, security systems, garage doors, electrical plugs and switches, motion sensors, video cameras, smoke and carbon monoxide detectors, and even more!

TIP If you want to use the Home app with your smart home devices, make sure that you see the "Works with Apple HomeKit" symbol on packaging or on the website (if you purchase the device online). Apple has an ever-growing list of HomeKit-enabled devices at www.apple.com/ios/home/accessories. You can also buy HomeKit-enabled devices on Apple's website: www.apple.com/shop/accessories/all-accessories/homekit.

Because there are so many ways to configure and use the Home app and so many different accessories you can control with it, it's beyond the scope of this book to cover the app in detail. Apple offers a great overview at www.apple.com/ios/home.

Translate Words and Phrases

I remember thinking how cool the Universal Translator was the first time I saw it in the original *Star Trek* television series. The Enterprise crew would meet a being that spoke a language unknown to them, but the Universal Translator would have them swapping jokes in no time flat. With the introduction of the Translate app, it would seem that Apple envisions the iPad as a step toward such a device in the early 21st century.

Translate allows you to, well, translate words and phrases from one language into another, supporting 11 different languages. Translate even helps you engage in conversations on the fly with its Conversation mode.

TIP

Translate currently supports English, Spanish, Mandarin Chinese, Arabic, Brazilian Portuguese, Russian, Korean, Italian, German, French, and Japanese.

To start translating:

1. Tap the Translate app icon to open it.

2. Tap the down arrow next to the button in the top center of the screen when viewing in landscape mode, as shown in **Figure 19-10** (or on the upper left in portrait), and then tap to select the language you want words and phrases translated from.

3. Tap the down arrow next to the button in the upper right and tap to select the language you want your words or phrases translated to.

4. Enter your words or phrases either by tapping the Enter Text area and typing or pasting your text, or by tapping the blue microphone icon and speaking your text.

   Translate displays your original text in white or black (depending on whether your phone is using light or dark mode) and the translated text in blue, as shown in **Figure 19-11.**

5. To hear the word or phrase spoken, tap the blue play icon under the translated text.

6. To save the translation to your Favorites, which is helpful if the translation is a common phrase that you'll need to refer to often, tap the small star under the translated text. To access your Favorites list, just tap All Favorites in the sidebar on the left (you may need to tap the Sidebar button in the upper left to open the sidebar).

7. If you'd like to see a comprehensive definition of a word, complete with usage examples, tap a word in the translation to highlight it, and then tap the dictionary icon below it.

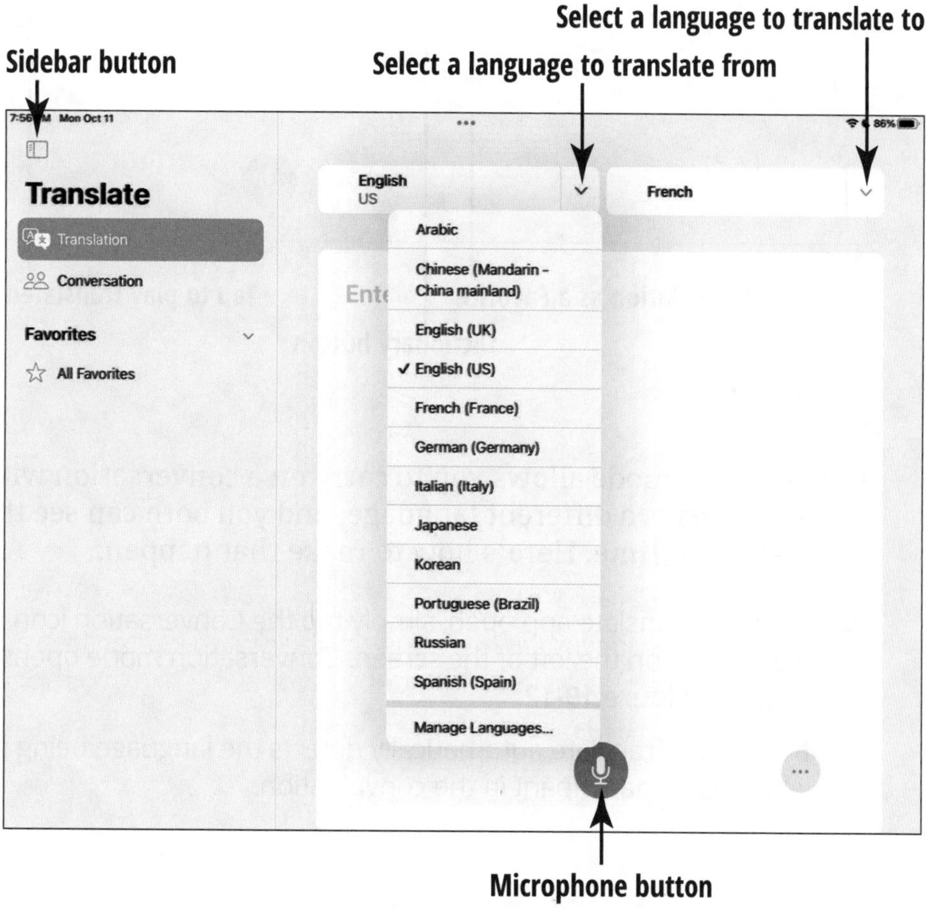

Select a language to translate to

Sidebar button   Select a language to translate from

7:56 AM Mon Oct 11   •••   86%

Translate   English   French
                             US

🄰🅍 Translation   Arabic

👥 Conversation   Chinese (Mandarin –
                             China mainland)
                             Ent
Favorites   English (UK)

⭐ All Favorites   ✓ English (US)

                             French (France)

                             German (Germany)

                             Italian (Italy)

                             Japanese

                             Korean

                             Portuguese (Brazil)

                             Russian

                             Spanish (Spain)

                             Manage Languages…

                                              🎤   •••

Microphone button

FIGURE 19-10

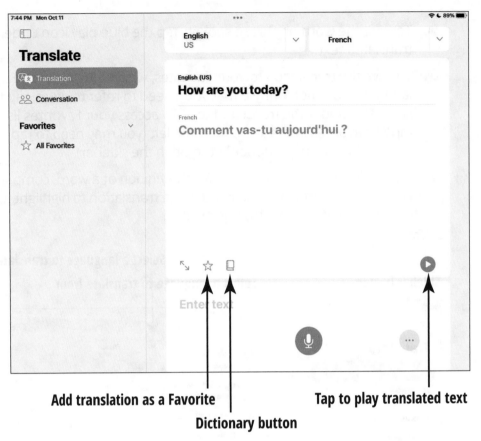

Add translation as a Favorite   Tap to play translated text

Dictionary button

FIGURE 19-11

Conversation mode allows you to carry on a conversation with some-one who speaks a different language, and you both can see the trans-lations in real time. Here's how to make that happen:

1. With the Translate app open, simply tap the Conversation icon in the sidebar on the left of the screen. Conversation mode opens, as shown in **Figure 19-12.**

   By default, Translate automatically detects the language being spo-ken by each participant in the conversation.

2. Take turns tapping the microphone icon and speaking.

When the speaker stops, the word or phrase is translated so that the other participant can read what the speaker said.

3. Tap the orientation icon (shown in **Figure 19-13**) to decide whether you and the person you're speaking with would like to translate the conversation side by side (the default shown in **Figure 19-13**) or face to face (shown in **Figure 19-14**).

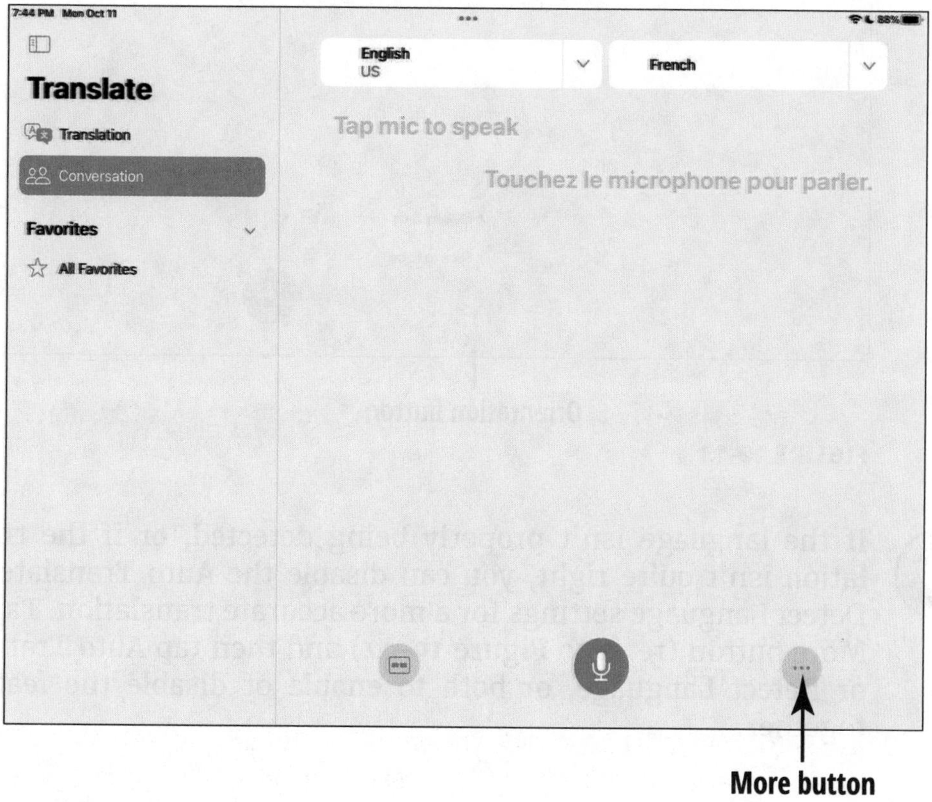

7:44 PM Mon Oct 11

Translate

English
US

French

Translation

Conversation

Tap mic to speak

Touchez le microphone pour parler.

Favorites

All Favorites

More button

FIGURE 19-12

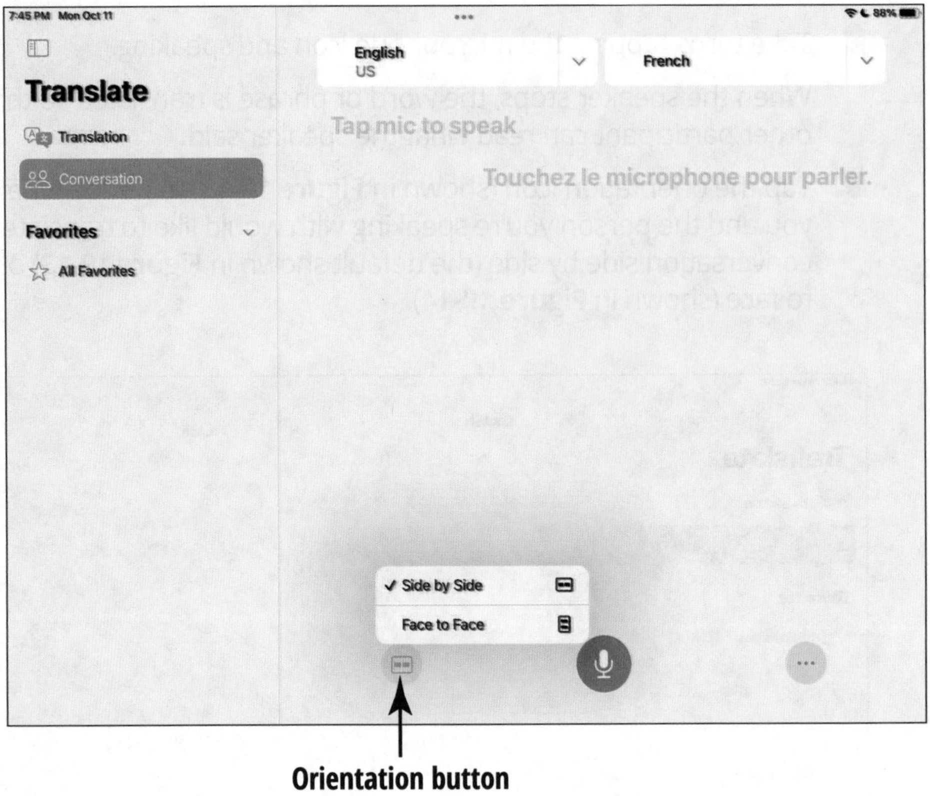

FIGURE 19-13

Orientation button

If the language isn't properly being detected, or if the translation isn't quite right, you can disable the Auto Translate and Detect Language settings for a more accurate translation. Tap the More button (refer to **Figure 19-12**) and then tap Auto Translate or Detect Language, or both to enable or disable the features together.

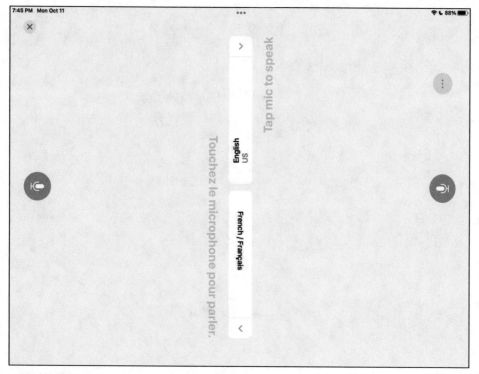

FIGURE 19-14

» **Fix a nonresponsive iPad**

» **Update the iOS software**

» **Get support**

» **Back up your iPad**

Chapter **20**

Troubleshooting and Maintaining Your iPad

iPads don't grow on trees — they cost a pretty penny. That's why you should learn how to take care of your iPad and troubleshoot any problems it might have so that you get the most out of it.

In this chapter, I provide some advice about the care and maintenance of your iPad, as well as tips about how to solve common problems, update iPad system software, and even reset the iPad if something goes seriously wrong. Finally, you get information about backing up your iPad settings and content using iCloud and the fingerprint reader feature, Touch ID.

Keep the iPad Screen Clean

If you've been playing with your iPad, you know (despite Apple's claim that the iPad has a fingerprint-resistant screen) that it can be a fingerprint magnet. Here are some tips for cleaning your iPad screen:

- » **Use a dry, soft cloth.** You can get most fingerprints off with a dry, soft cloth, such as the one you use to clean your eyeglasses or a cleaning tissue that's lint-and chemical-free. Or try products used to clean lenses in labs, such as Kimwipes (which you can get from several major retailers, such as Amazon, Walmart, and office supply stores).

- » **Use a slightly dampened soft cloth.** This may sound counter-intuitive to the previous tip, but to get the surface even cleaner, very (and I stress *very*) slightly dampen the soft cloth. Again, make sure that whatever cloth material you use is free of lint.

- » **Remove the cables.** Turn off your iPad and unplug any cables from it before cleaning the screen with a moistened cloth, even a very slightly moistened one.

- » **Avoid too much moisture.** Avoid getting too much moisture around the edges of the screen, where it can seep into the unit. It isn't so much the glass surface you should worry about, as it is the Home button (if your iPad is equipped with one) and the speaker holes on the top and bottom of the iPad.

- » **Don't use your fingers!** That's right, by using a stylus (or an Apple Pencil, if your iPad supports it) rather than your finger, you entirely avoid smearing oil from your skin or cheese from your pizza on the screen. Besides the Apple Pencil, a number of top-notch styluses are out there; just search Amazon for "iPad stylus," and you'll be greeted with a multitude of them, most of which are priced quite reasonably.

- » **Never use household cleaners.** They can degrade the coating that keeps the iPad screen from absorbing oil from your fingers. Plus, you simply don't need to use such cleaners because the screen cleans very easily with little or no moisture at all.

TIP

Don't use premoistened lens–cleaning tissues to clean your iPad screen! Most brands of wipes contain alcohol, which can damage the screen's coating. Be sure that whatever cleaner you do use states that it's compatible with your model iPad, because there are differences in screen technology between models.

Protect Your Gadget with a Case

Your screen isn't the only element on the iPad that can be damaged, so consider getting a case for it so that you can carry it around the house or travel with it safely. Besides providing a bit of padding if you drop the device, a case makes the iPad less slippery in your hands, offering a better grip when working with it.

Several types of covers and cases are available, but be sure to get one that will fit your model of iPad because their dimensions and button placements may differ, and some models have slightly different thicknesses. There are differences between covers and cases:

» **Covers tend to be more for decoration than overall protection.** Although they do provide some minimal protection, they're generally thin and not well-padded.

» **Cases are more solid and protect most, if not all, of your iPad.** They're usually a bit bulky and provide more padding than covers.

Extend Your iPad's Battery Life

The much-touted battery life of the iPad is a wonderful feature, but you can do some things to extend it even further. Here are a few tips to consider:

» **Keep tabs on remaining battery life.** You can view the amount of remaining battery life by looking at the Battery icon on the far-right end of the status bar, at the top of your screen.

» **Keep iPadOS up to date.** You can find out how in "Update the iPadOS Software," later in this chapter.

» **Use standard accessories to charge your iPad most effectively.** When connected to a recent-model Mac or Windows computer for charging, the iPad can slowly charge; however, the most effective way to charge your iPad is to plug it into a wall outlet using the Lightning-to-USB cable and the USB power adapter that come with your iPad.

A third-party charging cable (the cable, not the block) usually works just fine, but some are less reliable than others. If you use a third-party cable and notice that your iPad is taking longer than usual to charge, it's a good idea to try another cable.

» **Use a case with an external battery pack.** These cases are very handy when you're traveling or unable to reach an electrical outlet easily. However, they're also a bit bulky and can be cumbersome in smaller hands.

» **The fastest way to charge your iPad is to turn it off while charging it.** If turning your iPad completely off doesn't sound like the best idea for you, you can disable Wi-Fi or Bluetooth to facilitate a faster recharge.

Activate Airplane Mode to turn both Wi-Fi and Bluetooth off at the same time.

» **The Battery icon on the status bar indicates when the charging is complete.**

Be careful not to use your iPad in ambient temperatures higher than 95° Farenheit (35° Celcius) because doing so may damage your battery. Damage of this kind may also not be covered under warranty. Charging in high temperatures may damage the battery even more. Although you can safely use your iPad within a wide range of temperatures, the optimal temps are between 62–72° Farenheit (16–22° Celcius).

If you notice that your battery won't charge more than 80 percent, it could be getting too warm. Unplug the iPad from the charger and try again after it has cooled down a bit. If getting too warm becomes a recurring issue, be sure that you're using a genuine Apple charger block and cable.

Your iPad battery is sealed in the unit, so you can't replace it yourself the way you can with many laptops or other cellphones. If the battery is out of warranty, you have to fork over about $99 to have Apple install a new one. See the "Get Support" section, later in this chapter, to find out where to get a replacement battery.

TIP

Apple offers AppleCare+. For $129 for iPad Pro models or $69 for all other iPad models, you get an extra year of coverage (on top of the original one-year warranty that comes with your iPad, extending coverage to two years from the date of purchase), which even covers you if you drop or spill liquids on your iPad. Apple covers up to two incidents of accidental damage every 12 months with a $49 service fee, plus tax. You can purchase AppleCare+ when you buy your iPad or within 60 days of the date of purchase. Visit `http://www.apple.com/support/products/ipad` for more details.

What to Do with a Nonresponsive iPad

If your iPad goes dead on you, it's most likely a power issue, so the first thing to do is to plug the Lightning-to-USB or Lightning-to-USB-C cable (depending on your iPad model) into the USB or USB-C power adapter, plug the power adapter into a wall outlet, plug the other end of the cable into your iPad, and charge the battery.

Another thing to try — if you believe that an app is hanging up the iPad — is to press the Sleep/Wake button for a couple of seconds and then press and hold the Home button. The app you were using should close.

You can always use the tried-and-true reboot procedure: On iPads with a Home button, you press the Top button until the power-off slider appears. For iPads without a Home button, press the Top button and either Volume button until the power-off slider appears. Drag the slider to the right to turn off your iPad. After a few moments, press the Top button to boot up the little guy again.

If the situation seems drastic and none of these ideas works, try to force restart your iPad. To do this, press and hold the Top button and the Home button at the same time (for iPads with a Home button) for at least ten seconds until the Apple logo appears onscreen. For iPads without a Home button, press the Volume Up button once, press the Volume Down button once, and then press and hold the Top button until the Apple logo appears.

TIP

If your iPad has this problem often, try closing out some active apps that may be running in the background and using up too much memory. To do this on iPads with a Home button, press the Home button twice, and then from the screen showing active apps, tap and drag an app upward to close it. For iPads without a Home button, swipe up from the bottom of the screen and pause momentarily until the active apps display. Then swipe an app upward to close it. Also check to see that you haven't loaded up your iPad with too much content, such as videos, which could be slowing down its performance.

Update the iPadOS Software

Apple occasionally updates the iPad system software, known as iPadOS (formerly iOS), to fix problems or offer enhanced features. You should occasionally check for an updated version (say, every month or so). You can check by connecting your iPad to a recognized computer (that is, a computer that you've used to sign into your Apple account before), but it's even easier to just update from your iPad Settings, though it can be just a tad slower:

1. Tap Settings from the Home screen.

2. Tap General and then tap Software Update (see **Figure 20-1**).

3. A message tells you whether your software is up to date. If it's not, tap Download and Install and follow the prompts to update to the latest iPadOS version.

TIP

If you're having problems with your iPad, you can use the Reset feature to try to restore the natural balance. To do so, go to Settings ➪ General ➪ Transfer or Reset iPad ➪ Reset, and then tap the function you want to reset when prompted.

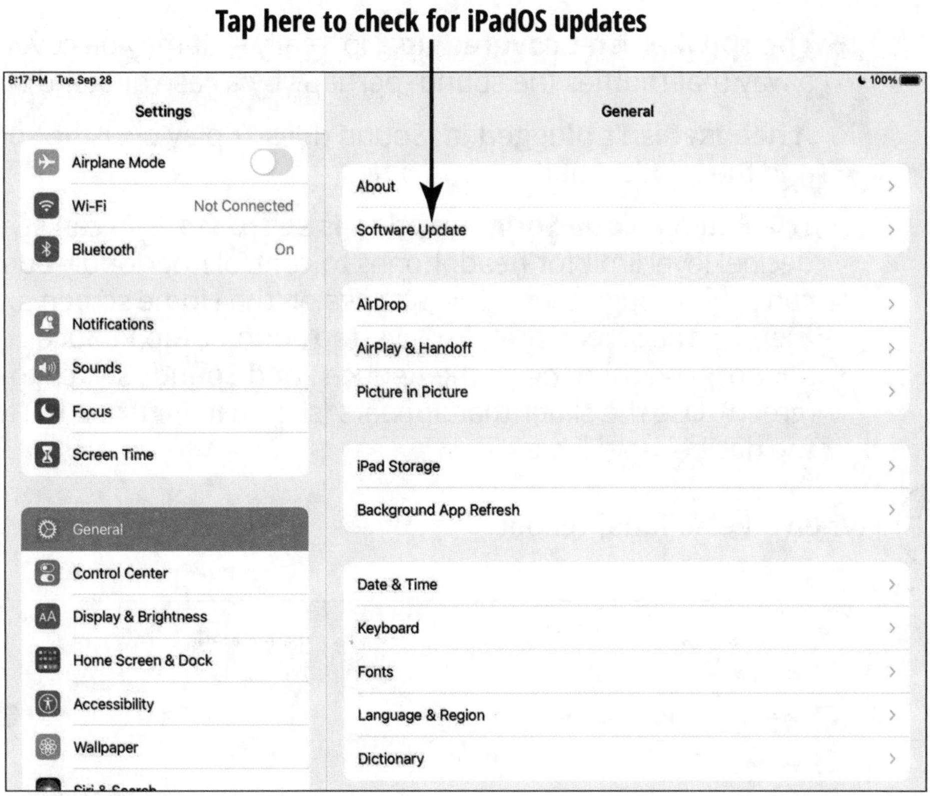

Tap here to check for iPadOS updates

FIGURE 20-1

Restore the Sound

My wife frequently has trouble with the sound on her iPad, and subsequently we've learned quite a bit about troubleshooting sound issues, enabling us to pass our knowledge on to you. Make sure that

> » **You haven't touched the volume control buttons on the side of your iPad.**
>
> Be sure not to touch the volume down button and inadvertently lower the sound to a point where you can't hear it. However, pushing the volume buttons will have no effect if the iPad is sleeping.

TIP

» **The speaker isn't covered up.** No, really — it may be covered in a way that muffles the sound (perhaps by a case or stand).

» **A headset isn't plugged in.** Sound doesn't play over the speaker and the headset at the same time.

» **The Reduce Loud Sounds option is set to On.** You can set the decibel level limit for headphones to control how loudly audio can play through them. Tap Settings on the Home screen and then, on the screen that displays, tap Sounds, tap Reduce Loud Sounds, and then toggle the Reduce Loud Sounds switch to On (green). Use the slider that appears (shown in **Figure 20-2**) to set the decibel level limit.

TIP

When all else fails, reboot.

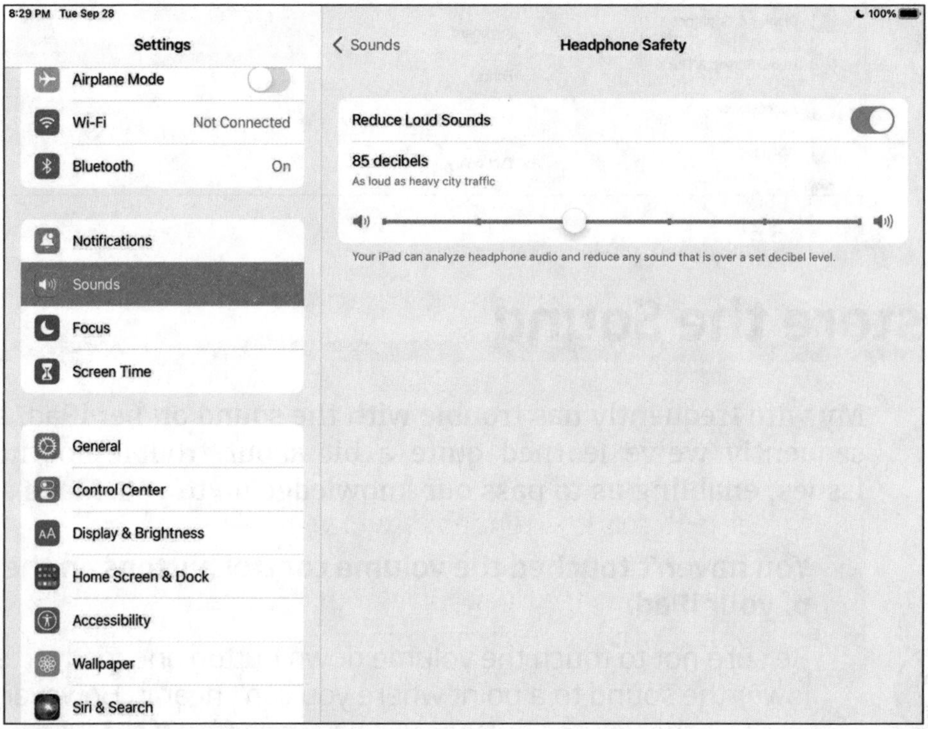

FIGURE 20-2

Get Support

Every new iPad comes with a year's coverage for repair of the hardware and 90 days of free technical support. Apple is known for its high level of customer support, so if you're stuck, I definitely recommend that you give them a try. Here are a few options for getting help that you can explore:

» **The Apple Store:** Go to your local Apple Store (if one's nearby) to see what the folks there might know about your problem. Call first and make an appointment with the Genius Bar to be sure you get prompt service. To find your local Apple Store, visit `https://www.apple.com/retail/` and enter your ZIP code.

» **The Apple support website:** It's at `http://support.apple.com/ipad`. You can find online manuals, discussion forums, and downloads, and you can use the Apple Expert feature to contact a live support person by phone.

» **The iPad User Guide:** You can download the free manual that is available through Apple Books from the Apple Books Store. Be sure to download the one for iPadOS! See Chapter 12 for more about Apple Books.

» **The Apple battery replacement service:** If you need repair or service for your battery, visit `http://www.apple.com/batteries/service-and-recycling` and scroll down to the iPad Owners section. Note that your warranty provides free battery replacement if the battery is defective during the warranty period. If you purchase the AppleCare+ service agreement, this is extended to two years.

TIP

Apple recommends that you have your iPad battery replaced only by an Apple Authorized Service Provider. Please don't take this warning lightly; you don't want to trust the inner workings of your iPad to just anyone who says they can work on it.

Back Up to iCloud

You used to be able to back up your iPad content using only iTunes on your Mac or PC, but since Apple's introduction of iCloud, you can back up via a Wi-Fi network to your iCloud storage. You get 5GB of storage for free or you can pay for increased storage (a total of 50GB for 99 cents per month, 200GB for $2.99 per month, or 2TB for $9.99 per month).

TIP

You must have an iCloud account to back up to iCloud. If you don't have an iCloud account, see Chapter 3 to find out more.

To perform a backup to iCloud:

1. Tap Settings from the Home screen and then tap your Apple ID at the top of the screen.

2. Tap iCloud and then tap iCloud Backup (see **Figure 20-3**).

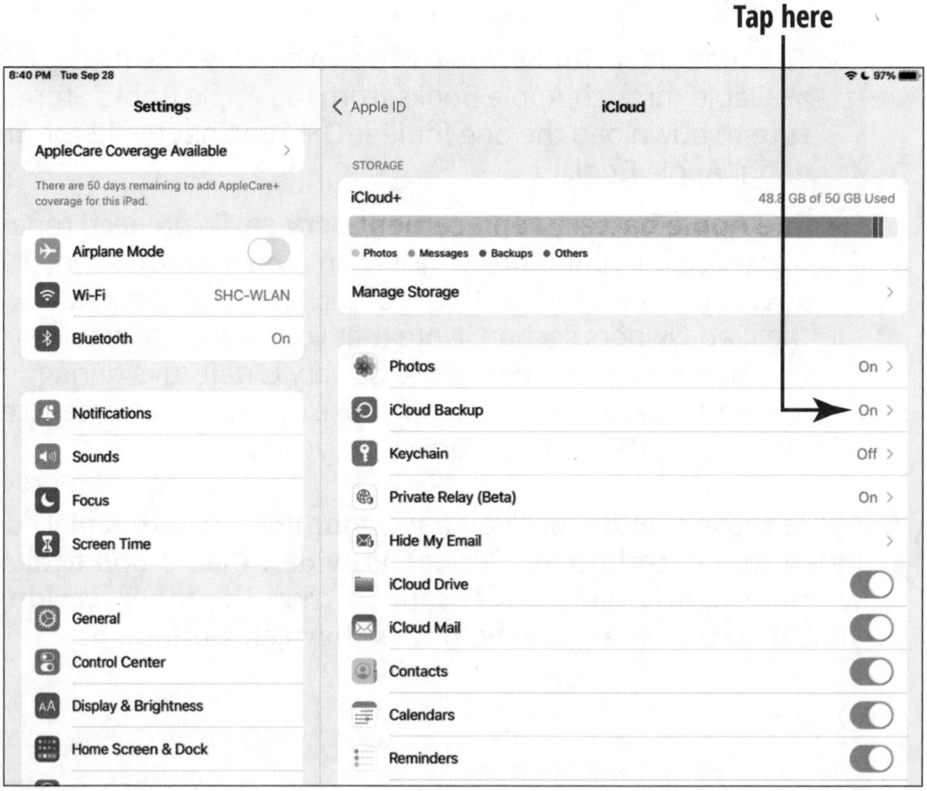

Tap here

FIGURE 20-3

3. In the pane that appears (see **Figure 20-4**), tap the iCloud Backup switch to enable automatic backups. To perform a manual backup, tap Back Up Now. A progress bar shows how your backup is moving along.

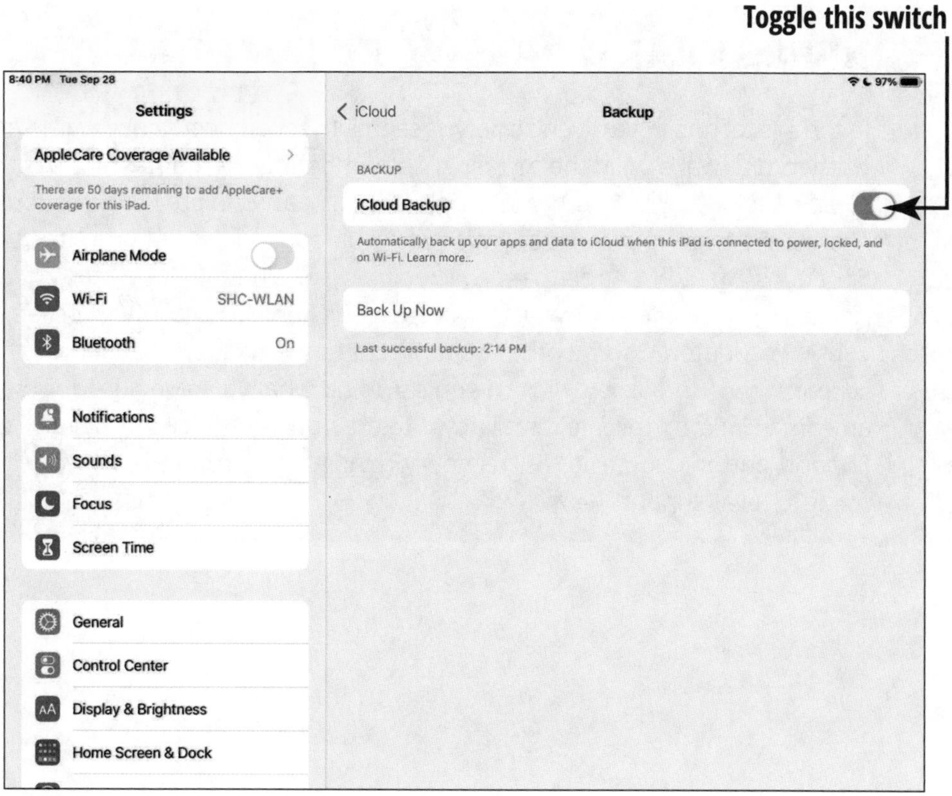

Toggle this switch

FIGURE 20-4

If you've been backing up your iPad to iCloud, you can get your content back if you erased it all because the iPad was lost. Just enter your Apple ID and password, and you can reactivate it.

You can also back up your iPad using Finder (for Macs running macOS 10.15 or newer) or iTunes (for PCs or Macs running macOS 10.14 or older). This method actually saves more types of content than an iCloud backup does, and if you have encryption turned on in iTunes, it can save your passwords as well. However, this method requires that you connect to a computer to perform the backup. If you do back up and get a new iPad at some point in the future, you can easily restore all your data from your computer to the new iPad.

APPLE ID AND PASSWORD SUPPORT

In today's technology-driven society, it seems that you need a username and password to wake up in the morning! Remembering usernames and passwords can be a daunting task, and your Apple ID and password are no exceptions. Thankfully, Apple is at the ready with your solution, but it's not one size fits all. Situations differ, but Apple is ready in every case. Whether you've forgotten your Apple ID, can't remember your password, your Apple ID account is locked, or you've encountered some other issue, Apple has your answer at `https://support.apple.com/apple-id`. If you can't find what you're looking for by using any of the links on the site, scroll down to the bottom and click the blue Get Support button under the "Tell us how we can help" section to connect with Apple's stellar support team.

Index

About the Author

Dwight Spivey has been a technical author and editor for more than a decade, but he has been a bona fide technophile for more than three of them. He's the author of *iPad For Seniors For Dummies*, 12th Edition (Wiley), *iPhone For Seniors For Dummies*, 10th Edition (Wiley), *Apple Watch For Seniors For Dummies* (Wiley), *Apple One For Dummies* (Wiley), *Home Automation For Dummies* (Wiley), *How to Do Everything Pages, Keynote & Numbers* (McGraw-Hill), and many more books covering the tech gamut.

Dwight's technology experience is extensive, consisting of macOS, iOS, iPadOS, Android, Linux, and Windows operating systems in general, as well as educational technology, desktop publishing software, laser printers and drivers, color and color management, and networking.

Dwight lives on the Gulf Coast of Alabama with his wife, Cindy, their four children, Victoria, Devyn, Emi, and Reid, and their pets, Rocky, Penny, and Mirri.

Dedication

To my children, Victoria, Devyn, Emi, and Reid. No dad could be more proud or grateful. It has been, and will always be, my honor to call you my own. Love, love, love, love you!

Author's Acknowledgments

Carole Jelen, my superb agent, is always first on this list. Thank you, Carole!

Next, the awesome editors, designers, and other professionals at Wiley are absolutely critical to the completion of these books I'm so blessed to write. I hope every individual involved at every level knows that I'm truly grateful for their dedication, hard work, and patience in putting together this book. As always, extra-special gratitude to Susan Christophersen, Elizabeth Stillwell, and Tom Egan.

Publisher's Acknowledgments

Acquisitions Editor: Elizabeth Stillwell

Project Manager and Copy Editor: Susan Christophersen

Technical Reviewer: Thomas Egan

Production Editor: Tamilmani Varadharaj

Cover Image: © Jose Luis Pelaez Inc/ Getty Images